Faithful in Adversity

Faithful in Adversity
The Experiences of Two Army Surgeons
During the First World War

A Surgeon in Khaki

Arthur Anderson Martins

A Surgeon in Belgium

H. S. Souttar

LEONAUR

Faithful in Adversity
The Experiences of Two Army Surgeons During the First World War
A Surgeon in Khaki
by Arthur Anderson Martin
A Surgeon in Belgium
by H. S. Souttar

FIRST EDITION

First published under the titles
A Surgeon in Khaki
and
A Surgeon in Belgium

Leonaur is an imprint
of Oakpast Ltd

Copyright in this form © 2014 Oakpast Ltd

ISBN: 978-1-78282-319-3 (hardcover)
ISBN: 978-1-78282-320-9 (softcover)

http://www.leonaur.com

Publisher's Notes
The views expressed in this book are not necessarily
those of the publisher.

Contents

A Surgeon in Khaki   7
A Surgeon in Belgium   199

A Surgeon in Khaki

THE AUTHOR OUTSIDE AMBULANCE HEADQUARTERS AT OUDERDOM.

Contents

Preface	11
From Peace to War	13
Le Havre and Harfleur	21
From Le Havre to the Bay of Biscay	28
From the Bay of Biscay to East of Paris	35
The Advance to the Marne	41
What I Saw of the Battle of the Marne	46
The Night of the Marne	51
From the Marne to the Aisne	55
The Aisne and the Tragedy of the Sunken Road	66
Missy on the Aisne	72
On the Aisne at Mont de Soissons	80
Field Ambulances and Military Hospitals	95
Goodbye to the Aisne.	105
The La Bassée Road at Château Gorre	122
Bethune	127
Some Medical Odds and Ends	148
We Leave Bethune	160

Over the Belgian Frontier	167
We Leave Belgium	189

Preface

In the following pages an attempt is made to record, however imperfectly, some of the scenes, and the impressions formed, during those great days of 1914 when our army was fighting so stubbornly and against such odds in France and Flanders.

The notes in many instances are disconnected, but the things seen presented themselves in a disconnected way, and if they are not all beautifully dovetailed one into another, they are at least given forth somewhat in the way in which I viewed and received them myself.

During the actual progress of this war, and when the war is happily over, much literature bearing on the great struggle will be produced, but I venture to think that of the personal narrative and the personal impression one cannot have too much.

The narrative includes my experiences at Le Havre, Harfleur, and the Battle of the Marne, the march to the Aisne, the wait on the Aisne, the move across France to the new lines behind La Bassée, and the final move to Flanders not far from Ypres.

Arthur A. Martin.

Chapter 1

From Peace to War

Early 1914.

In April 1914 I left my practice in New Zealand for a short tour through the American, British, and Continental surgical clinics.

After having visited all the important clinics in the United States—the famous Mayos of Rochester, Murphy's at Chicago, Cushing's at Boston, and others at Cleveland, Baltimore, and Philadelphia, I finally arrived at New York.

When visiting the clinic at the German hospital at Philadelphia, I, with other visiting surgeons, principally Americans or German-Americans, was invited to tea and cake, or cake and beer, in the reception-room of the hospital.

As the day was very hot we all drank iced German lager beer, and, when leaving the room, were presented with a gilt "wish-bones" holding ribbons of the German national colours.

All of the American and German-American doctors wore the ribbons on their coats, but I put mine in my pocket as a curio. I could not wish to be thought to have German sympathies, although I had drunk their lager beer. In Now Zealand the Germans have never been appreciated as they have been in England. Perhaps the air of the Pacific gives one a truer perspective of some things as they are.

At New York I delayed sailing two days, in order to avoid a German boat, and reached England by the Holland-American boat *Rotterdam* in July. We had on board the *Rotterdam* a very large number of Germans, and as usual they were chiefly noticeable for their great prowess at meals, and for their noisy method of eating. They drank much "good German beer" and filled the rooms with German smoke and German gutturals. They are not attractive fellow-travellers.

On arriving in England I proceeded to Aberdeen, where the annual meeting of the British Medical Association was being held, and to which I was a delegate.

At Aberdeen we had a very large number of foreign surgeons and physicians and men from nearly every part of the world. As usual there were many Germans and a few Austrians.

We were struck by a very curious incident towards the end of the meeting—last day of July. The president of the Association, Sir Alexander Ogston, gave a reception to all the delegates from the British kindred and affiliated associations, and to the foreign representatives. Although the German and Austrian had been about in. the morning, not one was present at the evening reception. They had all departed silently, and had said goodbye to no one.

Germany and Austria had sent out their messages, and the medicals returned with all speed.

We were then, on the eve of war, but none of us at Aberdeen thought that we would be in it, or that we were then rushing swiftly to great events.

The Austrian note to Serbia was being discussed. Germany's action was doubtful. Russia plainly said that she would not stand by and tamely see Serbian Slavs humiliated by their powerful neighbours. In spite of the cloudiness of the political atmosphere and the slight oppressiveness none really expected lightning and thunder, or that any spirit would

In these confines with a monarch's voice
Cry Havoc! and let slip the dogs of war.

On the 3rd August Sir Edward Grey, in the House of Commons, in a serious speech, reviewed the European situation. With convincing eloquence he showed how anxiously he had striven to maintain peace, and exactly defined England's attitude in certain possible contingencies.

The excitement all over the country was tremendous. The air was electrical with coming events, a spark would set the firmament ablaze. One could almost see the peoples of Russia, Germany, Austria, France, Belgium and Serbia gaze questioningly, anxiously, across the Channel at the Island Kingdom, and wondering in that tense moment, What would England do?

Then flaring headlines in the press told that Liége, the great eastern fortress and arsenal of Belgium, had been furiously bombarded by the

German artillery, and that Bethmann-Hollweg, the German Chancellor, had declared that a solemn treaty guaranteeing the neutrality of Belgium was of no more value than a scrap of paper.

Then England declared war against Germany, and on the 4th of August we knew that England was to take her place in the titanic world-war and step into the all-engulfing struggle.

So here it was at last. War with Germany! The restrained hostility of years was now no longer concealed, the long-pent-up passions were now let loose. Men seemed to breathe easier, and an air of relief pervaded the country.

England was like a sick man after a consultation with the surgeons. He looks eagerly and anxiously at the surgeons, hoping that no operation may be necessary, but dreading and expecting that it may. Once told by them that an operation is necessary in order that he may live, his doubts and hesitation disappear, and he agrees to submit and to undergo the drastic measures and emerge a strong and whole man. There is a relief that he has decided and the mind becomes tranquil.

The gravity of the issue was realised in England in those early August days. Those entitled to speak with authority pronounced that the war would be a big war—the greatest since the beginning of time—and that the men and women of our day and generation would have to pass through sorrow and tribulation and wade through dark and troubled waters before the end would be finally achieved.

The justness of England's quarrel was everywhere acknowledged, except in the land of the enemy, and the exposure of the tortuous and insidious German diplomacy stirred up the English sense of straight dealing and fair-play.

On 6th August I motored down from the Highlands to Edinburgh, through the Pass of Killiecrankie and some of the loveliest scenery in Scotland.

Everywhere were signs of mobilisation. Khaki soldiers and "mufti" recruits at every depot and around recruiting sergeants. The price of petrol had suddenly risen—why, nobody quite knew, but somebody was making money out of it, we were sure. At one town I paid ten shillings for a two-gallon tin.

In the evening I reached Queensferry, but was not allowed to cross at that hour. As the ferry would not be going again till next morning I motored back to Dunfermline, and having stopped the night there, returned early in the morning to the ferry. This time I got across with my car. The Firth of Forth presented a very busy scene that morning.

Torpedo boats and naval craft of all sorts and sizes were dashing about, and in the distance were the large dark outlines of big ships of war.

From Queensferry a rapid run brought me to Edinburgh, where the whole talk in hotel smoking-rooms, at table, and on the street, was of war. The kilted soldier was looked at with more interest as he walked the streets, and appeals were placarded on every prominent place for new recruits.

The morning papers announced that the House of Commons had passed a war vote of one hundred million pounds, and that Kitchener had asked for five hundred thousand men to join the army.

The Cabinet, like a good physician, was giving the nation its medicine in small doses during these early days. Doctors will tell you that small doses frequently repeated are so much better than a big dose taken at one wry mouthful, for a big heroic dose taken at one gulp often causes nausea. The hundred million pounds and the five hundred thousand men made the first teaspoonful of the national physic which was to help get rid of the fatty degeneration and change our sleeping, sluggish strength into the crouch and spring and hit of the prize fighter.

Next day I took train for London in order to offer my medical service to the War Office. There was an urgent demand for surgeons to volunteer for active service, and at this particular juncture good surgeons who were free to go were not very plentiful. As I was on a tour of surgical clinics at this time I decided to do my bit for the country and the men in the field. Having nothing to do when I reached London that evening, I strolled into a music hall and heard "God Save the King," "Rule, Britannia," the "*Marseillaise*," the Russian, Belgian, and Serbian national hymns—all blared out to cheering and shouting crowds, who seemed to thoroughly enjoy "being at war." It was reminiscent of the days of the Boer War in 1899:

'*Alea jacta est*'—The die is cast.

Early next day I visited the Medical Department of the War Office at Whitehall, and volunteered as a surgeon with the Expeditionary Army to France. Two days afterwards the War Office sent me a note requesting me to call at the office and be examined to see if I was physically fit. So I did. The physical examination was carried out with amazing celerity, and I was handed on as "fit." The genial old army doctor appointed for this duty of examining his younger colleagues made his diagnosis on sight almost, and toyed easily with his stethoscope while he inquired about the state of the teeth and the digestion.

I was then ushered into another office and was duly appointed a Temporary Lieutenant in the Royal Army Medical Corps.

All the civilian surgeons accepted for service with the army—with the exception of a few consulting surgeons—were given the rank of Temporary Lieutenant. Seniority or special skill or previous war experience mattered nothing. I had already served as a Civil Surgeon, attached to the Royal Army Medical Corps during the South African War, and had a medal and four clasps from that campaign, and since that period had been surgeon to an important hospital in New Zealand, and was a retired captain in the New Zealand Medical Corps. That, however, did not entitle me to hold any higher rank than the young medical man who had completed his medical training only a week ago. Many able medical men all over the country had voluntarily left lucrative practices and important surgical and medical staff appointments in big London and provincial hospitals and were enrolled as Lieutenants in the Royal Army Medical Corps, on the same footing as junior medical men who had perhaps been their pupils but a few weeks before. We all ranked below the regular officers of the Royal Army Medical Corps. Volunteers for combatant commissions who had had previous experience were given rank accordingly.

Some discrimination was made in the combatant arm, and rightly so. No discrimination was made in the medical service, and undoubtedly that was a mistake. The same lack of organised control was exhibited at every turn in the medical service. Men with imperfect professional skill and experience were given duties which should have been entrusted only to men fully possessed of those qualifications. This criticism is not merely a destructive one. Criticism is absolutely necessary at certain times, and there are some mistakes in policy which should be freely ventilated. This same policy was pursued by the Army Medical Department during the South African War, and was very openly discussed. This led to drastic changes in the organisation of the Royal Army Medical Corps, following on the Commission of Inquiry set up by Mr. Brodrick (later Lord Midleton). In this war, I regret to say, the old leaven has again appeared, and its re-appearance has aroused considerable comment and been a cause of inefficiency.

After having been given my commission I was told to procure a uniform—Sam Browne belt, a revolver, blankets, and other campaigning kit—and to be prepared to move in forty-eight hours. With great difficulty I managed to get some sort of equipment together. The military tailors were working at high pressure, and when asked to make a coat or breeches in a certain time simply said, "It can't be done." By skilful diplomacy I got a coat in one place, a pair of riding breeches in another, *puttees* at another, leggings elsewhere, and so on. One could not then obtain khaki shirts or ties in London. I did not get a revolver, although this was on the list of things necessary. Neither did I purchase a sword. Why a medical officer should be asked to carry a sword and a revolver, and at the same time wear a Red Cross brassard on the left arm, I am at a loss to understand. I have asked many senior medical officers of what use a revolver and sword were to a doctor on active service, and the only reply I could get was that they were useful to defend the wounded.

It would have been much more sensible for the War Office to tell each medical officer to get several pairs of rubber gloves for dressings and operations. I sometimes wondered if the War Office expected the surgeons to perform amputations with a sword. However, I did not get a revolver, and I did not get a sword. Later on, in France, I have seen mild-looking young surgeons arrive at the front armed to the teeth, with swords, revolvers and ammunition, clanking spurs, map cases, field-glasses and compasses strung all round them, and on their left arm the brassard with the Red Cross. We called them "Christmas trees."

At last my equipment was complete, and I received orders to go to Aldershot and report to the Assistant Director of Medical Services for duty.

I was now a "Surgeon in Khaki" and part of that great military hammer—the British Expeditionary Force.

When I arrived at Aldershot the town seemed deserted. The majority of the big barracks were empty. We were told that the British Army had just left for the Continent, and that the Aldershot command, under General Haig, had gone to a man. Aldershot was rapidly preparing to receive and train recruits, mobilise reinforcements, and keep up a steady flow of men to replace casualties. This was great news. When we left London we did not know that the British Expeditionary Army had gone.

The A.D.M.S. (Assistant Director of Medical Services) put me on duty at the Cambridge Military Hospital at Aldershot, while awaiting orders for the front. Several surgeons awaiting orders were already here, and we all billeted at the Victoria Hotel. We were soon at work examining and passing recruits, inoculating troops against typhoid, and vaccinating all who had no conscientious objections. Some had "conscientious" objections to inoculation. Soldiers should not be allowed liberty of conscience in these matters. They should be made immune against typhoid and smallpox at "the word of command" in spite of the screechings of fanatics suffering from distorted cerebration.

Our duty at the recruiting depots was a very amusing one. We here came in contact with the first hopefuls of Kitchener's new army. The first call to arms generally brings in a very motley crowd. The best of the recruits do not turn up during the first few days, as these have generally some domestic or business matters to arrange. It was the "First Footers" we got in these days at Aldershot.

Another medical officer and myself took over one depot. We arrived at 8.30 a.m. Standing in a straggling two-deep line before the depot door were about three hundred men of the most variegated texture—some lean, some fat, some smart, some unkempt, but all looking very cheerful and hopeful. A smart R.A.M.C. sergeant is waiting at the door with a list of their names. It is our duty to examine physically this first batch of three hundred, to see if they are fit enough to train to fight Germans. Ten men are marched into the depot. Each doctor takes five at a time. At the word of command they strip and the doctor begins. He casts a professional eye rapidly over the nude recruit. A general look like this to a trained eye conveys a lot. The chest is examined, tongue, mouth, and teeth looked at. The usual sites for rupture are examined. About three questions are asked: "Any previous illness?" "Age?" "Previous occupation?" A mark is placed against the name, the nude Briton is told to clothe himself, and the examination is over.

It is done at express speed, and although the examination is not very thorough it is sufficient to enable an experienced man to detect most physical defects. If a man passed, he was put down for foreign service. Some had slight defects and were put down for home defence. Some had glaring defects and were turned down altogether. We had all sorts of derelicts turn up. One weary-looking veteran, unwashed and with straw sticking in his hair, indicative of a bed in a haystack the previous night, was blind in one eye and very lame. A draper's assistant from a London shop had a twisted spine, an old soldier had syphilitic ulcers on the legs, some had bad hearts from excessive smoking, some bad kidneys from excessive drinking, some young men were really sexagenarians from hard living, and so on. They were old men before their time. The occupations of our recruits were as diverse as their shapes and constitutions—a runaway sailor, a Cockney coster, a draper's assistant, a sea cook, a medical student, a broken-down parson, an obvious gaolbird, and a Sunday-school teacher.

Cook's son, duke's son, son of a belted earl,
Son of a Lambeth publican, they're all the same today.

Before the doctor the son of a prize fighter makes a better showing than the son of a consumptive bishop. We had orders not to be too strict with our physical examination. We were not to turn a man down if he could be usefully employed in any State service during the war. For instance, many of the "weeds" amongst the young men, the cigarette victims, the pasty-faced, flat-chested youths, those who had lived down dark alleys and in unhygienic surroundings all their lives, were all capable of being made into better men. Regular meals, plain food, good quarters, baths, cleanliness and hard work, marching, drilling and gymnastics, made these slouching, dull-eyed youths into active, smart men. They then held their heads up, breathed the free air, lost their sullenness, and became cheerful. Some of the recruits were not fit to be made into soldiers, and work could always be found for them. There are so many openings for the willing man at this time, be it cook's assistant, mess servant, officer's servant, orderly, or bootmaker's help.

It was always an interesting sight to see the sergeant and corporal drill these clumsy recruits, and show them how to walk, and where to place their feet. The army drill sergeant has a very caustic wit and a wonderful fund of cutting comments. He knows his audience well, and with a few crisp epithets can galvanise a sluggish recruit or a slouching company into something instinct with alertness.

On 21st August, six surgeons, including myself, were ordered to hold ourselves in readiness for service abroad. We were told to overhaul our kits thoroughly, think out all necessary things, and not to have any excessive baggage. None of us had. The Wolseley valise held our little all.

The last goodbyes were said, and at 4 p.m. we entrained at Aldershot for our journey to "somewhere in France." We were all very glad to be off. We were all very curious to see and take part in the romance and adventures of the great battles that we knew would be sure to take place.

Romance! Adventure! Very soon we were up against cold facts, and there was no romance or pomp and circumstance then.

CHAPTER 2

Le Havre and Harfleur

At 12 p.m. we detrained at Southampton, hungry and thirsty. Owing to lack of foresight we had had nothing to eat since breakfast. The night was a beautiful one, and a voyage across channel sounded very inviting. We marched our 350 R.A.M.C. orderlies on to our transport, the *Braemar Castle*, and the officers tried to find a place to sleep. We managed to get some corners in the smoking-room, and curled up as best we could in the cramped places. The ship was packed full of troops, and we learned that we were the first reinforcements for the Expeditionary Army. We had two generals on board and the head-quarter staff of a new division. Our destination was to be Le Havre. At 2 a.m. we steamed out, followed by several other transports crowded with soldiers. Torpedo-boat destroyers kept watchful eyes on us across channel, and twice a huge searchlight played all round us from far out at sea. The navy was watching on the deep waters.

The soldiers on board slept on the deck, on hatches, anywhere, and they were all up and cheerfully carolling at dawn. When a soldier wakes his first thought is for food, and at 5 a.m. they were all discussing bully beef and biscuits. The ship's cook had prepared cauldrons of tea,—and Tommy loves tea. One wag after breakfast stood on a hatch reciting, "Dearly beloved brethren, the Scripture moveth us in sundry places," to a congregation of grimy-faced soldiers.

At 12.30 midday we sighted Le Havre, and in two hours were tied alongside the wharf. The disembarkation rapidly followed, and at 4 p.m. we were on the march through Le Havre to our encampment. As we steamed into Le Havre there was a scene of the wildest enthusiasm, and the whole harbour front was a mass of cheering men and women and children. "*Vive l'Angleterre!*" "*Vive Tommy!*" "*Vive l'entente cordiale!*" Flags and handkerchiefs were waved from every window, and the picture of enthusiastic welcome was most inspiring. Our men seemed to thoroughly enjoy it, and cheered and yelled their throaty greetings as loudly and as heartily as the French. One would call in a bull voice, "Are we downhearted?" and the reply, "No" from thousands of throats, echoed and reverberated over the sea front.

Then would come a piping voice, "Do we like beer?" followed by a unanimous roar of "Yes." The French welcome was a spontaneous and enthusiastic one, and Le Havre, gay with bunting and twined flags, shouted itself hoarse that day. I visited Le Havre some months later and saw a crowded British transport arrive. There was no cheering, no flags, no excitement. At the wharf was a big hospital ship, and wounded soldiers were being carried aboard by stretcher-bearers. The French had, since August, passed through some days of disappointment and despair, and the German was still in France. The frenzied ecstasy of that welcome of August, the gifts of flowers, of fruit, of wine were no longer there, but deep down there was still the same welcome, unspoken but warm and sincere.

A dusty march of eight miles on a hot, blistering road brought us to our camp at Harfleur. We were indeed on historic ground. Close by were the remains of the old Castle of Harfleur that Henry V. and his men-at-arms stormed in the long ago.

On this same field Henry is said to have addressed his soldiers:

And you good yeomen,
Whose limbs were made in England, show us here
The mettle of your pasture; let us swear
That you are worth your breeding.

It was on this field and at that time that old Bardolph said:

Would I were in an alehouse in London.
I would give all my fame for a pot of ale and safety.

So here again, in the twentieth century, were some thousands of good yeomen whose limbs were made in England, and a pot of ale would have been relished by all, for the day had been a thirsty one.

Our arrival at camp was not expected. The commandant seemed very surprised to see us, but told us to make ourselves at home. We had no kits, no blankets, no tents, no food—all had been left on the wharf—and no hot water was procurable. We made a meal off our "iron rations," which consist of a small waterproof cover holding a tin of bully beef, biscuits, pepper and salt and tea. Pipes were lit and we then lay down as we were, under the lee of a haystack, and slept till bugle-call, when we awoke, cold and damp with dew. The nights were very cold at this time and the days terribly hot.

The camp at Harfleur had about five or six thousand men, composed of representatives of all arms of the service—Highlanders, Guardsmen, Engineers, and details from dozens of other regiments. We were reinforcements. Rumours were coming through at this time that all Was not well with our army, and we were disquieted to hear that it was being steadily pushed back and fighting desperately. The retirement of our army occasioned anxiety at Le Havre, our principal base at that time, and the reinforcements at Harfleur could not be joined up till the position became clearer.

At Harfleur we got little authentic news. We lived on rumours, and some of these were of the most extraordinary kind. There was one rumour that came through, and the Tommies fully believed it. It was said that the Germans cut off the right hand of every captured stretcher-bearer, and killed every prisoner of the combatant rank. Our men were quite determined to die fighting, and the stretcher-bearers asked for guns. The day after our arrival in camp we were given tents, and these were pitched in the morning. Twelve men were put to each tent, but blankets were few and we could only give four blankets to each tent. Next day the tents were struck and packed away for some unknown reason, and that night we all had to sleep in the open. The officers' kits arrived on the second day, and on the fourth day we were told to take from them only what was absolutely necessary.

It was said that our kits were to be either packed away or burned. It was said also that the whole camp equipment, tents, blankets, etc., were to be burned. Later in the day this order was countermanded and we again took possession of our kits. We guessed from all these various orders that the position at the front was uncertain, and, as history has since shown, such was the case. On our fourth day at Harfleur a flying man arrived in his aeroplane from England, and we all crowded round to know what the latest news was. He had none to give, but told us that he had flown over a part of the German army. I think that he brought some important information, for that afternoon the whole camp was set to work digging trenches right across the front of the camp. We had more rumours of "tremendous British losses," "breakdown of French mobilisation," "stubborn fighting," but nothing authentic reached us.

However, work proceeded feverishly in the camp. Harfleur was on

A ROAD OBSTRUCTION NEAR HARFLEUR.

HARFLEUR—OUR SLEEPING QUARTERS.

the main road leading from the north to Le Havre. It was said that the Germans were advancing, and this was true. A raiding force of 20,000 men—one German division—of cavalry, gunners, and infantry—the latter on fast motor-lorries—was certainly moving on Le Havre, and the intention was to destroy the British base depot, burn our huge stores, and capture and sink all the shipping and blow up the railways. Our camp was to delay this raid till the French could move up some divisions. Accordingly, lines of trenches were dug across the turnip fields and meadows. The farmhouses were surrounded by trenches and put into a state of defence. The doctors and stretcher-bearers were ordered to occupy an orchard about 500 yards in rear of the trenches. There was an extraordinary resemblance between one old farmhouse adjoining the camp and the famous farmhouse of Hougoumont at Waterloo. There was an old chapel in the centre of the farm, near to the big two-storied stone dwelling. Behind the chapel were the wine cellars and stables.

To the right of the house was a long orchard surrounded by a stone wall about 5 feet high. The farmhouse and farmyard were surrounded by a high stone wall. Also there was a big gateway as at Hougoumont. Inside and lining the stone walls were tall pine trees. Our men soon began to make some alterations in the quaint old Norman place. The lower branches of the trees were lopped off. Trenches were made inside the stone wall and stones were pulled out of the base for loopholes for rifles, so that our men could lie in the ditch and fire through the bottom of the wall. The same thing was done in the orchard, and men of the Rifle Brigade were told off to line its walls when the time came. This farm, if exposed to artillery, of course would have been a death-trap, but against infantry or cavalry would have been a very hornet's nest for the enemy to attack. The gateways were pulled down, barricades were placed across the gaps, and machine-guns controlled the angles and were able to sweep the open spaces, should a rush be made, with a hail of lead.

All was ready for a second Hougoumont, and the picture was completed by the old farmer's wife, who was ordered to leave the farm, but who firmly refused to budge. Had the Germans come, like her ancient prototype on that June day at Waterloo, she would most likely have taken shelter at the foot of the cross in the chapel.

But the Germans did not come, and history is deprived of a moving and stirring story.

It was tragic but ludicrous to see the blank despair and consternation on the face of the old farmer when we started to lop down some of his trees, dig trenches round his farm and through his turnip fields. Knowing very little about the war, and only vaguely interested in the invasion of France, he was deeply concerned about his turnips and his trees. Everything, however, was put right for him before we left.

When all our preparations for defence were complete two German aeroplanes passed over us going towards Le Havre. Here they were fired on, and they then returned to have a further look at Harfleur and circled slowly over our camp. As we had no aircraft guns they descended fairly low, and I think must have seen everything there was to see. We had field-glasses out and could easily discern the black cross painted on the wings of the Taube.

So there we were in our trenches commanding the roads to Le Havre, with a Hougoumont and an orchard, and stone walls lined with riflemen. History, so far, has not recorded how we "held the gate" to Le Havre without firing a shot and without losing a man, but I am sure that it was our preparations, seen by the enemy aeroplanes, that deterred the Germans from coming on. It was a raiding German force, and a raiding force has no time to tackle defences and strongly held positions. A brigade of French cavalry moved across our front and rode as a big cavalry screen towards the advancing raiders. Fifteen thousand French troops followed them; and when twelve miles from our camp the Germans turned back, the menace was over, and we breathed again.

A fast scouting motorcar containing three Prussian officers ran headlong into a barricade cleverly placed across a road about ten miles from Harfleur. A ditch, broad but shallow, was made across the road near a curve, and artfully concealed with gravel laid on thin planking across the top. The car rushed right on to this and was upset. Some concealed French cavalry then rode up and captured the party.

The French officer who made the capture told me that the German officers were livid with anger when he and his men rode up with drawn sabres. One of the German officers had a revolver in his hand, which he flung violently at the head of the chauffeur.

This defence of the road at Harfleur was one of those minor incidents of the war which has been forgotten or ignored in the swirl of the big happenings at that time. The situation of Le Havre and Harfleur was then one of grave peril and gave rise to considerable anxiety. One need not have been on the spot to grasp the dangerous possibilities. Our defence of Harfleur ended tamely. We were told one day that Lord Kitchener was at Le Havre and had ordered the evacuation of the big base by the British. That night we were ordered by our commandant to strike the camp, move into Le Havre, and embark on transports for a destination unknown.

The day before we left Le Havre some British stragglers from our retreating army turned up in camp. About twenty-five dirty, grimy, footsore men, with unkempt hair and stubbly beards, wandered in and told us that they had lost their regiments and their way after Mons. Since then they had been gipsying through France towards the coast. Sometimes they got a lift on a farmer's cart, but mostly they walked. They said that the French people had treated them very well, and they certainly did not look hungry. As usual, they told most harrowing tales. One man said that the whole army had been captured by an army of twenty million Germans!

On the morning of our last day at Harfleur we were all thrilled by the visit of a German spy. I have said previously that when the trenches were being dug at Harfleur the medical detachment was sent to an orchard in the rear. A road led past the gate of this orchard. At the gateway we had two of our men on sentry-go. Farther down the road was a French sentry with a fixed bayonet. At 3 a.m. a powerful two-seater automobile dashed up this road and pulled up at the gateway. The driver had on a heavy khaki motor overcoat and a khaki cap. His face was muffled in a khaki scarf. An officer, also in khaki, stepped out and began questioning our men at the gate. He asked how many men were in the camp; were there any big guns, and where were they? Had any ammunition been brought up that day? Our sentries were heavy north countrymen, recently enlisted, and did not tumble to the fact that it was an unusual thing for a British officer to put such questions to a private on sentry-go. The officer then got on his car and went back in the direction of Le Havre. We were all agreed that the strange officer was a spy dressed up to look like a British officer. The French told us that Le Havre was full of spies at this time, and that they had made many arrests of suspects.

CHAPTER 3

From Le Havre to the Bay of Biscay

We knew that serious events must have happened when K. of K. had personally visited Le Havre and had ordered its evacuation. It was Napoleon who said that it was a disastrous thing to attempt to change an army's base during the actual progress of a war. But in this war old maxims and trite sayings go by the board. Anyone having the most elementary knowledge of war, and what an army in the field signifies, will agree that even if changing a base may not lead to disaster, it is nevertheless a very formidable and a very risky move. Le Havre at this time was a huge base from which our army in the field was receiving its supplies. Transports conveying all the necessaries for a fighting army unloaded their cargoes on its wharves.

From there the supplies were sent by train to the advanced base in the centre of France, and from there onward to the various refilling stations. The destruction of Le Havre, or its temporary loss as a base, would have been a calamity. The army would have ceased to receive food, waggons, ammunition and equipment, guns, horses, forage, reinforcements, hospital supplies, etc. An army without ammunition and food is no longer of any fighting value. Think also of the quantities of material necessary to supply an army of 70,000 men, and this will give some idea of the immense war depot Le Havre was at this time. Circumstances must have indeed been serious to have necessitated a change of base. It meant also that the railway arrangements so carefully thought out, and which had so far been in operation, would have to be suddenly changed. Supply trains would have to be sent to the front from some other base, and returning empty supply trains and hospital trains would have to be diverted from Le Havre to the place chosen as the future base. The task was a gigantic one, and was rendered more so because it had to be completed in a hurry.

We reached Le Havre from Harfleur in the late afternoon. A large convoy of Belgian ambulances full of wounded was moving through the streets towards the wharves, and a French Infantry Division passed us in full panoply of war going east. Six large transports with steam up were lying at the wharves. The wharves were a scene of unparalleled activity, and when one got right down amidst this activity and looked around, one could realise that things were very chaotic. Every one was shouting and cursing; contradictory orders were given; some stores which had just been loaded in one of the holds of one transport were being again unloaded. Through careless handling a huge crate of iron bedsteads for a military hospital fell into the sea between the ship and the wharf. But as the stores were government property—therefore nobody's property—no one seemed to mind very much. The stage between the ship and the big sheds was packed with all sorts of goods in inextricable confusion. Here were bales of hospital blankets dumped on kegs of butter, there boxes of biscuits lying packed in a corner, with a forgotten hose-pipe playing water on them.

Inside the sheds were machine-guns, heavy field pieces, ammunition, some aeroplanes, crowds of ambulance waggons, London buses, heavy transport waggons, kitchens, beds, tents for a general hospital, stacks of rifles, bales of straw, mountainous bags of oats, flour, beef, potatoes, crates of bully beef, telephones and telegraphs, water carts, field kitchens, unending rolls of barbed wire, shovels, picks, and so on. All had been brought into the sheds and left there in a higgledy-piggledy fashion. An Army Service man was trying in despair to get some forage on board; a colonel of the Medical Staff was trying to get his Base Hospital on board. There was apparently no single brain in control, and the loading of the ships went on in the most extraordinary way. Things nearest the ship's side were put in first. Part of a Base Hospital was put in with part of a battery, followed by bundles of compressed straw fodder and boxes of soap.

The transport *Turcoman* was full of troops. There seemed to be thousands of them on board, and the decks were packed with men. On walking up the gangway I was met by the officer commanding the troops, and he told me that I could not be allowed on board with any men as the ship was already overcrowded. I told him that my orders were to embark on the *Turcoman*, but the reply, "Very sorry indeed, but it can't be done," settled the matter.

So I descended, and with difficulty picked my way along another wharf and found another transport, the *Cestrian*, also a centre of the same scene of bustle and activity as the *Turcoman*. The *Cestrian* was crowded with soldiers, and was being frantically loaded up with all sorts of goods, from aeroplanes to bandages.

I got my men on board and told them to make themselves as comfortable as they could on deck, and after some searching round at last found a corner of the smoking-room which would serve me for a bed for the night. Here my servant dumped down my valise.

I was unable to find out the destination of the *Turcoman*; nobody seemed to know, but there were rumours that it was to be "somewhere in the Bay of Biscay." Nobody knew where the *Cestrian* was going. As my orders were to travel by the Turcoman, and as I was really on the *Cestrian*, I was anxious to find out if the destination of the two boats was to be the same port. But nobody could tell me, so I lit my pipe of tobacco, leaned over the ship's side, and never troubled any more about my orders. I really did not know whether the *Cestrian* was going to England or another part of France, or the Black Sea for that matter.

The scene on the *Cestrian* was a strange one. It was now quite dark and the loading of the cargo was carried out under electric flares. There were on board 2600 soldiers and 600 horses. These unfortunate horses had been put on board twenty-four hours before the troops embarked, instead of the other way about, and the smell from the hot, stifling horse-boxes was overpowering. Why these poor beasts were not embarked last of all, was a mystery. Imagine 600 horses cooped up in narrow boxes during a long, hot, stifling summer day, when they could easily have been kept at the horse depot close by till the last minute!

One horse died before we started, and was slung out by ropes on to the wharf.

This horse episode was the occasion of much scathing comment amongst senior officers and old cavalry and artillery non-coms.

It is a pity that some of the higher command—those responsible—could not have heard the remarks of these knowing old non-commissioned officers.

At last the ship's holds were full. Gangways were up and we dropped slowly down the locks to the Seine mouth, and so out into the Channel. We were met by a fierce, gusty head wind and welcomed it for the horses' sakes. Large wind ventilators were arranged to allow the fresh air to reach the horse-boxes.

Our men slept on the decks, and there were so many of them that to step one's way over them would have been almost impossible.

The dining-rooms, cabins, and smoking-rooms were full of sleeping or dozing officers. I managed to commandeer an old sofa cushion, and lay on that in the corner of the smoking-room and went to sleep, and dreamt of thousands of horses looking reproachfully at me out of boxes.

At break of day we were all up at bugle-call and soon washed. The ship's cook was a man of some eminence in his profession, for he had provided porridge and milk, ham and eggs, bread and butter and tea for our breakfast, and, filled with amazement, we sat round to enjoy it. Generally of meals on a transport there are none. A big cruiser was seen after breakfast to be bearing rapidly down on us, and the usual "optimist" present, after carefully observing her through a telescope, pronounced her nationality as German, and that it was now a watery grave in the Bay of Biscay for 2600 men and 600 horses. As she came nearer we showed our flag, and she displayed the French ensign. We gave her our number and dipped our bit of bunting, and the great ironclad sheered off. It was a relief to know that she was about, and looking after our transports.

On the way out from Le Havre we passed the United States battleship *Tennessee*, and our men seeing some of her sailors standing in a group gazing at us, gave a cheer and the usual "Are we downhearted? No!" greeting. The American sailors gave a real good hearty cheer, and yells of "good luck"; but an officer then ran up to them and said something, and they became suddenly silent, and only waved their hands. They had probably been told by their officer that they were "neutrals," and belonged to the battleship of a nation friendly to all the belligerents. But we knew that they were with us "inside," and anyhow the Americans have not been neutral in their hearts. They are all "for us" and "for the Allies."

Life on board our transport was uneventful. We smoked and slept and ate. There was no room to walk about. I never saw such a crowded ship.

We had on board the complete personnel of a Base Hospital, and the medical officer commanding told me that he had orders to pitch his hospital at once at Nantes in order to take in wounded, as there was a big demand for more beds. In spite of his utmost endeavours he could not get his hospital equipment on the *Cestrian*.

All the instruments, dressings, and X-ray apparatus had been left behind for another boat, and he thought that he might not be able to get them for another week, or perhaps longer.

This was but another example of the lack of control at Le Havre during the change of base; a hospital was badly wanted at Nantes; all the personnel and half the equipment were sent away, and the other half left on the wharves. We learned later that the holds of our boat the *Cestrian* were not full when she left Le Havre, but that she had been ordered to leave on account of the horses being in such a bad state from the hot, stifling atmosphere in their quarters below decks.

It was necessary to proceed to sea to get a current of cold air down the ventilating shafts to the horses' cribs. This senseless blundering over the horses led to the death of several of the poor beasts, and besides crippled a Base Hospital at a time when it was urgently needed. Over and over again during this war one has met with instances of a want of reasoned judgment on the part of senior controlling officers. In certain emergencies they have been unable to "orientate" themselves—to use an Americanism—or to "envisage" a situation.

Blunders, slips, miscalculations, carelessness, in time of war mean the loss of valuable lives. We want alert, clear-brained, thinking men in all responsible posts. If a senior officer shows himself lacking in these essentials—then he must go. Many of the responsible French army officials at the beginning of the campaign proved themselves lacking in initiative and judgment. Joffre sent these officers to "Limoges." We should send our incapables to "Stellenbosch." Both places are indicative of a quiet retirement, where they can live without thinking, where there are quiet clubs, cigars and cocktails, and comfortable chairs for an afternoon nap.

The good ship *Cestrian* was a very fine steamer, but a very dirty one at this epoch. She badly wanted a cleanup. The lavatories and water-closets were indescribably filthy and foul, and acrid ammoniacal fumes permeated the ship. No attempt was made at ordinary cleanliness, and no disinfectants were employed. Words could hardly describe the appallingly filthy state of the urinals and closets. It would have been so very simple to have made things cleaner. A sanitary squad could have been arranged in a few minutes to keep these places tidy and to maintain some control. But what was every one's business was nobody's business, and nothing was done during the three days and nights we were at sea.

As our ship approached the mouth of the Loire we saw three large transports ahead of us and four more were following up behind. We slowly steamed through the narrow lock entrance to St. Nazaire and, af-

Transport "Cestrian" in the Bay of Biscay.

The "Cestrian" at St. Nazaire.

ter the usual delay in getting alongside, finally tied up to the wharf. The day was stiflingly hot and dusty, and we were glad to leave our ship and get on shore. The horses were at once unloaded, and very bad the poor beasts looked. It was pleasant, however, to see them, once they were on land, looking round and neighing with evident pleasure.

The troops were marched out to a large field or a dry salt marsh some few miles out of town. A rest camp or camp for army details was being rapidly arranged, and areas were being marked out for the various units,—gunners, engineers, and infantry regiments, and there was considerable bustle. No tents had yet arrived and the camp was quite exposed. Fortunately, the weather was good and sleeping out was no hardship. I reported my arrival to the camp commandant, and he said that he did not know where I had to go or what I had to do. He told me to "wait round and see what turned up." At this period one's arrival was always unexpected. We always got a smile of welcome and were always told to "wait round." There was never any demonstrative hurry. John Bull on the job doesn't make much fuss. I think that he does not make enough. As there was nothing to do apparently, and as nobody seemed to Want me, I strolled back to the city of St Nazaire and had afternoon tea in a pleasant *café*.

As I was leaving the *café* I met the A.D.M.S. (Assistant Director of Medical Services). He asked me what duty I was on. I told him that I had just arrived and had reported my arrival, and was really wondering myself why I was at St. Nazaire. The A.D.M.S. said, "We are wanting medical officers urgently at the front. Would you please come with me." On our way to the office he explained that "the medical service had received some losses—casualties and missing, that there were a lot of wounded and a lack of hospital necessaries." He asked me if I had any "bandages, wool, or lint with me." I had none, of course, and the A.D.M.S. said that he had none to spare for the front. I thought of the Base Hospital on the *Cestrian* landed with only half its equipment, and of what a wonderful nation we are, and what a magnificent organiser John Bull is when he is really "on the job."

I received written orders from the A.D.M.S. to proceed by train at 4 a.m. next day to Le Mans, and report arrival and await orders there. Le Mans was the "advanced base" of the British Army. I learned here also that our gallant army was retreating towards Paris, and fighting stubbornly against overwhelming numbers of Germans flushed with victory, and I was very glad to get orders to join up with my countrymen and get a chance of "doing my bit" also,

Chapter 4

From the Bay of Biscay to East of Paris

After having received these definite orders I got my kit again conveyed to the *Cestrian* transport and slept that night in my old corner of the smoking-room. At 2.45 a.m. the surgeons detailed to join the army were up. A hasty cup of coffee and an apology for a wash—and we were down the ship-side, and on the way to the *gare*. The railway station at St. Nazaire at this time looked quite picturesque in the early morning. Its platforms were covered with straw, and rows of sleeping French soldiers lay comfortably around, while a stolid Grenadier sentry stood propped against the wall. There is no hurry at a French military station. The train was timed to start at 4 a.m., but that did not matter. At 5 a.m. it was quite ready. "*C'est la guerre.*"

There were five of us travelling together—all medical officers—two Scotchmen, one Irishman, one Englishman, and one New Zealander. A very gruff Railway Transport officer gave me a military pass for the party. This gave us permission, we noticed, to travel to Paris *via* Le Mans. The pass was signed by the French authorities, but we were never asked to show it again. The khaki uniform proclaimed we were British, the Sam Browne belt and stars showed we were officers, and the red-cross brassards on our left arms indicated our particular line of business. As the train moved off we wished our Railway Transport officer—an Englishman—a good morning, but this seemed to offend him, for he glared at us. Our Irish surgeon remarked that all Railway Transport officers were queer fish and very unpopular.

Perhaps their particular specialty makes them so, but I have never heard an R.T.O. referred to in any other but denunciatory terms. A sanguinary adjective is always prefixed to the mystic trinity R.T.O. It is said that they lead unhappy lives and generally die of long, lingering illnesses. We soon settled down comfortably in our luxurious first-class carriage and tried to get to know each other. No very difficult task amongst doctors, who are generally most sociable animals. One of us was a specialist in fevers and had passed most of his days in typhoid and scarlet fever wards. One was a neurologist, with pronounced views on the power of suggestion in treating cases of incipient insanity. One was a pure physician, who said that the surgeons were not men of science but merely craftsmen, and were too fond of using the knife.

The surgeons, as became their calling, treated all criticism with good-humoured complaisance. We talked a lot about the duties of the doctor in this war, and we were all very curious to know the role played by a doctor when he was attached to a cavalry regiment, to a battery, or to a field ambulance. None of us knew very much about it, but we all were agreed that we had somehow to get alongside Mr. Thomas Atkins when he was wounded in battle, get him to a safe place, and give him of our best. Curiously enough, although we were all scattered later on to various units of different divisions, I met all my fellow-travellers again one time or another in the firing line. One of the Scotchmen I met just as he came out from under heavy shrapnel fire, and I asked him how he liked it. His reply is not printable. One I met in a field ambulance later with sleeves rolled up and busy dressing the wounds of a crowd of men just brought in from the firing line. One I met in a town in northern France looking cold and wet and miserable, and asked him also how he liked the war. He gave an expressive shrug. I have not met anyone yet who liked the war, except artillery officers.

Our train travelled slowly from St. Nazaire along the Loire to the capital city of Nantes. This charming city is situated on the banks of the delightful river. We had a lot of khaki and French soldiers on board the train, and as usual they fraternised well together. Tommy Atkins gets on amazingly well with the French *piou-piou*, and the French grenadier chaffs Tommy a lot and enjoys his company. When they get together they exchange caps for a time. This is a sign of unalterable friendship.

To see a French *cuirassier* wearing a khaki cap and a Highlander in kilts wearing a *cuirassier's casque* with its flowing horsetails always excited the merriment and loud "*vives*" of the French people. The kilts of our Highlanders are also greatly admired by the French. They were consumed with curiosity to know if the Scotchmen wore any trousers under them. Khaki was a great novelty along the Loire valley at this time, and our appearance roused tremendous enthusiasm and applause. At Nantes the good people brought us baskets of apples, and little French flags which we duly stuck on our coats or caps and wore till the train steamed out of the station.

Crowds of people rushed down to the railway platform to see us and cheer us on our way. Tommy's "Are we downhearted?" and its stentorian "No!" had a very optimistic sound, and the French liked it.

At Angers the train stopped two hours, and the officers strolled round the town. The men were not allowed off the platform. Angers, the ancient capital of the old Counts of Anjou, is a delightfully sleepy city. A princess of Anjou was in the long ago a Queen of England, and a fine statue to her memory stands in the centre of the town. It was dressed with an intertwined Union Jack and the Tricolour when we were there.

The old castle of Angers, with its deep moat and castellated towers, has withstood the ravages of centuries and is one of the finest examples of mediaeval military masonry. Our walk through this city excited considerable comment and notice. It was Sunday, and a big congregation just leaving church stopped to stare at us and possibly to wonder why khaki was in Angers. As we passed a cafe crowded with, loungers sipping wine and coffee at the little tables on the street, all stood up to look at us. We felt very embarrassed and did not much like the novel experience, so sat round a small table ourselves, and while drinking our wine turned round to look at the people also.

A French colonel caught our eye, and one of our party held a glass towards him, saying, "*Vive la France!*" The effect was theatrical: all jumped up, and lifting their glasses shouted, "*Vive l'Angleterre!*" "*Vive l'entente cordiale!*" Several French, officers and citizens with ladies pulled up their chairs to our table, and we all drank wine very sociably together. One of our party of surgeons had been educated as a youth in Belgium and was an excellent French linguist. The people were all very anxious to hear the latest news. We had none to give except that large British reinforcements were coming over, and that England was now fairly on the job. In these early days of the war, when everything in France was "electrical," such sentiments were always cheerfully received. We drank a good many toasts before we left, and had our photographs taken three times.

Just before the train started crowds of gentlemen and ladies, old and young, shook hands with us in the usual French way, with the left hand as often as the right. One beautiful and sparkling little French lady embarrassed one of us by a sudden warm embrace and a sisterly kiss on the cheek. The surprise of the khaki man was only momentary, and the lady, in return, was well and truly kissed on the lips. We were all sorry to leave Angers, the city was charming, the wine was excellent and the people were most entertaining.

After Angers we had a long and dreary night ride to Le Mans. One curious incident occurred during the night. Our train was pulled into a siding at a small station and held there for three hours. At the end of this time a train, made up of forty-one huge locomotive engines, thundered by at sixty miles an hour going south. We were told that these were Belgian engines sent south to escape capture by the Germans.

In the cold shiver of a dark morning we bundled out at Le Mans, and at once made a dash for the railway buffet and got hot coffee and rolls. I then found my way with some difficulty in the darkness to the quarters of the A.D.M.S., to whom I had to report our arrival. He was in bed when I arrived, but got up and took my report. As usual he was surprised to know we were coming, and our visit was naturally an unexpected pleasure. He told us that we should have gone right on to Paris, as surgeons were badly wanted with the army which was retreating on to Paris. We were always being told that doctors were urgently required and were always delayed. We had definite orders to get out at Le Mans and report. The orders were in writing. No one was more anxious than we were to push rapidly on, and we chafed at the continual delays. The A.D.M.S. could not tell us when we would be able to get away from Le Mans as the train service was erratic. We were advised to "hang about the railway station" till "some train" started for the front. As this was highly unsatisfactory, I tried to find out how matters stood myself.

The stationmaster did not know when a train would start for Paris, as the line was blocked farther on by the military mobilisation. I found out, however, that a supply train conveying provisions and supplies for our men was to leave from Maroc some time during the day. Maroc was a small siding five miles from Le Mans. Here trains were made up for the various Army Corps. Maroc is a desert of sand and a truly desolate spot. We got our kits and a box of medical supplies—obtained with great difficulty at Le Mans—conveyed to this miniature Morocco, and we camped on the sand under the doubtful shade of the only two trees the place possessed, till 4 o'clock that afternoon. The only excitement was seeing a huge locomotive run off the track and block shunting operations for two hours. At last our huge supply train was ready. We all got into an empty guard's van and disposed our valises in the various corners. Two officers of the Royal Flying Corps joined us here and found accommodation in a waggon loaded with bags of wheat. We all clubbed together for mess, and laid in a stock of sardines, bread, butter, and a dozen bottles of red wine and cider. We learned from our flying friends that the army was retiring every day, and was supposed to be making for Paris.

We got some definite news for the first time of our big engagements at Mons, Landrecies, and Le Cateau,[1] and how our army was furiously attacked and compelled to fall back, and that although the retirement at first was precipitate it soon became ordered and steady. We were also told that there were over 15,000 casualties, and that the medical arrangements had quite broken down. However, we had a sublime faith in our own countrymen, and knew that they would come out all right, somehow, somewhere.

At daybreak our train reached Tours, and at Blois we had a welcome wash and a decent cup of coffee. Our quarters in the guard's van had been most cramped and uncomfortable, and we were all anxious to leave the old tortoise of a train. At midday we passed through Orleans, and here French officers told us that the Germans were advancing on Paris, and in spite of prodigious losses were hacking their way through by weight of numbers and numberless batteries of artillery. We were told that the British Army was to form part of the garrison of Paris, that Paris was fully prepared for a long siege, and that President Poincare and the Government were at Bordeaux. All these rumours gave rise to keen discussions, and they certainly helped to while the time away in our dreary old van.

During the night we passed through Paris, and at break of day pulled up at the railway siding of Coulommiers.

The railway siding was full of ambulance trains, British and French. All the trains were frilled with recently wounded men, and we got our first information that we were close to the actual scene of fighting. One French medical officer had rigged up a small dressing station on the station platform. An upturned box held his dressings, instruments, and antiseptics, and he had about twenty-five wounded Frenchmen all round him patiently waiting their turn. Most of them were slight

---
1. *Guns at Le Cateau* by A. F. Becke & C. de Sausmarez is also published by Leonaur.

cases, for the serious ones had already been put aboard the hospital trains.

Coulommiers at this time was the refilling point for the Army Service Corps, and our supply train was emptied here.

Chapter 5

The Advance to the Marne

Coulommiers at this time looked a little bit degage. It had been occupied by the Germans some days previously, and now the British had it. The French inhabitants were in Paris. The narrow old streets looked very cheerful and inviting when I passed through, for our Army Service men had several fires merrily blazing at the side of the pave, and the smell of frying bacon and roasting coffee beans was inviting and appetising. Signs of the German occupation were everywhere apparent. Bound the ashes of their fires in the side streets and square were the charred remains of old and valuable furniture—a carved leg of an old chair, a piece of the frame of a big mirror, a bit of a door, and so on. I think the German soldier enjoyed the novel sensation of cooking his food over burning cabinets and tables and chairs made in the times of the Louis' of France. Our men were extremely careful to avoid damage to French property and made their fires of chopped wood logs. Tommy has good feelings and is always a gentleman, and he genuinely pitied the French in their despoiled towns.

My orders were to report to the principal medical officer of the 5th Division of the 2nd Army. I could not find out where the 5th Division headquarters was, but ascertained that the 2nd Army headquarters was at the small hamlet of Doui, three miles away. My next problem was how to get there with my kit. Luckily, I found a motor-car driver about to start for the headquarters and he offered me a lift. This driver was one of the many gentlemen of leisure who had volunteered for service at the beginning of the war. He took out his own car at first and it broke down during the retreat, so he abandoned it by the roadside and got another car, the driver of which had been killed. We set off from Coulommiers at a rattling pace and passed part of the 3rd Division on the way.

The headquarters of General Smith-Dorrien, the commander of the 2nd Army, was a little cluster of houses by the roadside, and when we arrived the whole staff were standing by the road, while the grooms stood near holding their horses. Smith-Dorrien with another staff officer was poring over a map and indicating some spot on it with his finger. The principal medical officer, Colonel Porter of the Army Medical Staff, now Surgeon-General Porter, was just coming out of a cottage, and I walked up, saluted, and reported my arrival. The colonel gave me a cheery greeting, asked if I had breakfasted, and noticing the South African War ribbon on my tunic, said that as I had seen service before I would soon be quite at home. He asked me where I came from, and when told that it was New Zealand, inquired if the trout-fishing was still good. New Zealand seems to be principally known in England for its excellent trout streams.

I was then told to report to the officer commanding a section of the 15th Field Ambulance, which was lying about 500 yards farther down the road. I reported to Major O——of the Royal Army Medical Corps, who told me that he was waiting to evacuate some wounded to Coulommiers before moving up to rejoin the headquarters of the ambulance which was advancing with the 15th Infantry Brigade. There were sixteen wounded British in a small farmhouse beside the road. They were lying on straw on the floor and the wounds of all of them had been dressed. When I entered they were drinking milk supplied by the old farmer and his wife. This old farmhouse had been occupied by the Germans two days previously, and the old farmer brought me through the house to show what the Huns had done. His two wooden bedsteads had been smashed. All his wife's clothes had been taken out of a chest of drawers and torn up, and the chest had been battered badly with an axe. The windows were broken and two legs of the kitchen table had been chopped off.

An old family clock lay battered in a corner, and an ancient sporting gun was broken in two. The farmer showed me one of his wife's old bonnets which had been thrown into the fire by these lovely Germans and partially burned. Fancy burning an old woman's bonnet! All the fowls and chickens had been killed. Two German soldiers got into the fowlyard and struck all the birds down with their bayonets. A fine Normandy dog lay dead at the garden gate, shot by a German non-commissioned officer because the poor beast barked at him.

The old-fashioned furniture and adornments of the house had been destroyed. All of the pictures were broken except two—one of these was a framed picture of Pope Leo XIII., and the other was one representing the Crucifixion. We guessed that the German troops must have been Bavarians, who are mostly Catholic.

I have described this wrecked home as it was typical of hundreds of others that I have seen in France. It all seemed so stupid, so senseless, so paltry, and mean. Conceive the frightfulness of burning an old lady's bonnet and smashing an old clock that had been in the family's possession for three generations, and had ticked the minutes to the farmer's folk and whose face had been looked at by those long since dead. The old farmer was in tears and very miserable. He said that the German soldiers were very drunk and had brought a lot of bottles of champagne with them, round which they spent a very hilarious night. One of the men had a very fine voice and sang a German drinking song, whilst the others hiccupped the chorus. There were certainly a lot of empty champagne bottles lying about, and I don't think that the old farmer's beverage ever soared above *vin rouge*, so the bottles must have been German loot.

About eleven o'clock, while we were still waiting for returning empty supply waggons to take off our wounded, we heard that some German prisoners were being marched in. This caused some excitement, and, speaking for myself, I was consumed with curiosity to see some specimens of this great German Army and observe what manner of men they were. Under a strong guard of cavalry three hundred prisoners with about ten officers were marched into a field close to our farmhouse. It was laughable to see our old farmer. He rushed frantically up the road, his eyes blazing with excitement and joy, and stood gazing at his country's enemies with an expression of malicious joy and delight.

I was struck with the appearance of these prisoners. They were very tired, absolutely done in, and marched along the road with a most bedraggled and weary step. Were these the men who had goose-stepped through Belgium's stately capital and had pushed the united armies of France and England before them in one of the most rapid marches in history? They were utterly broken down with fatigue, and their famished expression and wolfish eyes betokened the hardships they had recently undergone. When they were halted in the field they simply rolled on to the ground from sheer exhaustion. On looking closer, however, one could see that they were fine soldiers, athletic, well-built, lean, wiry fellows, with shaven heads and prominent features, slim-waisted and broad-shouldered, clothed in smart, well-fitting, bluish-grey uniforms, well-shod with good serviceable boots, each with a light waterbottle clipped to his belt and a haversack over the shoulder; certainly no fault could be found with them as specimens of muscular and active soldiery.

The officers, disdaining to show fatigue, sat by themselves in a group apart and smoked pipes and cigarettes. The famished men were supplied with British bully beef and biscuits, and buckets of water were brought to them for drink. They at once threw off their exhaustion and simply rushed the food. We realised that they had been marched to a stop, and that the commissariat of that particular Army Corps must have broken down. The augury was a good one. Amongst them were some slightly wounded men—principally hand, scalp, and face wounds. These we dressed, and the men seemed very grateful to the medical officers for what was done. One of my men, with a slight shrapnel wound of the wrist, after I had dressed and bandaged it, seized my hand and kissed it. That is the German way, perhaps, but unBritish, and I do not love things German or unBritish today.

One of the men had a slight wound, but a very painful one owing to a small shell splinter sticking on to a nerve. Lieut. M'C—— administered a few whiffs of chloroform while I extracted the fragment of iron. Poor M'C—— remarked to me that this was the first anaesthetic that he had administered during the war, although he had been through the whole retreat from Mons, and that it was for a German. I say poor M'C——; this splendid young doctor was killed later on in Flanders while gallantly attending wounded in the trenches under a hellish shrapnel fire. This group of prisoners belonged to the *Jägers* of the Prussian Guard, one of the best infantry units in the German Army. We were all very pleased that they had been bagged, and I don't think that they worried much about it themselves. The officers, however, seemed very sullen—that also pleased us.

Shortly after the arrival of the Guard *Jägers* some empty motor supply waggons, returning from the front, were stopped. We packed plenty of straw on them and put our wounded British and Germans comfortably on top, and sent them all off to the hospital train at Coulommiers. Then our commanding officer, Major O——, gave the order to our ambulance drivers to harness up the horses and prepare to trek. We knew that our army was making a stand at last, and that the long retreat from Belgium was over.

All the morning heavy firing was heard on our front towards the River Marne, and we were not sure what was happening. We knew that our cavalry was at work somewhere, for the Guard *Jägers* had been bagged by our horsemen, but more than that we did not know. However, we were soon on the road, and following Napoleon's maxim to his generals—always to march on the firing. The roads were terribly dusty, the day was hot and sultry, and a blazing sun beat mercilessly down upon us. We all cursed our caps, and certainly the present khaki cap supplied to our officers and men deserves a curse. It gives no protection to the head or neck in summer, and in rainy weather it is soon soaked.

Marching on foot behind lumbering ambulance waggons on a dusty road, and under a hot sun, is no picnic. Eyes get full of dust, throat gets parched, feet get hot, and the khaki uniform wraps round one like a sticky blanket. So for many miles we marched, and all the time the sound of the guns became more and more distinct and intense. We passed St. Ouen and by St. Cyr, and at 4.30 o'clock we seemed to be in the centre of the artillery thunder area. Great guns were screeching and roaring all round us, and some of the enemy's shells were bursting to our left front near the road along which we were moving. We were then ordered to pull our waggons off the road and bivouac them under a clump of trees near at hand in order to conceal them from enemy aeroplanes, which were hovering high up in the blue.

The reason for at times concealing a Field Ambulance is that when a column is on the march the Field Ambulance has a definite position in the column; generally it is behind the ammunition column. The ambulance waggons, with their big white tented covers and conspicuous red crosses, are often the most prominent features on the road. The enemy flying-man when he sees a Field Ambulance knows that there is at least a brigade consisting of four battalions and an ammunition column in front of it, and he can then direct his gunners to plant their shells in front of the ambulance and so get the ammunition column and the brigade. Hence the necessity for sometimes hiding the whereabouts of a Field Ambulance.

After we had bivouacked, our section cook managed to light a fire in a hollow in a clump of trees, and soon brought us a much-desired mess of fried mutton, good bread and marmalade, and a can of tea. We rushed this as badly as the German prisoners did the bully beef earlier in the day.

It was an odd meal, as we sat by the roadside viewing a desperate artillery duel, and between sips of tea snatching up field-glasses to gaze at the bursting shells on the ridges held by the angry Germans.

Chapter 6

What I Saw of the Battle of the Marne

In a battle one really sees very little and knows very little of what is going on, except in the near neighbourhood. The broad perspective, the great view of a battle, cannot be seen by one pair of eyes. This can only be understood and appreciated afterwards when facts and events are gathered together and dove-tailed to form the battle story. When I was sitting by the roadside on this August afternoon, amidst the crashing and shrieking of the guns, the bursting of the shells, the furious crackling of the rifles, and the snarling notes of the machine-guns, I guessed that a battle was in progress and that we were blazing furiously at an enemy who was blazing furiously back at us. Beyond that, I did not know very much. During the night I learned a good deal more of the day's events. But the whole story was not connected up till many days afterwards. I am quite sure that the people of London knew more about the Battle of the Marne from the war bulletins than I did, although I was one of the humble units present in the actual fighting.

On this sultry summer day our ambulance section was resting by the side of the dusty road that stretched in our rear towards Paris and on our front towards a lovely green valley at the bottom of which meandered the River Marne. It wound its sinuous way from our far right to our near left. Directly before us, and on the distant side of the river, was a steep ridge, part of a low chain of uplands which rolled hazily away to the right and stopped abruptly in clear-cut lines in our front. The road beside which we sat, dipped into the valley and crossed the river on a fine stone bridge and continued through the undulating country beyond to the north. Small villages were scat-

AMBULANCES AT THE MARNE

tered about—Mery to the right, Saccy at the bridgehead, and small clusters of houses and farms on the countryside over the river. Some squadrons of dismounted cavalrymen were standing by their horses in a meadow near the bank of the river. These horsemen had been busy earlier in the day, and had done some hard riding, cutting off stragglers from the retreating German Army Corps. Infantry were hidden from view in the depths of the valley. Batteries on our left were sending a plunging fire of shot and shell on to the ridge and dips beyond the river, and the road leading from the bridge. With a field-glass, moving dots, and what looked like waggons, could be made out on the road and the field alongside. It was on these moving dots that our guns played, and cloud-bursts of earth and dust showed that our gunners had the range beautifully.

General French passed us twice in his limousine car. General Smith Dorrien passed twice—General Sir Charles Ferguson passed—all in motorcars travelling like mad. Gallopers with messages spurred up and down the road. Guns thundered into position, unlimbered and were quickly in action. Infantry marching rapidly passed down the road into the valley where a tornado of rifle-fire was going on. One could make out the distinct note from our own rifles and the muffled one from the more distant German Mausers. Two German shells burst short of the battery on our left and uncomfortably close to us. We were in an odd position for an ambulance—in front of our own battery, which was pelting shot into the Germans and which a German battery was trying to locate. When the enemy shells fell short they fell near us. Our position, however, was a dress circle box seat as a viewpoint, so we stopped where we were. It was not every day that one could look on at a real live battle. Before dusk came on, an aeroplane appeared over the ridge flying towards us, and was shot at by enemy aircraft guns. The shells burst all round it, but it sailed triumphantly through them all, and to our intense relief landed safely in our lines with some valuable information.

I was much interested to see our generals on this day dashing about in powerful automobiles. A general is always interesting at the front, be he a brigadier-general, a general of division, or an army corps general. One gets a fleeting glimpse of a "Brass Hat" in a motorcar and asks, "Who is that?" Someone with a keen eye or a nimble fancy will enlighten. "That's Haig, 1st Corps," or "Smith Dorrien, 2nd Corps," or "Ferguson, 5th Division," "Wonder what's up?" is the next usual query, for a general moving around means that "something's up."

Smith-Dorrien[1] is a general well worth seeing. It was "S.-D." who handled the 2nd Army Corps from Mons during those terrible hard-fought days of the retreat, and he was now commanding the 3rd and 5th Divisions on this day on the Marne, when they forced the passage and deployed on the other side.

When the action was at its hottest and every gun was busy, a car raced up from the valley in a swirling cloud of dust. The brakes were jammed hard down opposite us, the side door opened, and out stepped a well-knit, muscular, lithe figure, looking physically fit, smart, and cool in a well-made khaki uniform and redbanded cap. The face was a burnt-brick red, the moustache white, the eyes alert, wide open, and "knowing." A savage, obstinate, determined chin dominated the face. It was the chin of a strong, stubborn nature, the chin of a prize fighter. This was Smith-Dorrien, the commander of the 2nd Army Corps, and at this moment the 2nd Corps were at grips with the enemy. With a few rapid strides he had reached the battery on our left, asked some question of the battery commander, and at once clapped field-glasses to his eyes and gazed long and intently at a spot on the other side of the valley pointed out to him by the battery commander.

Our party of officers, filled with curiosity, also got out field-glasses and focused in the same direction. Our shells could be seen bursting on a far ridge, and after a long stare we managed to make out what we thought were some guns, but we were not sure. A few more words to the battery commander, a careless salute, and Smith Dorrien was back in his car, which was rapidly turned and disappeared "eyes out" down the dusty road up which it had but just come.

As the car disappeared a tremendous rifle-fire broke out all along the valley beyond the stream. It made one's pulses beat with excitement. The 2nd Army Corps was fighting hard in the valley at our feet, and Smith-Dorrien was down in the valley with his men.

When the devil's din was at its loudest, another powerful Limousine coming from the rear pulled up opposite us. "Go on, go on," shouted a voice from the inside, and the car again sped on. Inside was Field-Marshal Sir John French[2] poring over a map held out with both hands over his knees. His car also disappeared into the valley, and we again surmised that there must be some big thing going on down below to draw thither field-marshals, corps commanders, and divisional

---

1. The autobiography *Smith-Dorrien* by Horace Smith-Dorrien is also published by Leonaur.
2. *1914* by Sir John French is also published by Leonaur.

generals.

An hour elapsed. All of the batteries except one had ceased fire, the cracking of our rifles was still heavy but more distant, and now two cars were seen coming slowly towards us from out the valley. In the front car were French and Smith-Dorrien. We augured that all was well, for the car was proceeding slowly, and the field-marshal was placidly smoking a cigar. Our augury was correct. We had forced the passage of the Marne, and were grimly in pursuit of the retreating foe.

Chapter 7

The Night of the Marne

When the long day closed and darkness shrouded us all, the firing ceased completely, and the world felt strangely silent. The batteries limbered up and took the road down towards the river, and our ambulances followed the same way. The only sound heard was the crunching of the waggon wheels on the road. All else was soundless and still, a great quiet reigned over the valley which a short time before had been so tormented by the earthquake thunderings of battle.

We went down deeper and deeper into the valley, and in pitch darkness entered the quaint old village of Saccy on the Marne. Saccy is an old, world-forgotten village of narrow cobbled streets and ancient stone houses. Situated on the south side of the bridge which spans the Marne, the old village has ambled sleepily through the centuries disturbing no one by its existence, and undisturbed itself by the big events of history. During the preceding forty-eight hours the old place was suddenly engulfed in a cyclone of movement, for a German Army Corps had retreated rapidly through its streets and over its bridge,—too rapidly to stay and sack the houses in the manner so loved by the German soldiers. Their big guns had hurtled their iron messengers of death over the town from one side of the valley to the other, and sweating, panting British infantry, the finest warriors in the world, had pressed steadily along the same streets and over the bridge so lately trod by the enemy.

Saccy had seen two armies pass through her, and had emerged safe and unhurt. When our ambulances entered Saccy the narrow streets were packed and congested with supply waggons, ammunition carts, guns, and marching infantry. The dull lights from shuttered windows or an open door and the occasional powerful glare from a big motor headlight lit up a scene of cursing drivers, struggling and straining horses, heavy lumbering waggons, and tired, thirsty, dusty marching men.

The headquarters of the 5th Division was established in a cafe on the main street, and when we passed through the staff were at dinner in the large front room opening on to the street. We saw plates of steaming potatoes, a roast leg of mutton, bottles of pickles, and many bottles of red wine. The headquarters' cook was evidently a man of resource and knew his job.

After passing through the village we turned abruptly to the right and then we were at the bridge, a splendidly built stone affair with a parapet and side walks. The bridge was fine and wide, but our crossing was a slow process, owing to the mass of waggons, buses, and equipment ahead. Some artillery and infantry had already bivouacked on the other side of the bridge, and their camp fires with dicksies of boiling stews and of coffee looked very cheerful. Some of the men were sitting or standing round the fires, smoking their ever-popular Woodbine cigarettes; others were engaged lopping off branches from the forest trees for the fire; many had taken off their *puttees*, boots, and socks, and were cooling their feet.

They all looked very happy, and cheerfully exchanged compliments and remarks with the drivers of the waggons, who still had some miles to go before they could rest. Our ambulances were, however, about a quarter of a mile farther on, swung up a narrow cutting into a field, and here we found the headquarters of the 15th Field Ambulance, with seven ambulance waggons, supply carts, water carts, horses, tent and hospital equipment. When we joined up the unit was again complete. We had crossed the Marne behind the 15th Infantry Brigade, but our work was not yet done.

It was now eleven o'clock of a pitch black night with threatening rain. Our ambulances were packed in a semi-circle in the field near an old farmhouse. A huge log fire was blazing about 200 yards away, and round this were sitting some of the medical officers of the ambulance and two chaplains. I made my bow to my new comrades and introduced myself as the latest medical recruit to the unit, and was given a box to sit on, and a cup of hot tea, bread and marmalade. All of these officers had been through Mons and Le Cateau, and were now veterans. One who had just come in from the front with some stretchers, said that our cavalry had done splendidly during the day, and had made a very fine charge, cutting off some companies of retreating infantry. Our lancers had ridden through a squadron of *Uhlans*, turned round, and galloped through them again, spearing and slaying on their two bloody passages.

We were in for a busy night, for all the stretcher parties from the various ambulances were out in the field collecting the wounded, whose arrival was expected now at any moment. An operating tent had been pitched in the field near by, and was brilliantly lit up with a huge acetylene lamp. The operating table was fixed in the centre of the tent and along each side were the instruments, basins, and dressings lying on the lids of the panniers, which made excellent side-tables. Very soon the ambulances lumbered up with the men picked up from the fields close at hand. The stretchers, each holding a wounded man, were taken out of the waggons and laid on a heap of straw near the door of the operating tent. Sixteen men were taken out and laid side by side. New stretchers were put in the waggons, which again set out to bring in more wounded. One surgeon stood on one side of the operating table, another stood opposite him, and a third surgeon was ready to assist or give an anaesthetic if necessary.

Quietly and quickly one wounded man after another was lifted on to the table, his wounds were speedily dressed, and he was again carried out and laid on the straw with a blanket below and another above him. Those with painful wounds were given hypodermics of morphia. All who were fit to take nourishment had hot soup, tea, bread and jam. Stimulants were given freely to those requiring it. The wounds were mostly from shrapnel, and only one case required an anaesthetic. He had a bad compound fracture of the thigh and was in terrible pain. We made some good splints and fixed up the limb comfortably and in good position. One poor devil had a bad abdominal wound for which we could do nothing. He was given a good dose of morphia and slept quietly and easily till five a.m., when he ceased to breathe.

At one o'clock in the morning wounded were still coming in, and the surgeon on duty was relieved by myself. So with coat off, bare arms and covered with an operating apron, I did my spell of surgical duty during that night on the banks of the Marne. Our stretcher parties at last were finished, and had all come in with the report that all the wounded had been brought in. They reported that there were large numbers of British and German dead on the roadsides and in the fields. At six o'clock our large list of wounded were sent off to railhead at Coulommiers on returning-empty supply waggons and under the charge of a medical officer. The operating tent was struck and all the panniers and equipment were packed. The Field Ambulance had done its "job." It had followed its brigade into action, had collected all the wounded of that brigade, had dressed their wounds and made them comfortable during the night, and had then loaded all the wounded on waggons and sent them to railhead to join a hospital train. Having done this the ambulance was again ready to follow its brigade and do the same again. The long night was over and a new day was upon us.

This was the only occasion on the march that our Field Ambulance had to pitch an operating tent in a field. Generally a house or *château* was made use of as a dressing station. The tent made an excellent first-aid dressing station, but of course was unsuited for any major surgical operation, and we tried to avoid as far as possible doing much in the way of surgery. We examined every wound carefully to see that no bleeding was taking place, and all the fractures were very carefully splintered with firm wooden splints. The men suffered very little pain comparatively, and were remarkably cheerful when they had been dressed and placed on the straw. They seemed anxious to talk and review the events of the day, and they told us great tales of the Germans running away.

One man said that he, with his company, was in a belt of trees lying down and watching an open space in their front. Some *Uhlans*, not knowing the British were so close, cantered up and halted; our men took careful aim and emptied twenty saddles with the first fusillade, and then fired on the panic-stricken, terrified horses who were careering off with the remaining Germans; when the horses fell the riders surrendered at once. The man who told me the story was slightly wounded later in the day, and had a *Uhlan* helmet as a souvenir of the affray near the forest.

CHAPTER 8

From the Marne to the Aisne

At 7 a.m. our Field Ambulance was ready to march. Breakfast was over, and we stood by awaiting orders. While waiting, some of us strolled back towards the bridge which we had crossed the previous night. It was now empty of men and vehicles. The ashes of the bivouac fires and the lopped branches of trees were all the tokens left of the passage of a German and a British Army Corps. The Marne is a deep stream with a slow current, and is a popular boating river. Two or three boating-club sheds lay pleasantly situated on the banks of the stream, bowered in foliage and trees. Up and down the river the scene was exceedingly beautiful. It was curious, when standing on the bridge, to think that in the previous forty-eight hours the tide of war had rolled over this lovely valley; that artillery had plastered the landscape with shrapnel and high explosives, and that riflemen had lined the banks where to stand exposed for one minute meant instant death; that many hundreds of men had died and many hundreds had been wounded and crippled for life. The ambulance lorries climbing out of the valley to the rear with the loads of wounded men were the aftermath of the glitter and panoply of war, and of the deadly struggle in the now peaceful valley.[1]

At eight o'clock we received our orders to follow on. So "Field Ambulance, fall in!" and away we went on the great walk to the Aisne. At this time I did not have a horse. Every ambulance medical officer is provided with a horse; but horses were scarce just then, and with three other doctors I "foot-slogged" the way. It was a beautiful morning. The night's rain had settled the dust on the roads, the sun was shining pleasantly, but drifting rain-clouds threatened a change. Major

---

1. *1914: the Marne and the Aisne* by H. W. Carless-Davis is also published by Leonaur.

B—— and myself marched at the head of the column on foot. Behind marched the men of A Company—the stretcher-bearers and orderlies, followed by the six ambulance waggons of A Company. Then the men and the waggons of B Company, followed by the men and waggons of C Company. Water carts, kit waggons, supply and equipment carts, brought up the rear.

Our personnel was about 250 men, and these with the waggons, carts, and horses made a fairly long column. Our road led in a snake-like way through the gradually rising uplands beyond the Marne on to the plain beyond. The countryside was typically French: clumps of forest were on our right, villages were dotted about everywhere, and there were many isolated farmhouses surrounded by belts of trees and orchards. The countryside was agricultural. The wheat and oats had been cut and newly-made stacks were standing in the stubble fields, and some of the fields still held the "stooks" of grain. About nine o'clock we came on the grim evidences of war. Our road led right through a country over which the Germans were retreating and we were pursuing. Two large motor-cars, broken down, were lying in a ditch beside the road. These were German staff cars. One had a badly burst tyre and that seemed to be all that was the matter with it. Farther on was a smashed French ambulance waggon, with a broken axle, and full of equipment and stores, abandoned by the Germans. This car had evidently been captured from the French during the German advance.

Four German soldiers of the Mecklenburg Corps were lying together in a ditch. All had been killed by shrapnel wounds in chest and head. It seemed as if the four men had sat down exhausted in the ditch by the roadside and that one of our shrapnel shells had burst right over them, killing them all outright. We removed their identification discs in order that they could be sent to Germany later on. Close by was another dead German lying face downwards on the earth and with both hands extended above his head. Shrapnel had caught him full in the back of the neck. In a small clump of trees to the left of the road were two more dead Germans. One was lying on his back with his left hand over a wound in the chest. The other soldier had evidently been trying to assist him, for he had been kneeling on the right side of the wounded man when he too received a mortal hurt and fell dead across his dying comrade. His head was lying in a deep puddle of coagulated blood.

The rifle of one lay some distance off, evidently violently thrown away by the first man when he received his chest wound. The rifle of the other soldier had been laid carefully against a tree within reach. The poor fellow did not reach out for it again. Two young Germans were found lying close together in a clump of vegetation. They had been sorely wounded and had crawled off the roadside into the friendly shelter of the trees. Left behind by their countrymen, grievously wounded and in dire distress, they had curled up together in the damp grass and died during the night. One had died from haemorrhage and one from a brain injury. Another group of four soldiers had crawled into a ditch and were lying close together in their last long sleep—killed by one of our heavy shells.

A small footpath at one place ran from the side of the road towards the gate of an orchard of apple trees. Two German soldiers were lying here dead, and with their rifles alongside them. One had just reached the gate and the other was close on his heels when a burst of British shrapnel stopped their further progress. Stragglers from the retreating army, they were making for the orchard to hide when death came suddenly upon them. So the grim picture went on. The German dead dotted the roadside, the clumps of trees, and the fields on either side. Thirty Germans were found killed on a small ridge to our right. Another one was found alive, but dying. His wounds were carefully dressed and we carried him into a neighbouring cottage to die. Our artillery at the Marne did deadly execution and our shrapnel must have made of that roadside and the fields alongside a perfect hell.

Our gunners had got the range of the road and plastered it and the adjoining land with a murdering hail of lead and iron. It was curious to note how badly wounded men seemed to try to escape from the open and crawl into the shelter of a ditch or a clump of trees.

A man wounded in the field would do as a wounded stag or rabbit would,—try for cover. Some men died after crawling away a few yards. Some got some distance away into the ditches and died there, a bloody trail marking their last painful journey.

The expressions on the faces of the men were on the whole peaceful. Some had a look of wild surprise in their upward, staring eyes. Some looked as if a great fear and terror had possessed them at the last awful moment. The expression on the face of one finely built German officer, with a clean-cut intellectual face and firm jaw, was that of a sublime contempt. His eyes and nose and the curl on his lips betokened a contemptuous regard that was curious to see in a dead man.

One burly young man killed by a shell wound in the abdomen

had lived some time after having received his mortal hurt, for he had plucked some straw from the wheat stack near which he lay and made a pillow of it. On this he had rested his head. His military cloak lay over him, pulled tightly round his neck. There he lay with one hand under his head and resting on his pillow of crumpled straw, and the other hand pressed on his wounded abdomen as if to give it some support. He looked like a man sleeping the peaceful sleep of utter fatigue, and when painlessly asleep his heart had ceased to beat. In his haversack there was a hard sausage and a piece of hard white bread. His water-bottle was empty and the cork had not been replaced, nor had the bottle been hooked on to his belt. Wounded, bleeding, thirsty, and exhausted, he had slowly crept off that awful field into the friendly shelter of the haystack.

The dead Germans were young sturdy men, strong-jawed and wiry. This was no canaille whom we were fighting, but a trained, determined soldiery who would fight hard and die gamely.

Our route for the remainder of this day lay through such scenes of blood and devastation. We passed abandoned ammunition trains, field guns, saddlery, field kitchens, and war equipment of all sorts. There could be no doubt about the precipitate retreat of the Germans, nor of the tenacious and pressing character of the pursuit. Large numbers of dead horses littered the roadsides and fields. Some had been wounded or killed by our fire. Some lay with outstretched necks and open mouths, dead from exhaustion, and some had evidently been shot as temporarily useless by the Germans themselves who did not wish them to remain alive for the enemy. One sorely wounded horse as we passed tried painfully to get up. We gave him the merciful dispatch with a revolver shot.

Rain fell heavily during the afternoon for about an hour and then the sky cleared again. Continuous heavy fighting was going on all day on our front and flanks, and muffled waves of artillery bursts could be heard from the far distance. The whole French and British Army was advancing in one wide semicircle, endeavouring to "roll up" two German Army Corps.

After a hard, gruelling march of twenty-two miles we reached Chiezy. It was then pitch dark and we were all exhausted, for we had been on our feet for over twenty hours, part of the time marching, and part of the time standing by waiting to go forward. When a column is marching along a road, pursuing an enemy who is every low and again making a temporary stand to get a brigade or a battalion out of a tight corner, the going is necessarily slow and there are many waits—sometimes for ten minutes, sometimes for an hour or more. The waits on the roadside are really more tiring than the steady marching. When one is "soft" and not accustomed to long walking, a day's march like this proves a torture. If such a "tenderfoot" sat down by the wayside for a few minutes, it was almost impossible to get the cramped body into the erect attitude again.

Towards the end of the long, long day, and in the darkness of the night, with feet swollen and sore, brain and body numbed with fatigue, one did not march, but only stumbled and lurched along the never-ending road like a drunken man. A tired brain induces muscular fatigue, aid physical exhaustion causes mental torpor. When our ambulances pulled into the stubble field at Chiezy, we had lost all interest in the war, and in everything else on this earth except a cup of tea and a long sleep.

However, certain duties had to be attended to before one turned in. The horses were looked after, the ambulances parked, and rations served out to the men. We had about twenty patients, all of them British soldiers with sore feet—men who had fallen out of the regiments on the march and lad waited by the roadside for the ambulance waggons. We always ordered these poor devils to jump into the waggons and take off their boots and socks This gave instant relief. The sores on the heels and across the instep were painted with iodine. In a few days the men were generally well and fit to rejoin their regiments.

On bivouacking this night we got at these "foot birds" to wash their feet. This was a novel experience to men who had marched from Mons without a wash or change of socks. The officers' cooks soon had coffee and stew ready, and our servants had spread straw on the ground, on which our valises were unrolled. The night was beautiful; about two miles away the guns were booming and the bright flashes of the bursting shells reminded us that war was close beside us. Without even taking off our boots we lay down on our valises and were asleep as soon as our bodes assumed the horizontal.

At four o'clock next morning we were roused by the penetrating voice of the O.C., Major X——. "Turn out, turn out!" There was no escaping that voice or the caustic remarks that would be sure to come if one did not "turn out." We all got buckets of water, and stripping in the open had a good morning bath in the buckets. It was cold, but bracing. Breakfast of coffee, bread, jam, and fried bacon. Day broke shortly afterwards and we found that we had camped on the scene of a struggle of the previous afternoon. Close by were a number of dead horses with their saddlery still on. Some newly-made graves were distinguished about 500 yards from our sleeping quarters. A German cavalry patrol had been bivouacked near a wood hard by our camping-place, and had evidently been very badly handled, judging by the signs of confusion, the litter left behind, the dead horses, the recent graves. In a small hollow I picked up a very fine German saddle and bit, and a good waterproof sheet. A bundle of letters was lying near in a small leather satchel, and on the cover of the satchel was stitched the photograph of a very pretty woman's face. Our O.C. had been educated in Germany, and being a good German scholar read the letters. They were of no military importance, and had been sent by the lady of the photograph to the owner of the satchel—evidently an officer. There were congratulations about his "promotion," and an earnest, loving message for his safe return.

Poor devil! We surmise that he must have been a young cavalry officer in command of the patrol. His "promotion" was short-lived, for he lay under one of the new mounds of clay, and the poor lady with the charming face would have some very sad hours when she learned from the German casualty lists that "Ober Lieutenant X—— was missing." One of our men picked up here a very fine pair of new German boots. As his own were a little the worse for wear he put on the German ones, and said that they were much more comfortable than the British military boot. I believe that his observation was quite correct. Amongst other souvenirs picked up at this interesting corner were a pair of field-glasses, a revolver, a good set of razors and mirrors, an ivory-backed hair-brush—all made in Germany.

Our greatest find was yet to come. As our ambulance was getting under way one of our R.A.M.C. corporals hove in sight marching proudly at the head of eleven fully-armed German prisoners. The corporal's tale was full of interest. He was searching in the wood for more "souvenirs" when he came suddenly upon the eleven soldiers lying together in a small clearing. The corporal thought that his last hour had come. All the tales of German atrocities he had heard unfolded rapidly in his mind, and when the German non-commissioned officer got up and approached him, speaking German, which our corporal did not understand, he thought that his death-sentence was being pronounced.

By signs, to the utter amazement of the corporal, he grasped the fact that the Germans wished to surrender. He beckoned the enemy to follow him, and the eleven hungry, tired, and very dirty-looking Mecklenburghers came docilely into camp. Our O.C. approached them, took their rifles, and ordered them coffee, bully beef, and biscuits. The prisoners set to without delay, and ate as only hungry Germans can eat. Three of them had badly blistered feet, and when we marched off these were accommodated in the ambulance waggons. The remainder marched behind the waggons of A Company, under charge of the corporal who "captured" them. Later in the day we handed them over to the Norfolk Regiment, as it was clearly against the etiquette of war for a Field Ambulance to have prisoners of war. We hadn't a gun amongst us.

The capture of eleven prisoners of war by our Field Ambulance was the occasion for much joy to our men, and the corporal was a very proud man. I don't know what the Germans thought when they discovered that they had surrendered to an unarmed party. The 15th Field Ambulance is so far the only ambulance which has taken prisoners of war, and I hope that the R.A.M.C. messes at Aldershot and Netley will duly treasure the fact in the archives.

Rain fell heavily when we left Chiezy, and we were soon soaked to the skin. The roads were quagmires of greasy and sticky mud, heavy lowering clouds made everything sombre and grey, and the countryside looked mournful and cheerless. Mile after mile we trudged in the pitiless rain. I shall always remember the march from the Marne to the Aisne, for its wet and mud. Shortly after leaving Chiezy we came upon some gruesome evidences of German savagery. Near a stable built on to a farmhouse we saw a Frenchman lying dead across a manure heap. The top of his head had been blown off, and his brains were plastered over his face. The man, evidently the proprietor, had been shot the previous day by a German officer. There was an old woman at the farm, and she told us this, and that she had seen him fall. What was the reason for the brutal murder she did not know. She said that the officer and the farmer seemed to be in conversation near the stable, and the farmer appeared to be protesting at something.

Suddenly the officer placed the muzzle of his revolver close to the farmer's forehead and shot him. The wound had been inflicted at close range, and we were filled with disgust at such a callous murder. About a mile farther on, we met another poor devil who had been done to death. A middle-aged man with a bald head, bare-footed, and dressed in an old pair of blue pants and a cotton shirt, was lying near a plough close to the road. His head had been battered in, probably with the butt-end of a rifle, and he had been dead for about twenty-four hours. Why the poor wretched man had been killed we did not know. The third instance of this fiendish villainy I saw later on in the day at Billy. This time it was a young man, a mere youth, and he lay face downwards at the door of a cowhouse, dead from a bullet wound in the chest. I examined the wound with some care, and would be quite prepared to swear in any court of law that the man who shot him had pressed the revolver against the dead man's chest when he pulled the trigger. This is the German way. These examples of nauseous and disgusting frightfulness amazed me. I had never before come up against such tragedies, and I felt an unholy pleasure that our big guns farther along the road were pouring shrapnel and shell amongst the living devils who did such things.

At Billy our brigadier-general, Count Gleichen, ordered us to bivouac for the night. Major B—— and I billeted in a small cottage abutting on a very smelly cowshed. At the cottage fire we dried our soaking uniforms, and dug dry underclothing out of our valises, which we spread on the kitchen floor and lay upon. *Madame* of the cottage was full of the latest war news. She was *très intelligente* and very satisfied with the progress of the war. She told us that our advanced guard had entered the village only six hours behind the retreating Germans; that the Germans were in a great hurry and were too tired almost to march; that their officers were angry and cursed and struck the men who lagged behind. She also assured us that some *Uhlans* had ridden through, and that they were very drunk and had bottles of champagne suspended in festoons round their necks. While making some tea, and boiling eggs, she cheered us up with the assurance that the war would soon be over, for Monsieur le Curé had told her so himself, bless his heart.

The *curé* opened his church and allowed our men to carry in straw and sleep there for the night. This was a godsend to our men during that night of pouring rain, and the *curé* got many a rough blessing for his kind act. The villagers at Billy were much heartened at seeing the British so close on the German heels, and one old fellow—he must have been a centenarian—got very drunk on the strength of it all, and assured us that he was a veteran of the *soixante-dix* and had killed many Germans at that time. He was too drunk to remember the exact number.

During the night I was awakened by a tremendous artillery fire. The batteries beyond the village had got the range of something and were giving them hot potatoes. *Madame* of the cottage was very alarmed, and thought that the Germans were coming back. Her confidence in the British was not as firm as she had led us to believe the previous evening.

We were all out and ready to march at five o'clock next morning, but did not move off till seven o'clock. Rain still continued to pour down and we were all miserably muddy and damp. Whenever a big artillery duel took place heavy rain was sure to follow. This was so on the Marne and on the Aisne, and someone with a meteorological bent had made the same observations during the Peninsular War. All day long we marched or waited on the muddy, sopping *pavé* with waterproof sheets tucked round our necks and shoulders, off which the water streamed. The advance now was very slow, and we were told that our men ahead were meeting with a more organised and steady resistance. We no longer met evidences of a precipitate retreat. There were no more German dead or abandoned material by the roadsides.

At 9 p.m. in the dark we entered the doleful village of Chacrise. For sixteen hours we had been on our feet and had only covered about eight or nine miles. The soft roads, ground down by our heavy waggons and guns, were in a bad state, and we walked through ankle-deep mud and slush. When we entered Chacrise we were told that all the billets had been taken up. The church, the *Mairie*, the shops, and houses were all occupied by our soldiers. It looked as if we should have to sit all night on the cobble-stones of the street, and what with the darkness, the incessant pouring rain, and the fatigue, we were all very sorry that we had come to France to fight Germans. But every cloud has its silver lining.

We found an unoccupied house down a dark alley. The windows were firmly shuttered and the door securely locked. The occupants had locked up their house and bolted when the Germans were known to be about. By a little skilful burglary with a jemmy we opened a window. One of us got in and opened the front door from the inside: very soon our cook had a fire lighted and a hot supper ready. We got all our men and horses under good cover, and our night at Chacrise, which promised so badly, turned out very happily. We were all given an issue of rum this night. Rum is an oily, nauseous drink, but given certain surroundings and a certain physical state it has a most excellent flavour. On the night at Chacrise everything conspired to make the rum very palatable.

At 4 a.m. next day our never-sleepy O.C. disturbed our dreams with his "Turn out, turn out!" and out we turned. We had no choice when he was stalking round. Again we stepped out on muddy roads, and under a heavy downpour of soaking rain, and marching and stopping, reached the village of Serches on the Aisne at eleven o'clock in the morning. The rain then ceased and a glorious, welcome sun appeared. The whole countryside was bathed in a delightful warmth, and we felt glad to be alive.

We were ordered to bivouac our ambulances in a field behind the village, and were told that the German rearguard was holding up our advance most determinedly along the Aisne banks, and that the enemy artillery was in great strength.

Our march from the Marne to the Aisne was accomplished, and we now entered upon a new and different phase of the great war game. Our brigade was in action on the Aisne banks, and we had to take up a position behind it and be prepared to receive its wounded and sick.

The Field Ambulance with a marching army takes its number from the Brigade which it serves. The 15th Field Ambulance followed the 15th Brigade; the 13th Field Ambulance, the 13th Brigade, and so on. Four regiments or battalions form a brigade, and all the other units attached to the brigade, such as cavalry or ammunition columns, are also medically attended by the Field Ambulance attached to their brigade.

Our brigade consisted of the Norfolks, Cheshires, Bedfords, and Dorsets, and the brigadier was Major-General Count Gleichen, now a General of Division.

It was from these regiments that we received most of our casualties on the Marne, on the Aisne, and later at La Bassée, and, as the following few notes will show, we were serving with regiments who had proved themselves doughty warriors in the past.

The Norfolk Regiment was created in 1685 in the time of the Stuarts to help suppress the rebellion of Monmouth. Their badge is the figure of Britannia, well won, in 1707, for their gallant bearing at Almanza. This great regiment has done sterling service in many lands, and has as battle honours, Roleia, Corunna, Peninsula, Sevastopol, Afghanistan, and South Africa. Their nicknames are three, "The Holy Boys," "The Fighting Ninth" (they were formerly called the 9th Regiment of Foot), and the "Norfolk Howards."

The Bedfordshire Regiment, with its badge of the united red and white rose, and its battle honours with the proud names, Blenheim, Ramillies, Chitral, was a magnificent unit in France when we joined it. The regiment had been raised in the last years of James II. in 1688, and from 1809 to 1881 was known as the 16th Regiment of Foot. The nicknames of the regiment are "The Peacemakers," "The Featherbeds," "The Bloodless Lambs." This regiment lost heavily at Missy on the Aisne, and at Ypres later on in the war it had over 650 casualties.

The Cheshires, with a united red and white rose for a badge like the Bedfords, were raised in 1689, and were in old days the 22nd Regiment of Foot. Their war record includes Martinique, Hyderabad, Scinde, and South Africa, and their nicknames are "The Two Twos," "The Red Knights," and "The Lightning Conductors"—when marching in Ireland about fifteen years ago the regiment was struck by lightning. The Cheshires have suffered terribly during this war, and at Missy we had a number of their casualties to treat, and many were buried near the old village on the Aisne.

The Dorsetshire Regiment has a proud motto, *"Primus in Indis,"* commemorating its great services in India; and the fact that it stands first in order of precedence amongst British regiments that have seen war there. The drum-major of this regiment still carries the staff of the *Nawab's* herald on parade. It was captured at Plassey, where the regiment was in action under Clive.

Sir Horace Smith-Dorrien, Commander of the 5th Division, "particularly mentioned the fine fighting of the Dorsets. They suffered no less than 400 casualties. Their commanding officer, Major Roper, was killed, but all day they maintained their hold on Pont Fixe." Their battle story is a great one, and includes Plassey, Albuera, Vittoria, Sevastopol, and Relief of Ladysmith. The 1st Battalion was raised in 1702. The "Green Linnets" is their nickname.

CHAPTER 9

The Aisne and the Tragedy of the Sunken Road

On arriving at Serches on the Aisne our ambulance pulled off into a sloping grassy field, and the tired horses were taken out, fed, and rubbed down. Fires were lit and we all prepared to enjoy ourselves by resting in the glorious sun's rays, washing, shaving, and smoking a pipe in comfort. For the past few days we could not smoke in the open owing to the rain.

A tremendous artillery engagement was going on at the front. Our batteries were posted behind a long ridge not far from where we were, and every gun was in action, making the air resound with the bursting charges. It was not by any means a one-sided affair, as we were soon to know. The enemy were firing from a ridge on the other side of the river, and they had got our positions very accurately. At one o'clock a Taube flew over our position and dropped three bombs. Two fell near us with a terrible clatter, one on the road to our left down which we had come, and one about 400 yards behind us in a belt of trees. The third one actually fell in our field, and plunged itself angrily into the soft turf. Our position was obviously not a safe one for a Field Ambulance, and we got orders to retire two miles farther back. We did not move off, however, till 5 p.m.

Major B—— and I walked through the village of Serches and turned up the road leading to the right behind a steep ridge which flattened out into a plain of about one to two miles' width. This plateau fell abruptly on its northern side right on to the Aisne River. When climbing up this road, which led to the summit of the ridge, we passed numerous stretcher-bearers bringing in wounded to the 13th Field Ambulance, which was also quartered in the village. The

Halt at Serches

men with slight hand or head wounds were walking, and the serious cases were on stretchers. The Germans had got the range of the ridge summit towards which our road led, and were freely plastering it with shrapnel and Black Marias.

On approaching the top of the rise we saw two of our batteries on our right, and three on our left well forward in the plateau, and busily engaged. Our guns at this date were not concealed from inquisitive Taubes by trees and foliage—that lesson had not yet been learned by the conservative Briton. German shells were bursting on the ridge in good line for our guns, but about a quarter of a mile short. Our road now took a direct turn for the far side of the plateau, and here it went through a deep cutting down to a bridge which spanned the river. On the left-hand side of the road at the cutting there was a large gravel pit or cave where road-metal was obtained. The road across the plateau was open and exposed, but from the cutting to the banks of the river it was lined with pine trees. Major B—— and myself were standing on the road at the top of the ridge trying to make out the German positions with our field-glasses.

A gunner officer, seeing the red-cross brassards on our arms, hurried up and said, "You are urgently wanted in the sunken road about a mile and a half down. Two doctors have just been killed and there are a lot of badly wounded on the road." We had no dressings of any sort with us. We had come thus far out of curiosity, not expecting that it was such a "hot corner." We, however, went forward at the double along this exposed road, passing upturned waggons, dead and dying horses, khaki caps and overcoats, overturned and smashed water carts. Out of breath, we reached the cave and found how urgently necessary we were. The scene defied description. The cave was a shambles of mangled forms. Nineteen wounded men were lying in the loose sandy gravel, having just been brought in by their surviving uninjured comrades. One was on the point of death from a shrapnel wound of the brain—the bullet had passed through the orbit. There were fractured limbs, shrapnel wounds of the chest, abdomen, and head, shell wounds and concussions. We did all we possibly could with first-aid dressings. We got the uninjured men to take off their puttees, and these we used as bandages; rifles were employed as splints for the lower limbs, and bayonets for the upper limbs.

One poor officer, Captain and Quartermaster M——, an old soldier with two rows of ribbons on his coat, had a badly shattered thigh and knee. He was suffering tortures, and his anguished face showed the strong efforts he made to control himself. Lieut. W——, R.A.M.C., a civil surgeon, had a smashed ankle-joint. We sent at once for ambulances and stretcher parties. These soon arrived, and the terribly wounded men were conveyed to the Field Hospital which had just been arranged at Serches.

Poor Captain M—— died that night, and was buried near a stone wall in the garden at the old farmhouse of Mont de Soissons, and the doctor had to have his leg amputated later. He was a very plucky man. Even when wounded and lying in helpless pain, he gave instructions about the other wounded men.

After the wounded were sent away I walked a few yards down the road to the place of the disaster. Here was a scene of ghastly horror. On the road lay mangled and bleeding horses, dead men lying in all sorts of convulsed attitudes, upturned waggons, smashed and splintered wood. Add to this the agonised groans of our wounded men, the shrill scream of dying horses, and that impalpable but nevertheless real feeling of standing in the face of the Creator—one can, perhaps, then feebly picture this scene of carnage, of the solemnity of death, and of the pitiless woe of this devastation. Where could one find here a trace of the glory, pomp, and magnificence of war?

The story of the incident is one not uncommon. A party of men of the West Kents were sitting by the roadside beyond the cutting, having a meal of bully beef and biscuits. As they were eating, a cavalry ambulance came up from the bridge over the Aisne. When the ambulance was abreast of the West Kents, a German battery landed a Black Maria on the ambulance, and at the same moment shrapnel burst right amongst them all. The heavy explosive and the shrapnel did terrible execution. Captain F——, R.A.M.C, was killed outright, the other doctor was badly hurt. Eight men of the West Kents met instantaneous death; eight horses were killed, and three horribly mangled and flung off the road by the violence of the explosion. On examining these dead men on the road it was noticeable that they had all received a multiplicity of wounds. One man, a burly sergeant-major, had a big hole in his head, another huge hole in his neck, a lacerated wound of the chest, and one boot and foot blown completely away. All had widely open staring eyes. The expression seemed to be one of overwhelming surprise and horror.

Poor fellows! Their moment of surprise and horror must indeed have been brief, for death is dealt out at these times with a lightning flash.

In describing events in this war one unconsciously has to turn to superlatives. "Devilish, hellish, bloody, awful, and terrible" are words that come most trippingly to the tongue. This war is superlative in all its moods and tenses. Superlative in the number of men engaged, in the extent of the battle front, in the duration of the battles, in the misery it is causing and has caused, in the awful loss of life, in the mutilating wounds caused by the shrapnel, in the number of the missing, in the atrocities, inhumanities, and blasting cruelties of the enemy, and in their wanton destruction of all that is sacred and revered.

Few few shall part
Where many meet.'

Gun teams at the Marne.

The way to the sunken road.

Chapter 10

Missy on the Aisne

We left Serches at 5 p.m. and retraced our road for about two miles till we reached the ancient *château*-farm of Mont de Soissons. This historic farm was our headquarters during September and till the date we left in October 1914, and it was during this eventful period that all the great stirring events "on the Aisne" took place. "On the Aisne," how much of tragedy and pathos, of great deeds, of gallant deaths, stubborn fighting, and indomitable courage are associated with those words?

On the night after our arrival at Mont de Soissons, the ambulance officers were sitting about eleven o'clock round a table in the old dining-room of the *château*, when an urgent order arrived from headquarters to send doctors, stretcher-bearers, and ambulance waggons with equipment to Missy. The orders were for the ambulances to get to Missy in the dark, pick up the wounded, and at all costs to come out again in the dark. To get to Missy, which was situated on the far side of the Aisne, we would have to cross the river, and,—reading between the lines of this definite order to get in under cover of darkness and get out again in the dark,—one could see that our night ride was to be a somewhat perilous one.

Section C, the section to which I was attached, was ordered to undertake the task, and at twelve o'clock, on a pitch-dark rainy night, our section was ready to move off. We had five waggons, with the complete personnel of one section. Major B—— was in command, with Lieutenant I—— and myself as the other medical officers, and with us *Monsignor*, the Catholic chaplain attached to our field ambulance, also came as a volunteer. *Monsignor* was the salt of the earth, and whenever he thought that he could be of service to our wounded men he was there. There was no demand on him on this wild rainy night to leave the comfortable shelter of the farmhouse and voyage out towards the enemy lines; but he had a strong sense of duty, and behind the priest there was more than a *soupçon* of the knight-errant, who warmed at the thought of a dangerous adventure.

We were not permitted to light our waggon lamps, and in the darkness we rumbled off, anxious not to lose any time over our mission, and if possible complete it under cover of darkness.

Misfortune dogged us from the start. We had but one map; and as nobody could give us any directions, that was our only guide. We mapped out the route, Mont de Soissons to Serches—Serches to Venizel on the banks of the Aisne, where was the bridge by which we were to cross the river—Venizel to Bucy le Long, and thence to Missy. Altogether, we reckoned that we had 7 or 8 miles at least to go; but it proved to be a *"long, long way to Tipperary."*

After being five minutes on the march we discovered that we were on the wrong road, and it took twenty minutes to turn the waggons on the narrow, muddy *pavé* and get on again. Passing through Serches, we turned to the left and followed the road through a valley leading to the banks of the Aisne. Here again we were nearly off on a wrong road, and lost about another twenty minutes righting ourselves. The country was intersected with roads not indicated on our map. We now got on to a narrow road dipping sharply down towards a clump of trees, and here one of our waggons slipped over the embankment, and one of the horses was killed. We could not get the waggon up again, so abandoned it and pushed on with our remaining four waggons, water cart, and supply waggon. The loss of this waggon was a serious blow to us, as events will show.

As we entered the forest we were challenged by a sentry of the Cameron regiment, who passed us on. A Cameron officer met us here and told us that we were going into a bad place, as late that afternoon he had lost some men from shrapnel at the very spot where we then were. Progress was very slow for the next 500 yards, as the road was barricaded with felled trees, and trenches had been dug alongside. After negotiating this nasty corner we got on quickly to Venizel.

We reached Venizel right on the banks of the Aisne, and learned to our chagrin that the fine stone bridge had been destroyed by the German artillery that day. The engineers with superhuman energy had just about completed a pontoon bridge. We were kept waiting here for an hour. Then, one waggon at a time, we got across. The bridge was very doubtfully lit at either end by darkened lanterns, and one seemed to be very close to the swift current of the Aisne, already in flood. At the far side of the bridge our progress was again very slow for some time, as we had to meander gingerly between the trenches dug for the men who were holding the bridge-end. As we left the pontoon an optimistic engineer lieutenant, in clothes dripping with water, cheerfully called out "Good luck. Hope you get back all right." In reply we warned him that he would get pneumonia if he didn't change his clothes, and that it was foolish to take baths in the Aisne with a uniform on.

Our road lay now along a flat plain, curving to the right. The night was very dark and ominously silent. Our men were forbidden to talk or smoke cigarettes, as we were approaching the enemy lines. Reaching Bucy le Long, we inquired the way from a Scottish officer who was standing near a stone well on the village street. All his men were alert and under arms and expecting an attack at any moment. The officer, speaking with the good Doric accent, indicated our way and told us to hurry on and get under cover, as Missy was very "nasty" just then and they expected a German attack.

We realised by this time that we might get into Missy in the dark, but by no possibility could we bring the wounded out in the dark; and by the serious preparations for repelling an attack in the village street we knew that we could not get out in daylight. It looked as if we were soon to be in the thick of that most sanguinary of all forms of war—street fighting.

So on we went, and after taking another wrong turn and losing another half-hour we got on to a straight road leading direct to Missy. It was extraordinarily difficult to find one's way, as the night was dark and everything was strange and unfamiliar. There seemed to be hundreds of roads, and the greatest care had to be exercised; for a wrong turning would land us very speedily in the German lines, and none of us wished our expedition to end in an inglorious pilgrimage to Germany.

As the first doubtful streaks of dawn appeared we reached Missy.

The main street of the village was full of men of the Norfolks and Cheshires, all up and armed, and awaiting the Germans. There had been a very hot skirmish outside the village on the previous afternoon, and the Norfolks and Cheshires had lost heavily. It was the wounded from this *mêlée* that we were to get to. A cheery Norfolk sergeant directed us down a small lane to the right of the street, telling us that there were a lot of badly hit men somewhere at the bottom of the lane. The lane was too narrow to admit of our ambulances, so they were parked in front of a baker's shop and the horses were taken out. We hurried down the lane and found the wounded men.

Dawn was breaking and shafts of grey light and shadow were thrusting through the darkness. Then, like a clap of thunder, the German batteries opened up, and from that moment till nightfall we lived through one of the most hellish artillery duels that any mortal man could imagine. A tornado of shot and shell swept across that beautiful Aisne valley. It seemed as if all the fiends of hell were let loose. The noise was deafening, ear-splitting, the bursting of the shells, the mighty upheavals of earth where the shells struck, the falling trees, falling masonry, crashing church steeples, the rolling and bounding of stones from walls struck by these titanic masses of iron travelling at lightning speed, the concussion of the air, the screeching, whisking, and sighing of the projectiles in their flight, made an awful scene of destruction and force.

Add to all this the snarling, typewriter note of the Maxims, the angry *phut* of the Mauser bullet as it struck a house or a gate, and the crackling roars from our Lee-Metfords—truly it was the devil's orchestra, and the devil himself was whirling the fiery baton. The steeple of the village church was struck fairly by a German shell, and with a mighty crash the stones were hurled madly on to the road down which we had but just passed, and killed one of our horses. Another shell plunged right into the old church and sent its roof in a clattering hail over the surrounding houses. A stone house at the top of our alley-way got another shell and was levelled to the ground, killing two women who were inside. The corner of the building in which we were located was struck by a passing shell and a huge hole was ripped out of the solid masonry. Shrapnel burst over the house, in the garden in front, on the doors of the house, on the roof, and down the alley. Our red cross flag and Union Jack were badly holed with shrapnel.

At the kitchen door a large piece of shell fell, sending mud and gravel against the windows and into the room. A railway line ran past the foot of our garden, and stretching from this railway line to the banks of the Aisne in the distance was a wide grassy meadow on which some cows were grazing. A thicket of tall trees, surrounding a small farmhouse, was situated to the right of the meadow. This house was the headquarters of Count Gleichen, the commander of the 15th Brigade.

The Germans evidently were aware of this fact, for the first shots they fired at break of day were at this house. We could plainly see one shot fall short of the house, but in a straight line for it. The second shot we thought had really got the house, but fortunately this was not so. It landed near the door, as we learned later. After this shot the headquarters galloped off: as hard as they could go, and the enemy tried to reach them with shrapnel, but without success. Alongside the railway line there was a line of trenches, and every inch of that line seemed to have been covered during the day by the German fire. Their artillery practice was perfect, and at this period of the war the enemy artillery mightily outclassed ours. Our guns from the ridge on the other side of the Aisne made but a feeble reply to the terrific German bombardment.

Now for the story of our wounded at Missy. When we got down our alley at dawn on this eventful morning we found eighty-four grievously wounded men. In a little stone fowl-house to the left of the alley, fourteen men were lying packed close together. There was no place to put one's foot in trying to walk over them. To the right of the alley a gate opened into a gravel yard of a fine two-storied stone house, a very old and solidly built building. The house formed three sides of a square; a beautiful flower garden with a rose pergola formed the fourth side. The gravel yard was in the centre. The lower story of this building, with the exception of the kitchen and an adjoining room, consisted of stables, granaries, saddlery rooms, and coach-house.

Lying on the floors of the stable, kitchen, etc., were wounded men. They had all been wounded the previous evening in an attack on the enemy concealed in a wood. The wounded in the small fowl-house were carried, under shrapnel fire, across the alley to the big house and placed in the room adjoining the kitchen and in the saddlery room. The cooks made up a big fire and soon had hot water boiling. The three medical officers were soon rapidly at work. The first case attended to was that of a young soldier of the Norfolks who had been struck by a shell in the abdomen. His intestines were lying outside the body, and loops were inside the upper part of his trousers. Under chloroform we did what we could. He died painlessly four hours afterwards.

There were many bad shell wounds of the head; one necessitating a trephining operation. One poor fellow had his tongue half blown off. The loose bit was stitched on. The compound fractures were numerous and of a very bad type, associated with much shattering of the bone. Four men died during the day, but our arrival and timely help undoubtedly saved many men. We made the poor fellows as comfortable as we could, and we were incessantly busy from the moment we entered this blood-stained place. I personally shall never forget the sight of these poor, maimed, bleeding, dying and dead men crowded together in those outhouses, with not a soul near them to help, and I am more than thankful that I was privileged to be of service and to employ my professional skill to help them in their dire hour of need. We knew that we were in a tight corner. We expected that at any moment we would be all blown to pieces; we did not know how we were to get these men back to our own lines; but we knew also that whatever happened we would stand by our helpless countrymen to the last, and if we failed to get them safely back it would not be our fault.

I mentioned previously that when our ambulance got orders to go to Missy, *Monsignor*, the Roman Catholic chaplain, volunteered to come with us. It is difficult to attempt to write of our brave *Monsignor*. He was the bravest of the brave. When the three medical officers were working hard with the wounded—dressing, operating, anaesthetising—*Monsignor* was very busy too. He made hot soups, hot coffee, prepared stimulating drinks, set orderlies to work to see that every man who could take nourishment got it. One man injured in the mouth could swallow only with the greatest difficulty. *Monsignor* patiently sat by this man, and one way or another with a spoon managed to give him a pint of hot Oxo soup and a good stiff nip of brandy. This splendid prelate carried straw with his own hands and made pillows and beds for our men. He took off boots and cut off bloody coats and trousers in order to help the work of the surgeons. He rummaged in a cellar in the house and discovered a box of apples. These he cut into slices for our men. He stood by our dying men and spoke words of cheer and comfort to the poor helpless fellows. He was absolutely reckless about himself. Exposed to shrapnel and shell fire many times during the day, he was too busy attending to the wounded to think about anything else.

Towards dusk, when our work eased off, we collected some pieces of shell which fell near him—as souvenirs. I looked at *Monsignor* many times during the day, and was struck with his expression of content and his happy smile. He was exalted and proud and happy to be where a good priest,—and what a good priest he was!—could be of such great service. I am not a Catholic, but I honour the Church that can produce such a man as *Monsignor*, and I very greatly honour *Monsignor*.

As darkness came on the hellish artillery fire quietened down and then ceased altogether. The rifle-firing continued intermittently for a little while longer and then it too ceased. We were now "up against" the last and greatest trial of all—the evacuation of our wounded. During the day some more wounded men had crawled into us, and we had now 102 men to bring back to our lines. We managed in the darkness to get two large French country carts to act as ambulances. Our four ambulance waggons were, of course, not enough, and even with the help of the country carts we could not accommodate 102 wounded men. Every man wounded in the head or arms who could walk, was told off to march with our stretcher-bearers. We packed the wounded lying down cases into the ambulance waggons and on to the country carts. Plenty of straw had previously been placed in these latter. We were compelled to load up our waggons and carts far too heavily, but our position was a serious one; we had to get the wounded out somehow, and we had no one to help us.

Our troops had retired from Missy during the day and we were left all alone in front of the Germans and quite at the mercy of their guns. The *via dolorosa* of our sorely wounded was on this night a very pitiable one. Exposed to rain, lying in the utmost discomfort, compelled to keep for hours a cramped position, they deserved our pity. The wounded men who had to march were also in a sorry plight. These poor fellows were not fit to march; weak with shock, pain, and loss of blood, they ought all to have been in bed; yet they had to march, for we could not leave them behind.

At last all was ready to start. Strict orders were given against lights and cigarettes. No talking was allowed, for the Germans were just "over the way," and they are people with "long ears."

Before setting out we buried four officers and five men in a grave by the railway, near the bottom of the garden. This mournful duty over, the ambulance moved off.

This time we anticipated no delay, as we knew the road—vain hope. The night was again very dark, and a drizzle of rain was falling. We had just emerged from the silent village on the road to Bucy le Long when the inky blackness of the night was cut through by the powerful beam of a searchlight played from the German lines. The light swept slowly up and down our column in a zigzag wave once, and then a second time, this time more slowly still. Every detail was illuminated with the brilliant glare. The light was then fixed ominously on our front waggon, which had a big red cross painted on its canvas sides. The column kept moving slowly on, but for ten minutes that sinister, baleful light played all round the first ambulance.

We all thought that our last hour had come—that after going through such a hellish day in the farmhouse at Missy we were to be finally scuppered on the muddy road. We knew that the Germans were only about 800 yards away. With strained nerves we waited, expecting them to turn a machine-gun on us. The searchlight played up and down the column once more and then was turned in another direction. My impression is that the Germans made out the red cross on the leading waggon and so let us pass. If they wished they could have destroyed us easily. We all breathed again and continued on our way.

After passing through Bucy le Long, where we again saw our soldiers, we came across some returning-empty motor lorries. We placed all our marching wounded on to these and eased off the pressure in the country carts by taking off a few men. At Venizel we were held up for five hours. The pontoon bridge had given way during the day under the weight of a piece of heavy French artillery. The gun had been fished out from the bottom of the Aisne with great difficulty, but the horses were drowned. The engineers were straining every nerve to repair the bridge. It was vitally important to hurry, as this bridge was the only artery of communication between our advanced troops and the ammunition supplies. At last we got across and reached Mont de Soissons, our ambulance headquarters, at nine in the morning. The wounded were handed over to the other medical officers. Men and officers were completely done up. We had been marching during two anxious, harassing nights, and had lived through a bad day, but—-we got out our wounded.

CHAPTER 11

On the Aisne at Mont de Soissons

Our Field Ambulance headquarters at the *château*-farm of Mont de Soissons was occupied by us till October. During this time our army was righting hard. Most of the days were rainy, and the trenches on the other side of the river suffered from this. To our right was Braisne on the river, and to our far right was Reims. To our left was Soissons—about eight miles away. We were about fifty-eight miles from Paris.

Our billet was a good one. Imagine a huge hollow square surrounded by stone buildings, and the square itself filled with an enormous manure heap. One side of the square was taken up by the two-storied old stone building containing kitchen, hall, sleeping-rooms, and offices. Stables for sheep, cows, and horses formed two sides. The fourth side was a truly beautiful and artistic one. It was formed by a wonderful old chapel, and remains of what was part of the refectory and cellars of a monastery. These buildings were in a splendid state of preservation, and were now used to hold straw and cattle fodder. The chapel had been built by the Knights Templars, and was in its day a place of renown. It is indeed a pity that such historic buildings are so neglected and forgotten.

In the lofts of the dwelling-house and in a shed outside we put our sick and wounded men. In a bedroom downstairs we put the wounded officers. We were principally concerned at this time in the transportation of sick and wounded to railhead. Although we were at headquarters of an ambulance, no preparation or effort was made for any special treatment. Very few of our cases remained more than twelve to twenty-four hours. Motor lorries arrived at Mont de Soissons every morning, and on these our men piled straw and placed the men, covering all with a huge tarpaulin cover raised tent fashion on upright sticks. This method of transporting wounded was crude and

Mont de Soissons, showing the old Templars' Hall and Church

brutal. There were no motor ambulances at this time. The first motor ambulance arrived after we had been ten days at Mont de Soissons. Why motor ambulances were not with us from the beginning of the war is a question which the Army Medical Department will have to answer when the war is over, and the necessary public washing-day arrives.

Several wounded men and officers died at Mont de Soissons and were buried in the garden alongside a stone wall. Wooden crosses mark each grave-head, and two of them have stone crosses erected and engraved by one of our orderlies. And the women of the house and neighbourhood attend to the graves, and place flowers on them. It is beautiful to see how reverently the French women look after our soldiers' graves. The old lady—the owner of this farm-*château*—has the names and dates of burial of all officers and men interred in this garden, and the relatives of these dead heroes will be able one day to visit this quiet corner of a garden in France and will see how beautifully the graves have been tended by the simple, kindly French peasant women.

Our life at this place was full of interest. In front of us were our own batteries, behind the ridge; then beyond was the river, and beyond that our advanced troops in the trenches. To our left, the French occupied Soissons. The French artillery was continually in action, pounding on every day *sans cesse* and generally also through the night, and it was excellent and well served; but our guns were silent most of the day. At eleven o'clock in the morning they would open up and leisurely plunge their shot across the valley at Fort Condé for half an hour; then remain silent till four or five in the evening, when another bombardment would commence and continue till dark.

Occasionally they seemed to wake up and become very angry, and on these occasions would bark and roar and screech for a couple of hours. The Germans never refused an artillery duel, and when our batteries seemed to wake up the Germans did too, and hurtled across their shot at a tremendous pace. The Germans at this time wasted an enormous lot of ammunition, but they nevertheless were extraordinarily formidable and effective with this arm. There was a small embankment outside our farmhouse, and this was a box seat *de luxe* every afternoon from four till half-past six o'clock. On our right, stretching on to Reims, and on our left towards Soissons, the artillery, German, French, and British, was then at its best. Sometimes the sound would be deafening all along the line, sometimes it would concentrate itself in our particular corner. Directly opposite us, on the far side of the river at Fort Condé, the Germans had a very strong artillery position. Their guns there outranged ours at first, and used on fine evenings, at the usual concert hour, to give us some splendid exhibitions.

First would come one shot to the right, and then one to the left. Then four flashes of yellow flame followed by huge cascades of earth would appear to strike the same spot, and a few seconds after the *dub-dub-dub-dub* of the explosions would reverberate and re-echo across the hills and valleys. They would sometimes pick out one particular area of ground on our front and simply cover every yard of it with bursting shells. At other times they would plant a line of shells right across a particular place. Again they seemed sometimes to go "shell mad," and would wildly send shells to all points of the compass. In the darkness of an autumn night the bursting of the shells was a terribly magnificent sight. We could see our shells, and especially the French shells, burst over the German positions. The French artillery always excited our admiration. The great guns, the men, the rapidity of fire, the noise, and the terrible bursting charges were all wonderful. No wonder France is proud of her big guns and her splendid gunners.

About ten o'clock in the mornings we frequently were surveyed by Taubes. Many of them were most daring. They were always pursued by our men and the French; and wonderful pursuits and flights were witnessed. Two of our aeroplanes often started together after a Taube. One would fly directly for the enemy craft, and one would circle into the upper blue and try to get above it. We were told that they used to fire at one another with carbines, but we never could hear the shots or see any smoke. The Taube always made off. Sometimes a Taube would be up alone, and after hovering and circling over our gun positions would make a sudden dash to directly above a battery, drop a smoke signal, and fly away; this signal would be rapidly followed by some German shelling.

The greatest spectacular effect of all was to watch the German shots from their anti-aircraft guns bursting round our aeroplanes. It was like pelting a butterfly with snowballs. We could see the burst and flash long before the sound reached us. The bursts produced white and black smoke balls, the black one appearing a little higher and later than the white. The white smoke balls unrolled themselves into a curious shape, very like a big German pipe. There was a huge bulb and a long, curling, thick stem. We stood often with "*our hearts in our mouths*" expecting that one of our daring flyers had been hit. Smoke-bursts would appear below, above, and round the craft, and then one shot would seem to actually hit it. But no; a minute afterwards we could make out the little machine flying higher or emerging swaggeringly from the midst. We watched our own bursts round a Taube with a different spirit, waiting eagerly for the *coup de grâce*, and having no humane thoughts for the daring pilot.

One afternoon we were certain that a Taube had been struck, for one burst appeared to be right on, but when the smoke cleared away the Taube was still going merrily. Then it began to slowly descend, then ascend again, and then suddenly plane away to our right. From the last shot she really had "got it in the neck," as Tommy Atkins puts it, and the machine plunged down behind the French lines. The pilot was killed, the observer got a fractured spine, and was dragged out of the wreckage—paralysed.

On the 19th September, orders from General French were read out congratulating the British troops upon their valour and tenacity at the Marne, and commending their courage on the Aisne. We were assured that by holding on to our present positions the enemy would be forced to retire.

On one Sunday, service was conducted by *Monsignor*, our Catholic chaplain, for Catholic soldiers, in one of the stable lofts at the farm. The preacher and the men had to climb up a ladder placed on the outside of the building, and get into the loft through a small door. The ladder was a crazy affair, but *Monsignor* tested it by going up first. He was a light-weight and very active, but a burly Falstaffian sergeant looked very hesitatingly at it, and it certainly creaked and bent considerably as he slowly mounted. The loft was packed with men, and we heard afterwards that the floor was not meant for a heavy weight. We were relieved to learn that there were no casualties at the service, and that *Monsignor* and his flock had not gone through the floor and startled the horses underneath.

I spent one forenoon in an advanced artillery observation post, and tried to make out the German positions through a telescope. We could make out some white waggons moving on a road far off, but they were out of range. The observation officer got to his post by walking up a cutting and then crawling into a hole, and there he stood for hour after hour patiently watching the other lines, while his sergeant sat close by, well concealed, and with a telephone receiver over his head. Any observations of importance were 'phoned back to the battery. These observation posts were dangerous "spots," for they were well within the reach of enemy shells and afforded very little cover. The observation officer here was an enthusiast, and I think he was familiar with the outline of every tree and rock on the other side. It requires some practice to be really expert with a telescope.

General officers occasionally came up to talk to our observer and peer at the opposite ridge. I met this artillery observation officer later on in the north of France, and this time he was a patient in hospital with a scalp wound. He had been in a house well in advance of our own advanced line, and had made a small hole in the roof through which he obtained a good view of the enemy dispositions, and directed the fixe of his battery. The German is a wily man, and evidently did not like the position of this house, for he shelled it out of existence. I was glad that the major got out with nothing more than a scalp wound, for good artillerists are worth much to our army today. Our artillery officers seem to enjoy war more than any other branch of the service. This major told me that one day his own and a French battery got fairly on to a German battery that had done considerable damage. The Allied guns destroyed the Germans, and the French were frantically delighted, their colonel coming over and warmly embracing Major X—— and kissing him on both cheeks. We told the major that he was a certain starter for the Legion of Honour. The major was a happy man when he was standing in a hole, or peering round a piece of rock, telescope to eye, and a sergeant lying near him with a telephone receiver strapped on his head.

One afternoon on the Aisne we heard that the Norfolks, who were in the trenches on our front, were hugely delighted. They had just killed a sniper. This particular sniper had become notorious, for he was a dead shot and had hit many of the Norfolk boys. Owing to the vigilance of this particular sniper they could not get hot tea into the trenches, and several of the Norfolk "Bisleys" were keenly anxious to bag him. One day a tree was observed to rustle after a sniping shot, and at once the Norfolks sent a hail of bullets into that particular tree. This brought the man down, for winged by Norfolk bullets the arboreal Prussian fell out of the branches like a ripe acorn, amidst the cheers of the men in the trenches.

It was said that these snipers on the Aisne belonged to the Forest Guards, who were rangers in the Imperial forests of Eastern Prussia, and were dead shots, accustomed all their lives to shoot wild pigs and wolves. They were highly unpopular amongst our men.

Sniping is quite in accordance with the rules of war, but the soldiers feel that sniping as the Germans play it is not "cricket." They naturally feel very angry with a sniper who gets up a haystack with some provisions and ammunition, and after having eaten all his food and fired off all his cartridges calmly emerges and surrenders.

Our men are extraordinarily good to wounded Germans and to prisoners, but these sniping sneaks stir their venom and ire. I saw one of these surrendered uninjured snipers at Ypres meet with savage scowls and epithets from some men of a company whose officer had been killed by him that morning.

About the last week of September I brought over some motor ambulances full of sick men to Braisne. This charming little town, situated on the Aisne and on the Marne Canal, was full of ambulances and clearing hospitals. Every house almost had a red-cross flag up, for the place was crammed with sick and wounded, and the clearing hospitals had been very busy with the big casualties. Three doctors had been killed a few days previously at Vailly when in action with their regiments, and another doctor had died the next day after having had his leg amputated for a bad shell wound. He was awarded the V.C., but did not live to enjoy that signal honour and distinction.

The clearing hospitals and ambulances were sending large numbers of sick soldiers down to the base *en route* for England—mostly cases of dysentery, lumbago, and rheumatism. Many of these men looked bad wrecks, and no wonder, when one remembers the rapid, arduous retreat from Mons and Le Cateau in the broiling summer heat, followed by the hard fighting and marching in the rain from the Marne to the Aisne, and how this was succeeded by the hardships, miseries, and discomforts in the wet sodden trenches at a time when it was impossible to give them hot cooked food and sufficient warmth. More men were wanted, and until they arrived the few had to do the work of many. The 5th Division had been promised a rest in reserve to recuperate, but not a man could be spared from the line we were so hardly holding, and so they simply had to "plug on," and, as cheerfully as they could, sing "It's a long, long way to Tipperary"; but they did not sing much at this time.

While we were at Mont de Soissons and a week after the arrival of our first red-cross motor ambulances, we were given instructions to look out for a mysterious red-cross motorcar driven by an officer in khaki who had a beard and wore a red-cross brassard on his arm. This car seemed to be very busy and was constantly travelling up and down the roads and always at high speed—too high a speed to be challenged.

Sitting at the front of the car and next the driver was a nurse, dressed in nurse's uniform, wearing a white cap, and also with a red-cross brassard on the left arm. We smelt something fishy about it all. Firstly, none of our medical officers wore beards; secondly, medical officers did not drive motor ambulances about; thirdly, there were no nurses with us. Nurses are not allowed in the fighting line. We watched for this car always, and always wondered what we would do if we did sight it, for none of us had arms, and this villain with the beard would be sure to have a loaded six-shooter near at hand.

Two days after our warning the car was spotted by a sentry, who challenged, but the driver went furiously past him. He was not out of the bush though, for a barricade had been erected half-way across the road at a very sharp turn, and to get round this the car had to slow down to "dead slow." A British sentry was here, and other soldiers were standing not far away. The bearded driver was ordered to stop and get out under cover of the sentry's rifle. The guard came up and the two motorists were arrested.

The man with the beard was a German spy right through, and he was handed over to the French, who shot him at daybreak next day. They say he died very gamely.

The "nurse" who sat beside him was not shot. We were told that "she" was really a man, a dapper little German waiter who had been on the staff of a leading hotel in Paris for some years. I saw the man with the beard shortly after he was arrested. He looked quiet and scholarly and somewhat meek, but *"still waters run deep."*

At 4 a.m. on the 27th of September we were all "turned out" by our O.C., who had just received urgent orders to be prepared to leave Mont de Soissons as the Germans "were over the river." After standing by for two hours we got word that it was a false alarm. Something had been irritating the Germans this morning, for at daybreak they opened a furious fire on our positions. As far as we knew it wasn't the *Kaiser's* birthday or the anniversary of any prehistoric German victory, so we put it down to nerves. Their gunners made a dead set on a field in our front just behind the ridge along the Aisne. Hundreds of Black Marias and shrapnel were sent on to that unlucky piece of ground, and it was wonderful to see the shot-ridden earth sent up in huge volcanic bursts. The enemy thought that we had a battery there, but we hadn't one nearer than half a mile, hence our enjoyment of the spectacle.

On the afternoon of this day we heard that Mr. Winston Churchill was with us and was dining with the Scots Greys. At least that was the rumour, but we hardly believed anything we heard out here. He was reported to have said that the war would last another eighteen months. This piece of information, following on an early morning's alarm and in cold wet weather, was distinctly cheering! However, as a kind of set-off, in the late afternoon we heard that the crown prince had been buried again, this time in the Argonne, and that it had been authentically established that he was quite dead before having been buried. We were glad to know this, because on the other occasions when he had been buried, he had not really been quite dead.

We were at this period suffering from the effects of a dislocated postal system. I had not yet received any letters from England, and did not know if mine had reached there. We were all anxious to get the London papers to "see how we were getting on at the front." We knew what was going on around us, but knew nothing more. One medical officer returned from Braisne, told us that he had heard a great rumour there. We were all agog to hear it. After whetting our appetites he gravely told us that a *padre* had informed him that, "*All Europe was in the melting pot and the devil was stirring the broth.*" This officer was duly punished by having his rum ration cut off.

One day on the Aisne I was an interested listener to a discussion between two British officers and three French officers on national characteristics, and this led up to a review of the way that the British, French, and German charge with the bayonet.

The French charge magnificently with the bayonet, but they charge in a state of tremendous excitement. When rushing across an open space to the enemy they shout and scream with excitement, "France!" "*A bas les Boches!*" "*En avant!*" They are uplifted with the wild ecstasy of the onfall. Men fall in the mad rush never to rise again. *N'importe*—all is unnoticed, on they go, an impetuous and irresistible avalanche of steel, yelling, stabbing, slaying, overwhelming. They are superb, these Frenchmen. I have seen them charge, and know from what I saw the splendid fellows they are. In the Argonne, on the Aisne, and in Flanders, the French soldier has carried out as resolute and daring bayonet charges as ever his fathers did under Napoleon, when they stormed the bridge at Lodi, swept over the field of Marengo, and hacked their bloody path at Austerlitz.

The British charge stoically and more grimly. They do not shout. I have heard them cursing. The British line advances as a sinister cold line of steel, in a sort of jog-trot. It is a line of cool-brained gladiators, alert of eye and thoroughly bent on slaughter. Our Briton sees his foe, and smites savagely with the calculating judgment of a good Rugby forward and with the bound of a wild cat. The disciplined valour and the savage relentlessness of the British bayonet attack has been heralded in story from Malplaquet to Waterloo, from Badajos to Inkermann, and historians will chronicle the undying glory of the 7th Division at Ypres when with rifle and bayonet it held the gate to Calais.

The German, in spite of what is often said to the contrary, is a brave and determined man with the bayonet. The German discipline is undoubted. It is a part of the people. It is the fibre of the nation. Discipline, subjection to authority, has not to be taught to this people; it is absorbed into their very being. The discipline of mind and body as we understand it is not the discipline of the German, for his is an obedience to authority only,—a "go" when ordered to "go," a "come" when ordered to "come." But it is also a "die" when ordered to face certain death. Men with whom this discipline is a message may not make saints or pleasant companions, but do make sturdy foes and stubborn fighters.

They charge well, advancing with a stooping, jerky trot, uttering hoarse guttural cries and "Hurrahs." On they come, in solid masses shoulder to shoulder, hoping by the weight and speed of the dense columns to get a momentum that nothing can withstand. When in a solid compact phalanx this German charge is very dangerous and formidable, and has been able, although at a frightful cost, to brush aside and overwhelm veteran British and French troops.

But if this compact line and solid column is broken, as it so often is today by shrapnel, rifle, or machine-gun fire, the sense of cohesion or "shoulder to shoulder" support is lost, and the heavy column is then no match for the lightning bayonet onfall of the French infantry or the weighty heave forward of a British regiment. The German infantryman is not an "individual" fighter, but he is nevertheless a brave soldier, and knows how to meet death. All three peoples have a great respect for each other when it comes to close quarters and take no chances.

A curious feature of French bayonet charges was told me by a French officer. He said that if the daily dispatches were read carefully it would be noticed that the Germans, when they attacked the French, generally made them vacate the first trench, but that the French always counter-attacked, retook their own, and carried the charge on into the German lines. He said that the Frenchmen are very easily surprised and are only at their best when they know what they are up against and what they have to do. They also require at times to be worked up to the "fire" of the business, and that this was specially true of younger troops. The officers know this, and when their men fall back from the front trench, they get them together, tell them that they must go forward again,—that France is watching them, that the cursed German has his foot in beautiful France, that the sons of the men of Jena and Wagram must still show their metal; then drawing his sword, and with "*En avant, mes enfants*," the officer leads forward, followed by his cheering men, and they are at these times irresistible.

There is a story told at the front of a famous Scottish regiment whose deeds have won admiration in nearly every battle in English history, which occupied some advanced trenches. The Germans rushed them in overwhelming numbers and drove them out with the bayonet. Another regiment, composed almost entirely of little Cockneys, was called up in support, and gallantly rushing forward drove out the Germans and took many prisoners. They then told the brawny Scotchmen that they could go back to their trenches again and if they felt anxious at any time the M—— boys from London would be only too pleased to come back and comfort them. Some weeks afterwards the Kilties helped the Cockneys out of a hot corner, so the odds are now even.

Talking of bayonet charges leads up to bayonet wounds. It is a curious fact, well noted amongst surgeons at the front, that there are very few bayonet wounds to treat. Yet bayonet charges are constantly taking place, and very bloody melees they are.

Where are these men who have been speared by the bayonet? The majority are dead, for the bayonet when it gets home is a lethal weapon. When it pierces the chest or abdomen it, as a rule, reaches a big artery; a rapid haemorrhage follows, and death comes speedily.

The majority of bayonet wounds are in the chest and abdomen, and ghastly terrible wounds they are. After the Bavarians and Prussians were hurled back at Ypres and La Bassée there were comparatively few bayonet wounds. Amongst the vast number of wounded men in the Clearing Hospital at Bethune I had personally to treat only one or two cases of bayonet wounds. These were, as a rule, simple flesh wounds, and were the lucky exceptions amongst the bayonet victims.

This feature about bayonet wounds was also noted by Larrey, the surgeon-in-chief to Napoleon during the great Continental wars, by M'Grigor, surgeon-in-chief to Wellington in the Peninsula, and by surgical observers at a later period during the Crimean War. A war correspondent in the Crimea wrote that a man who has been bayoneted dies in great pain, that his body and limbs are twisted and contorted by the last agonised movements preceding death. This belief is fallacious. Men who die speedily from a sudden loss of blood die easily and quietly. They go to sleep.

The German bayonet is longer, broader, and heavier than that of the Allies. The French bayonet is not a blade, but is shaped like a spear or stiletto. The British bayonet is a blade, short and light. It is not, however, the blade or the stiletto, it is the man behind that counts.

I mentioned before that our sick and wounded were housed in a loft of the farm-*château* of Mont de Soissons and in a shed outside. This shed or lean-to was a most uninviting place for the sick. One side was formed by a stone wall, from the top of that a roof projected, and this roof was held up by wooden pillars. There was no floor and there were no other walls. It was quite open to every wind that blew, except for the protection of the stone wall and the roof. Straw was laid on the ground of this lean-to and this straw, owing to the constant rain and the very muddy, filthy state of the roads and yards round about, got very sodden at times. New straw was then put on top of this old straw—that was all. It wasn't very much, truly. Yet badly wounded men were brought in in large numbers from the trenches and kept lying on this sodden straw for hours, and in some cases for a whole day and night. If the wounded man arrived after eleven o'clock in the morning he had to put up with a night on the straw in this lean-to.

If the man was sick from one of the usual diseases prevalent at this time—lumbago, rheumatism, and sciatica—he was led up to the loft in the main house. If he had a slight wound he was also led up to this place, but if he had a compound fracture or an abdominal injury it was necessary to carry him up on a stretcher, and the stair up to the loft was so narrow that the task was an extremely difficult one, and full of pain and misery to the patient. The loft was a draughty hole and not fit to accommodate a sick mountain goat. But it was a Buckingham Palace to the Whitechapel lean-to on the stone wall outside. Yet on this dirty sodden straw I have dressed foul, septic compound fractures, have elevated a fragment of loose bone pressing on a man's brain, and have stood by men dying from gas gangrene, and from pneumonia due to exposure from lying out in the rain and cold after having been wounded.

And every time I saw men lying out in that open shed I have asked,

"Why have we not motor ambulances at the front?" Every morning empty lorries returning from distributing their supplies at the front called in at Mont de Soissons and took our wounded down to railhead; and this method of transportation of the wounded was one of the horrors of war. Our wounded and sick did not arrive according to any time-table, and if they arrived at midday or in the afternoon or evening, they had, willy-nilly, to be accommodated at the *château*-farm, and the only accommodation we could offer was the windy, inhospitable loft or the straw-covered lean-to outside. If we had had motor ambulances all of this would have been avoided. Then the patients would not have had to be sent to our headquarters at all, but could have been carried to railhead at once. Why did we not have motor ambulances at the outset of war? God knows. Had anyone asked me five years ago what was the best way of transporting a wounded or sick man with an army in the field, I would have answered at once, "By motor ambulance, of course."

If a man is wounded in the streets of London or any other city in the civilised world he is conveyed to the nearest hospital by an ambulance motorcar. When the Army Service Corps had to arrange its transport for this war, they naturally thought of nothing else than motor traction. Yet in spite of the lessons of army manoeuvres in this country, and of the dictates of reason, our Army Medical Department sent Field Ambulances to the front with the old horse-ambulance of the days of Napoleon and Wellington, and did not have a solitary motor ambulance where they were so vitally necessary. The position was so odd and incomprehensible that I wrote about it to Lord ——, who, I knew, would look at the matter from the view-point of common sense and humanity. Lord—— has a great name in the Empire, and has been one of the best and ablest of governors of one of our Dominions beyond the seas. I knew that if I wrote to him, and he chose to act as I was sure he would, something would occur. I did not, owing to army postal delays, get his answer till long after, and it was worded as follows (allowing for considerable deletions of some parts of it, and for names):

> My Dear Martin,—I received your letter in London on Wednesday night. Within half an hour of its arrival I hunted up Mr. ——. I found him in a state of great indignation because of the obstacles put in the way of —— giving the assistance they desire to the wounded at the Front. I understand, however, that

LOADING WOUNDED AT SOISSONS.
THE FIRST MOTOR AMBULANCE ON THE AISNE.

THE LEAN-TO AT SOISSONS. UNLOADING WOUNDED.

sixty motor ambulances will be ready on Wednesday next, and that further ambulances will be provided later. Your letter has been read by Lord Kitchener. It arrived at an opportune moment, when the great want of motor ambulances at the Front was being realised here. I hope that even before you receive this letter the scandal which makes you so righteously indignant may have been removed and that proper arrangements are now in successful operation for the treatment of the wounded.

Please let me hear from you from time to time how things are going, and always remember that I shall be more than pleased if I can give you the slightest assistance in getting those things done which you may think necessary.—Believe me, yours sincerely,

Shortly after this, motor ambulances appeared, and the position eased, to the infinite and lasting benefit of our wounded officers and men. I still, however, often wonder why motor ambulances were not landed in France with the other motor vehicles when our Expeditionary Army disembarked. Many lives would have been saved, and much suffering would have been avoided.

CHAPTER 12

Field Ambulances and Military Hospitals

The military medical unit known as a Field Ambulance deserves some description.

The Field Ambulances are officially designated as Divisional Troops under the command of the Assistant Director of Medical Services. A Field Ambulance consists of three sections, known as A, B, and C sections, and each of these sections is divided into a "bearer" and a "tent" subdivision.

The personnel consists of a commanding officer, generally a major or a lieutenant-colonel of the Royal Army Medical Corps, who is always in one of the tent subdivisions, and of nine other medical officers and a quartermaster, generally an honorary lieutenant or captain, of the R.A.M.C. In addition there are 242 of other ranks, bearers, orderlies, cooks, Army Service Corps drivers, officers' servants, dispensers, clerks, washermen, etc. The personnel is fairly evenly divided amongst the three sections, so that on occasion a section of a Field Ambulance can carry on a limited but complete service. As will be seen later on at Bethune, one section of our ambulance did this, and for a time acted as a Clearing Hospital and passed thousands of wounded through its hands. B and C sections have three four-horsed ambulance waggons, and A section has four, making a total of ten waggons for the transport of wounded. The other transport of a Field Ambulance consists of six general service waggons, three medical store carts, three water carts, a cooks 5 cart, and an extra cart for odd jobs. The drivers and grooms have about one hundred horses to look after.

The Field Ambulance carries a complete hospital emergency equipment. Theoretically, if necessary a serious abdominal operation, a trephining operation, or an amputation could be carried out at an ambulance station by skilled surgeons surrounded by the latest and best of surgical instruments and in antiseptic surroundings. I said theoretically, but as a matter of fact such a state of affairs is not achieved, and the surgery performed at Field Ambulance stations is crude and temporary.

A Field Ambulance station is a first-aid station, and surgery is avoided as much as possible. The equipment of our Field Ambulance today leaves very much to be desired, and I earnestly hope that during this war the whole organisation will be thoroughly reviewed, reorganised, and remodelled, and that there will be evolved a medical unit more in consonance with the modern conceptions of good clean surgery. The Field Ambulance should receive the wounded from the brigade which it serves, and as long as it holds these wounded it should be able to give them the very be surgical and medical help. It must send the wounded as speedily as possible to the hospitals and stations in the rear, and keep the fighting line, of which it is really a part, as clear of wounded as possible. It must conform to the demands of the military situation; for after all war is war, and the purpose of a war is to beat the enemy with sound troops and get the wounded out of the way. A Field Ambulance can do all this and must do all this, and yet it need not be too obsessed with the idea that immediately a badly wounded man is brought in he must necessarily be bundled off to the base, irrespective of the nature or magnitude of his wounds.

The future of very many battlefield injuries depends on the first treatment received, and a skilled surgeon surrounded with familiar tools and appliances to ensure absolute cleanliness can be a god of mercy and confer health and power on many a stricken man. A blundering, incompetent amateur, lacking the divine essence of knowing his own imperfections and courageously taking responsibilities which are skyhigh above him, can inflict a lifelong wrong and deprive a man of his power to earn his livelihood in the future. The cautious and conservative surgeon is ever the boldest when boldness means success. In every Field Ambulance in this war and in future wars, let us see to it that we have a cautious and conservative surgeon. The medical officer is not as a rule a good horse master.

From my experience (and I am speaking both from what I saw in the South African War and in this war), the medical officer is a very indifferent horse master. He will do his best, as he always does in all circumstances; but it is clearly unfair to ask a doctor, who knows as much about horses as a monk does about antelopes, to take charge of a unit comprising about one hundred horses, sixteen four-horsed waggons, and seven or eight two-horsed carts, Army Service Corps drivers, and a miscellaneous lot of grooms. I have seen an amiable and competent army medical officer dismayed when he was compelled, owing to some duty, to get on a horse's back, and the horse seemed to know and enjoy it, for, usually a docile, mild-eyed beast, he at these times became exceedingly sportive. Yet this officer may have, owing to his rank, to assume charge later of a hundred horses and a lot of waggons. A shoemaker should stick to his last, and a doctor is only at home with his own professional work.

The remedy is to put Field Ambulances under trained officers of the Army Service Corps. They are experts in the management of convoys and transports, and could manage the field work of an ambulance to the infinite satisfaction of everybody. Leave the doctors to the purely professional work. There is enough of that to be done. Doctors are too valuable as doctors to spare them for work which A.S.C. subalterns and young captains can perform. The arranging of advanced dressing stations, the choosing of buildings as hospital sites, can be done by the A.D.M.S. of the division, and the purely workman's part of the job can be done by the A.S.C. officer and his men.

The transportation of wounded from the fighting line has been extraordinarily well carried out by the Royal Army Medical Corps and the Red Cross since our army took up its present fighting line in France and Flanders. During the great retreat the transportation was ineffective, and there is no doubt at all that many of our wounded who had to be left behind could have been rescued if we had had motor ambulance convoys as we have today.

On the Marne, and for the first week on the Aisne, the transport of the wounded to the base was most imperfect. Who is to blame for this is a matter that will have to be thrashed out when the piping days of peace arrive, and we have time once again to put our house in order and profit by the lessons of the war. The only means of transport previous to the arrival of the motor ambulances was by transport lorries belonging to the Army Service Corps. These waggons brought provisions and supplies to the front, and on returning empty had to call at the various ambulance stations. Straw was laid on the floors of these lorries, and the wounded were packed tightly on the straw. This method of transportation for a man suffering from pneumonia or compound fracture, a chest wound or a wound in the abdomen, was a terrible ordeal, and undoubtedly added intense suffering, misery, and discomfort to our badly stricken soldiers. Things improved directly on the advent of the comfortable, well-sprung motor ambulance. From the firing line to the horsed or motor ambulance the man is carried on a stretcher by hand, but all future transportation is by motor ambulance, train, river-barge, and steamer.

When a man is wounded at the front he is brought in by regimental bearers to the dressing station of the medical officer of the battalion. This is generally either a "dugout" or is situated in a cottage a little way back or sometimes behind a stone wall or near a clump of trees. Here the regimental doctor simply dresses the wound, as cleanly as possible under the circumstances, stops all bleeding and applies rough splints to fractured limbs, and administers morphia if there is much pain. These regimental aid posts are dangerous places well within shell fire, and the wounded are got out of them as quickly as possible, and generally at night. They are carried on stretchers to the ambulance waggons—horse or motor—which are drawn up on some point of a road, or sometimes in a village farther back. From here the wounded man is conveyed to the headquarters of the ambulance in a village or *château* or church, and his wounds are again dressed, if necessary, but as little handling as possible is done, although the soldier thinks that his wounds should be frequently dressed.

At the ambulance headquarters urgent operations, often of a serious character, have sometimes to be carried out, but no operation is done if the case will permit of safe transportation farther back. The next rest-house for the wounded man is the Clearing Hospital or Casualty Clearing Station, and through this pass the wounded of many ambulances. Many wounded are brought direct from the trenches to a Casualty Clearing Hospital without calling at all at the ambulance headquarters. All urgent operations are performed at the Casualty Clearing Station, and this station should be thoroughly well equipped in staff and personnel as well as with all the modern appurtenances so necessary for the safe performance of intricate and dangerous surgical operations.

For obvious reasons the Clearing Hospital or Casualty Clearing Station could not fulfil its destiny during the retreat of our army from Belgium to the east of Paris. If the army is retreating, the Clearing Hospital must go. It is part of the line of communications and would impede and cumber the fighting divisions as they fall back. If full of wounded at this time, it would of course be captured by the advancing enemy, as the Clearing Hospital has no transport of its own, and depends on the regular transport department of the army. There ought to be a transport attached to a Clearing Hospital and solely under the control of the commanding officer, and it would be of great advantage to have the whole Clearing Hospital under the command of an Army Service Corps officer of experience, a man accustomed to the transportation of supplies and to commanding drivers of vehicles and mechanics. To put a Clearing Hospital under the command of a doctor as is now done is as absurd as it would be to place a large civil hospital under the control of a doctor.

Our civil hospitals are governed by Boards and a Secretary who has the whole administration at his finger-ends. The medical staff do not control or govern a civil hospital. They are busy enough in their own sphere, which is a purely professional one—the treatment and cure of the sick inmates. So with the Clearing Hospitals, the Army Service Corps officer should be in charge of the hospital, and the purely professional part of the hospital, the treatment of the wounded, should be entirely and absolutely under the control of the medical staff, and completely outside the range of action of the administrative chief. The evacuation of the wounded from the Clearing Hospital to the hospital train and base could be controlled also by the administrative lay head of the hospital, and all that the medical officers would be concerned with would be the cases suitable to evacuate and when they should be evacuated. There would at first be considerable opposition to this course by the regular Army Medical Corps, but they could not advance any cogent arguments against the devolution of administrative authority from them to the Army Service Corps.

The Royal Army Medical Corps is, or should be, a professional body of men. Anything that impairs their professional efficiency is bad. The control of Field Ambulances and Clearing Hospitals is not a professional man's *métier*, and he does not shine in this position. Too much military control or command changes the army medical officer from a doctor to a military officer, and this change is not to be desired.

In civil life the more experienced a doctor is, the bigger becomes his practice and the wider becomes his sphere of professional usefulness. In military life, experience means promotion to higher rank, and the higher the rank the less the professional work and the more the administrative work.

In war time, as witness South Africa and this present war, civil surgeons have to be called in large numbers to undertake important surgical work. The experience of medical officers of the army in peace is professionally a poor one. They are rarely called upon to perform serious surgical operations, for a man requiring an important surgical operation is no longer of use as a soldier, and is invalided out of the army. This man then necessarily comes under the civilian surgeon, who sets about to cure him, if possible, of his affliction. An urgent appendix operation, a rupture, the removal of a loose cartilage in a knee joint and varicose veins in their various manifestations—these, roughly speaking, compose the experience in surgery of the army doctor in times of peace.

In advanced and intricate surgery in the abdomen he gets no practice, and yet it is just the experience gained in this branch of surgery that is so vitally important to surgeons at the front to-day.

A surgeon at the front should be a man of ripe judgment and a good operator. He should know when to operate, and what is equally important, when not to operate. He should know whether a wounded man should be operated upon at once without exposing him to the risk of further transportation, or whether he could be transported to a Base Hospital without endangering his safety. And if the case demands immediate surgery at the front, this surgeon should be able to undertake the operation himself. Surgeons of approved judgment and skill are not hard to find, and every Base Hospital, every stationary Hospital, every Casualty Clearing Hospital, every Field Ambulance should have one officer on its staff possessing the qualities and attributes mentioned. And such a distribution is the easiest thing in the world to effect.

These men can be drawn from the civil side of the profession, as the military side, the Royal Army Medical Corps proper, cannot provide them.

There are of course able surgeons in the Royal Army Medical Corps, men who, were they in civil life, would have large consulting practices and great reputations, but these men are few and are of that surgical bent which will rise superior to its military environment, and keeping touch with modern work, will absorb all that is good and new in the methods and technique of surgery.

This lack of appreciation of the requirements of modern surgery has been evidenced in so many instances at the front with our Field Ambulance and Clearing Hospital equipment.

One day early in the war I had a number of wounded men to treat, all with dirty septic wounds. The method of sterilising our hands was inefficient and I asked for rubber gloves. Rubber gloves for the hands of the surgeon are absolutely essential when dealing with a number of septic cases. After handling septic cases he may be called upon at any moment to operate on a case requiring the strictest antisepsis or asepsis to give the wounded man a fighting chance of life. I asked a senior medical officer of the ambulance for these rubber gloves. Judge of my consternation and amazement when he said that "There were no rubber gloves in the ambulance equipment, and *he did not believe in the necessity for rubber gloves.*" When the ambulance was being equipped previous to leaving this country at the outbreak of war he could have obtained as many pairs of rubber gloves as he wished, but because he did not think them necessary, they were not obtained. He did not realise what war surgery would be like and had not been accustomed to operate on a large scale. This blunder on his part was inexcusable and serious, and the one who suffered from such a blunder was not himself but a wounded officer or man.

In a Clearing Hospital in a small town in France to which I was temporarily attached for some days, again I could not obtain rubber gloves, although I had there to operate on profoundly septic cases, on the cases of appalling gas gangrene and also on recent wounds of knee joints, of brain, and abdomen. I asked for rubber gloves and was promised them. None came. On my own initiative I wrote to a London surgical supply establishment and obtained three dozen pairs of rubber gloves by return mail. Was this fair to our wounded? At another time I had a difficult bowel operation to do, and the only fine needles in stock could not be used as the finest silk available there would not go through the eyes of the needles. The examination of the silk and the needles had not been carried out when the equipment was being put together in England. At this same place I had nothing strong enough to ligature blood-vessels at the bottom of deep septic wounds, except silk. The catgut was too fine and brittle to hold a big blood-vessel, yet any surgeon will tell you that to put a silk ligature on a vessel in a foul wound is very bad surgical technique. Yet it had to be done.

Again, in a dangerous operation on the knee joint I could not get any sterilised towels nor an aneurism needle nor a pair of scissors. The only scissors had been lost, and only one aneurism needle, which had also been lost, was supplied in the instrument case. The patient was an officer who had been struck by shrapnel at the back of the knee, on the shoulder, and on one foot and one hand. He bled smartly and was admitted to this Clearing Hospital with a tourniquet round his thigh to control the bleeding temporarily. I opened up the wound behind the knee and secured the large bleeding artery and veins there, and all I had to ligature these vessels with was silk. There was no stout catgut, as there ought to have been. Also I could only get two sterilised towels, and these I had to boil myself. This was in a Clearing Hospital at the front in November last year. There were no gloves. There were none of the things round one to treat shock from which the officer suffered after the operation. It made one despair. Yet all of these things should have been at hand, and could have been easily obtained by the exercise of some forethought. No wonder the wounds in so many cases were at this time sent back to England in such a foul and septic condition. It was not the military authorities who were to blame. The military chiefs did all they could to help the medical department and always have done so. The fault lay at the door of the Royal Army Medical Corps chiefs, and after the war these things will again be reviewed in order to prevent a future repetition.

My criticism is meant entirely for the good of our wounded officers and men. They deserve the best, and it is the duty of the Army Medical Department to give them of the best. It is only by pointing out defects that improvement can follow, and the only man who can point out these medical defects is a surgeon who has actually had to operate on wounded men in a Field Ambulance or in a Clearing Hospital under adverse surroundings.

It is an easy matter to arrange for a modern surgical equipment for a Field Ambulance or a Clearing Hospital. Sterilisers for instruments and towels and dressings are not cumbrous appliances and do not take up much space. The surgical instrument case at present in use by the Royal Army Medical Corps is out of date and requires a complete revision and overhaul by a surgeon who is accustomed to operate, and not by a committee of senior or retired officers of the Army Medical Staff. The younger officers of the Royal Army Medical Corps and the "professional" men amongst the seniors recognise the defects of the present system, but naturally they cannot say much. This lack of medical equipment and the "unreasonableness" of the medical department is a common subject of conversation at the front amongst civilian medical officers, and I have seen some of these men indignant beyond measure at what they have seen and met with.

The Clearing Hospital, in addition to being a "rest-house" on the *via dolorosa* of the wounded, is also a sieve. It has to sift the lightly wounded from the seriously wounded and the serious cases from the desperate cases. In this process of sifting a large collection of wounded men, it discriminates between those who are fit to be sent to the Base and those who must remain for a longer or a shorter period. Many claim that the Clearing Hospital is not a hospital *per se* but holds a purely administrative position. I feel sure that it will become more and more a hospital as time goes on, and that its present surgical and medical equipment will necessarily undergo a complete reorganisation. Today its equipment is little more than that of a Field Ambulance. It is not equipped to deal with extensive and serious operations, and yet serious operations have been performed and will necessarily continue to be performed at the Clearing Hospital.

There is no shadow of doubt that many of the men operated upon at Bethune in the *Hôpital Civil et Militaire* later on in the war owe their recovery in a very large measure to the excellence of the complete sterilising equipment and cleanly surroundings. No trouble can be too great and no expense should be spared to make the surgical stations at the front up to date in all that makes for surgical cleanliness.

It is even more necessary to have the skilled surgeon at the front than at the Base, but we have any amount of skilled surgeons for both places. A skilled operating man of experience should not be attached to a regiment as regimental surgeon while a recently qualified man is deputed to blood his 'prentice hand at a major operation in a Clearing Hospital. Yet this has been done, and I know of an instance where a recently qualified man performed his first trephining operation on a soldier with a bad head injury whilst a few miles away there was an experienced operator engaged solely in first-aid work as regimental surgeon.

I was told by a senior officer of the R.A.M.C. that in the city of X—— before the war he had as assistant in his military operating room a very clever young R.A.M.C. orderly. This man was well trained in the sterilisation of instruments and dressings and in the preparation of a room for operations. When the ambulance was mobilised in this city on the outbreak of war the medical officer applied for this man, who would have been invaluable, to be appointed to the tent section of the Field Ambulance. Here the training and knowledge of this orderly would have been of great service. Instead of that, the man was appointed to look after the water waggon of an infantry regiment and was killed early in the war. Any untrained man would have done for the water cart, but a lot of training is necessary to make a good hospital room assistant.

At the Clearing Hospital the wounded man meets for the first time the army nurse. This is the nearest point to the firing line that our nurses are allowed to go, but I know lots of them who are extremely anxious to go into the trenches. The nurse is a welcome sight to both officers and men, and no man nurse can adequately take the place of a trained woman. The presence of nursing sisters in a hospital is good and wholesome, and where they are the hospital work is carried on infinitely better and the patient is well looked after. R.A.M.C. orderlies do not like our nursing sisters. The sister makes the orderly work, will not allow him to smoke in the wards, makes him wash his hands and keep tidy. To the slacker, of course, these things are highly unpalatable, and there are many slackers about. Our British nursing sisters are splendid women, and work ungrudgingly and sympathetically always. It is good to see a bright-faced, white-aproned nurse amongst the wounded, and she is extraordinarily popular with her patients.

The hospital train in France is a well-run unit. The accommodation for the sick and wounded is excellent, trained nurses accompany each train, and the medical arrangements are controlled by three doctors, generally a regular army medical officer in charge and with two temporary lieutenants or civil surgeons to assist him to do the actual professional work. No surgical or medical work worth mentioning is done on hospital trains; they are simply means to an end—the end is the Base Hospital.

The Base Hospitals in France are well-run units also. There are here big medical and nursing staffs, a large number of orderlies, and any amount of equipment. I was for some time Surgical Specialist at No. 6 General Hospital at Rouen, and this hospital was splendidly administered by the commanding officer, Lieutenant-Colonel ———. In the Base Hospitals there are good operating rooms, and in fact every modern appliance that one could desire. It is a pity that the same care in administration and equipment had not been carried farther up and nearer our soldiers at the front.

CHAPTER 13

Goodbye to the Aisne.

Early in October, and at night, the ambulance again took the road—we turned our back on the Aisne and with the 2nd Army Corps began the famous move across the French lines of communication to the Belgian frontier and into Flanders. This change of position will be written up in the future as one of the most masterly episodes of the war. It was a formidable task to move the British Army and its supplies across the French lines and bring them into an entirely new position on the front. It had to be carried out with the utmost secrecy. None of us knew where we were going. Each day the secret orders were issued and the various brigades and columns carried out the indicated programme, while the French took up our positions and trenches as we retired from them. This was done also with great secrecy. I can imagine the perturbation of the Saxons and Wurtemburgers on our front on seeing French *képis* and uniforms where for weeks they had seen the khaki. The 2nd Corps moved off first. The 1st Corps left a week later.

On the first night we marched through Nampteuil and reached Droszy about midnight. It was a beautiful starlight night with a biting frost. We billeted in a spacious *château*, with plenty of cover for the ambulance waggons and with stables for the horses. The men slept in stable lofts and the officers on the floor of the marble hall. The hall was a beautiful room, containing some valuable old furniture. The walls were covered with relics of the chase of the days of Louis xiv., and old hunting horns, knives, and boar spears. Part of the *château* was modern, and part consisting of a wonderful old tower, loopholed for arrows, was evidently all that was left of the keep of a strong feudal castle. The proprietor was an old rear-admiral of the French Navy and he received us with the greatest courtesy; the Norfolks arrived an hour after us and quartered in a big house and yard close by. Our brigadier, Count Gleichen, arrived early in the morning and slept in our *château*.

A Taube was seen approaching in the morning and every one was ordered to get under cover or stand stock-still. This Taube was evidently trying to find out the reason for the absence of British in the old trenches and the presence of the French in their place. We surmised correctly that the Teutonic curiosity was considerably aroused. A few hours afterwards another Taube appeared—or it may have been our first visitor—and flying very fast, for a French airman was in hot pursuit. Both soon disappeared into the upper blue, but we laid our odds on the Frenchman.

At 6.30 that night we again got under way and had a magnificent night march to Longpont, arriving there at 10.30 p.m. Longpont is a wonderful old place. The Château Longpont dates back to very early times and contains some marvellous old tapestry. It is the home of the Comte and Comtesse M——, and they were in residence at this time and entertained as their guests on this day General Sir Charles Ferguson and his staff. Sir Charles was the commander of the 5th Division of the 2nd Army Corps. The *comte* and *comtesse* had as guests, some weeks previously, General von Kluck, Commander of the right wing of the German Army, and had some interesting anecdotes to tell of this hard-fighting General and his staff.

Abutting on the *château* were the famous ruins of the abbey of Longpont. The remains of the old abbey are so historic that they are known in France as "*Les Ruines.*" It was built by the Cistercian monks in the twelfth century, and in the adjoining priory over three hundred monks were accommodated in the days when the Church was omnipotent in France. During the Reign of Terror the beautiful old abbey was destroyed by the revolutionaries, but the massive character of the pillars and walls proved too much even for these iconoclasts, and stand today, clothed in ivy and moss, the monuments of a glorious past. The venerable and stately majesty of these ruins, where every stone seemed to speak of the grandeur of other days, impressed the imagination of all who gazed upon them.

The day following our arrival at Longpont was a Sunday. Divine service was conducted at 10 a.m. round the old broken altar by our Church of England chaplain, and Sir Charles Ferguson, the Divisional General, read the lessons. *Monsignor* conducted the Catholic service at 11.30. Both services were largely attended by our own men and by

Château of Longpont.

Village of Longpont

French soldiers occupying the village. In imagination one could see the princely abbots and the cowled monks who, during a period of six hundred years, had chanted their litanies and passed in procession inside the beautiful abbey, gazing wonderingly at the simple military services held round the tumbled masonry of the ancient altar.

After the services we spent the day wandering through the old-fashioned village of Longpont, examining its ancient gateways adorned with the crests of the kings of France, or strolling through the fine woods bordering the lake. Heavy artillery fire from the French batteries could be heard all the day. We were now right behind the French lines.

I cannot pass from Longpont without describing our sleeping quarters on the night of our arrival. The officers of the ambulance had to sleep on the straw of an old stone stable. The stable looked comfortable and inviting, and it was not till we had crawled into our valises that the "fun" commenced. We had just lain down and blown out the candles when we felt curious obscure movements under our valises. Then a rustling of straw and a scampering of some objects over our beds. One doctor at once yelled out, "Good Lord, the place is full of rats." He turned on his electric torch and immediately there was a wild scurry and stampede to cover of hundreds of rats. The torch was turned off, and after a little while the scampering and squeaking started again. The rats were either enjoying a game or were upset by our occupation of their stable.

At one end of the stable was a feeding trough, and sitting in a row on the edge of the trough were innumerable rats. Conspicuous amongst them was one enormous fellow, about the size of a cat— someone said he was as big as a calf—with huge grey moustaches and very knowing eyes. This was undoubtedly the leader. We christened him Von Hindenberg. Somebody threw a bottle at him, but the cunning old rascal dodged it by making a tremendous leap into the middle of the stable and disappeared. One young doctor then said that he would rather sleep out in the open than amongst the rats, and he carried his valise outside. The rest of us decided to stop where we were, but we all pulled our blankets well over our heads. Our childhood horror of rats still remained, and we were just a little bit afraid of them—especially of Von Hindenberg.

From Longpont we had a hard gruelling march of fifteen to eighteen miles through the night, and arrived at Lieux Ristaures at 6 a.m. We were stopped a long time on the road at the little village of Corey by hundreds of motor vans, waggons, and buses containing French troops. We realised on this night what "crossing a line of communication" actually means. The French were hurrying up heavy reinforcements to strengthen a part of their front which at that moment was withstanding a most resolute German attack, our brigade was moving as quickly as possible to another point of the front. The roads of the two armies crossed at Corey, and of course one had to wait till the way was clear. It all looked very confusing and chaotic, but it was really very cleverly managed. Our road at first led through a forest, and anyone who knows the forests of France knows the beauty and charm of the tall trees. Little could be seen, however; high overhead one could make out a few stars, but the track itself was in Cimmerian darkness. About 2 a.m. we reached Villars Cotterets and marched through the old cobbled streets without a pause. This old town looked interesting, and one would have liked to have explored the birthplace of Dumas.

After Villars Cotterets our road lay through more open country and a grey dawn made things clearer. We were all dog-tired with the long march and the constant halts; marching at night was more monotonous and fatiguing than day marching. On the way from Villars Cotterets to our next bivouac, Lieux Ristaures, at night time, when we were all feeling very done up, a most surprising rumour reached us. Far ahead on the long column we suddenly heard distant cheering which grew in intensity as it travelled quickly down to us preceded by a message shouted from one to another, "The *Kaiser* is dead. Killed yesterday morning. Pass it on." When the message reached us we laughed, and did not pass it on. Cries came out of the darkness in front, "Pass the message on. It's official. The *Kaiser's* dead." So we passed it on, and the cheering travelled back across country to the marching men far behind. It cheered the men up wonderfully; they were delighted.

It of course turned out to be a fake, cleverly engineered by some wags at the head of the column. Of rumours there was no end. The crown prince had been buried in Flanders, in the Argonne, at Soissons. But he always got out of his grave. We buried Von Kluck, Hindenburg, and Bulow, and each burial was related with a wealth of detail that left nothing to the imagination. The most accepted rumour of all, and one which is still believed by many, was the harrowing story of the prince with the velvet mask. This story had a distinctly Dumas flavour, and it had a great vogue. It was related to me first on the Aisne by a doctor in a Scottish regiment, who had had it from the colonel, who had received it from somebody higher up. I, of course, passed it on lower down the social scale, and our division knew it that afternoon.

The crown prince at this time was said to be living in a richly furnished cave opposite Reims. On dull days he would sit on a chair outside and order the shelling of Reims Cathedral, while he gazed through a powerful glass at the falling masonry. One day the Prussian Nero was missing from his cave, and the story then shifts to Strasburg, whither in the dead of night a wounded officer of apparently august rank was conveyed in a motor-car. Two powerful limousines accompanied this car, one before and one behind, and these were full of highly placed army officers. A special train with steam up was awaiting the arrival of the cars, and as the wounded officer was carried across the platform on a stretcher, closely surrounded by generals, it was noticed that a velvet mask covered his face. The mask fell off as the body was lifted into the train and the crown prince's face was exposed to view. I believe that this story was afterwards circulated in the French press. We certainly did not hear of His Imperial Highness for many months afterwards.

Another rumour circumstantially related by a field chaplain and duly passed on with the *imprimatur* of the Church, was that Prince Albrecht of Prussia, son of the War Lord himself, had been wounded and taken prisoner into Antwerp by the Belgians. He was operated upon by Belgian surgeons in the presence of two German medical officers, and a bullet was extracted from his spine. The bullet was a Mauser—a German one. The prince died and his body was handed back to the Germans.

On the way to our next bivouac we also heard that Arras was being bombarded by the Germans and that they were investing Antwerp. We had quite a lot of war news to discuss for the remainder of our road, and until we pulled our waggons under the trees round an old mill at Lieux Ristaures. The men were billeted in outhouses and wood sheds belonging to the mill, and the officers were cordially welcomed by the hospitable miller and his kind-hearted womenfolk. They prepared coffee, bread and butter, and eggs for us, and we had the use of two bedrooms and a small office. A rapid mill race ran through the garden and under the kitchen floor of the house to the orchard beyond. When the miller's wife wanted fresh water, all she had to do was to lift up a trap on the kitchen floor and dip the bucket into the tumbling water below. Lieux Ristaures has a fine old ruined church all to itself, but it is disfigured by some modern attempts to restore it to its ancient

On the road to Compiègne

grandeur, and these attempts have spoiled completely the beauty of the ruins. At Lieux I received my first mail since leaving England. It was now October, and I had left England in August. This will give an idea of the marvellous work of our Army Post Office, but as no department has received such abuse as this one, I will spare its feelings and say no more.

A fine contingent of French cavalry passed by on this day. The men and horses looked splendid. The brass helmets, plumes, and *cuirasses* caught the sun's rays, and we described the passing as a "gorgeous cavalcade." The helmets and *cuirasses*, however, seem to belong to old-world armies, and look stagey amongst the simpler uniforms of this age.

We stopped two nights at the quaint old farm of Lieux with its rushing mill race, and at three o'clock on the second day marched to Bethisy St. Martin, where we had an excellent tea at a cosy house in the town—butter, eggs, bread, cold beef, and pickles. We sat round a table with a tablecloth! our first since August. The good woman who prepared the meal made us very welcome. We slept on the floor of the *Mairie* in the centre of the town till 5 a.m., when we again took the road to Santines and Verberie, passing near Senlis. Verberie showed many evidences of the Prussian sign manual—shelled houses and smashed walls. We reached the river Oise at 10 a.m. and crossed by a pontoon bridge, as the fine old stone bridge had been blown up; marched through Rivecourt and bivouacked for three hours by the wayside. It was a glorious morning, the going was good, and everybody was cheerful and looked very hard and fit. At Halte de Meux, where was a railway siding with troop trains, we received orders to embark on one of the trains for a destination unknown.

The train by which we were to travel had to carry the Norfolk Regiment also. When the Norfolks were all on board we found that there was not room enough left for the Field Ambulance, with its ambulance waggons, supply waggons, horses, and men. C section, with its waggons and equipment, had to be left behind, and get on as best it could by some other train; so we of C section took the road to Compiègne. We reached this charming and historic city in the dark, and found that there was no train for us. We crossed the Oise again on a bridge of moored barges, as the magnificent stone bridge spanning the Oise here was in ruins, destroyed by the French during the German advance. The night was desperately cold; we slept, or tried to sleep, on the boulevard alongside the river bank, but had to get up and march about to keep up the circulation. The men lit a fire under the trees of the boulevard and sat round it all night. There was no reason really why we should have slept out on the open boulevard, for there was a large, half-empty infantry barracks about 20 yards away and the French offered us the use of it for the night. Our commanding officer, however, decided otherwise, and consequently we passed a most miserable night.

Compiègne, situated on the Oise, is one of the most charming and fascinating cities in France. In the palace, Napoleon Bonaparte and the Empress Marie Louise, Louis Philippe, and Napoleon in. frequently resided. The tower where Joan of Arc was imprisoned, the sixteenth-century *Hôtel de Ville* with its belfry tower, and the old church of St. Jacques well repay a visit. The city appeared on the surface to be leading a normal life except for the large number of French soldiers and the many Red Cross Hospitals. Compiègne was at this time a favourite afternoon call for the Taubes, and they frequently dropped bombs, meant no doubt for the old palace. Old historic *châteaux*, cathedrals, and churches have a strange fascination for German artillerists and bomb-droppers.

I must now relate an episode of some interest that occurred on the march up to Compiègne—nothing less than seeing General Joffre, the commander-in-chief of the Allied Armies. I had dropped behind from my ambulance, and had given my horse to my groom to lead behind my section on the march. A marching regiment was coming up behind us, and as I knew the doctor I waited till the regiment came up, and then joined in and walked alongside my medical friend. A large *château* was situated on the side of the road some distance on, and as we came up we saw a large group of French officers standing at the old gateway. A whisper travelled rapidly down the line that this was the French Headquarters Staff and that Joffre himself was there. At once the subalterns "tightened up" the marching men, heads were lifted, shoulders squared, the step became smarter and rhythmic. Low muttered commands snapped out: "Smartly there," "By your right," "Keep your distance, men."

As we came abreast of the group at the gateway, the sharp, clear command rang out from each platoon officer, "Eyes right!" the officers saluted smartly, and with a parade swing the fine regiment marched past. I gazed long and interestedly at the officer at the gateway who took our salute. He was easily distinguishable as Joffre, for he was exactly like the pictures seen of him in every shop window in France, or rather the pictures were faithful representations of Joffre. When I got past, I stepped out of the company I was marching with on to the far side of the road, and while the remainder of the regiment was still passing by I had a good long look at the man who means so much to France, and in whom France is so sublimely confident. He was dressed in a well-fitting but easy blue tunic, with stars on the sleeves near the curl indicating his rank of general, and with a gold band on the shoulders, the familiar red French trousers, and black polished cavalry jack-boots. On his head he had a gold-braided *képi*.

Joffre is of middle height, strong and sturdily made, broad-shouldered and with a figure stout and heavy. His face is full, genial, and attractive, browned like the faces of men who have lived and worked in the tropics, and with a white moustache which gave a somewhat benevolent air. He was evidently interested in the march past of our regiment, for he walked three or four paces forward from his staff and towards us, and seemed to take in all the details of men and equipment as his eye scanned up and down. His salute was given with the careful exactness and ceremony always bestowed by the French upon this act, which the British officer goes through so casually.

Joffre did not look the dazzling military leader of romance, but he looked very business-like. Here was not the lean figure and the hawk nose of a Wellington, the glittering swagger of a Murat, or the inscrutable pose of the little Grey Man of Destiny. Yet this broad, homely, comfortable, and democratic figure standing by the roadside and carefully observing us, is the most powerful man in France today—the man against whom no political criticism is levelled, the idol of the soldiers, and in whom the people of France have such a simple faith. He is called "Our Joffre," and the possessive phrase indicates the pride the people and army feel in him. The French will tell the following story, which has gone the rounds, with great gusto. After a big battle in Poland, Von Hindenberg's Chief of Staff contracted a "political illness" and was sent to Berlin to recover his health.

The *Kaiser* wired to Hindenberg, "Whom do you nominate for your new Chief of Staff?" The reply came back, "Would like Joffre."

French officers at the front will tell you that Joffre is an Aristides the Just; that he ordered the shooting of four French generals early in the war because they were traitors to France, and that he has "retired" all the old generals who are slow to think and too fond of cocktails to be good campaigners; that he speedily rewards ability and initiative by promotions on the field, and is merciless on an officer—no matter of what rank—who shows incompetence.

Joffre was met early in the War of the Trenches by an old friend, who greeted him with, "Well, how are things going?" The general's eyes twinkled humorously as he replied, "*Laissez-moi faire, je les grignotte*" ("Leave me alone, I am nibbling them"). A French surgeon who knows Joffre, told me that he is a good sleeper, and that during the worst days he never missed one night's sleep. It was Shakespeare's Caesar who said, I think, to Mark Antony:

Let me have men about me that are fat,
Sleek-headed men and such as sleep o' nights.

Joffre has never interested himself in politics, and he is one of the few great Frenchmen who have avoided the glamour of the political stage on which so many ephemeral reputations have been made and so many good ones blasted. Joffre, like most men who "do "things, is a silent man. I am glad that I have seen "Joffre *le taciturne*," and been privileged to salute him.

Joffre and French are both over sixty years of age. Pau, the one-armed French general, known as the "Thruster," is a veteran of the war of 1870. Gallieni, the "rock of Paris," the general destined to hold Paris when Von Kluck was bearing so hastily down on the capital, is an old man. Von Hindenberg, the pride of Germany, is sixty-seven. Von Kluck, the commander of the right wing of the German Army, who so furiously hacked his way almost to the gates of Paris, and was rolled back in a crushing defeat, is over seventy years of age. Napoleon and Wellington were forty-six at Waterloo. Nelson died at forty-seven. Ney was thirty-five when he was shot. Von Boon, the German Minister of War in the Franco-Prussian War, was sixty-seven when the campaign began.

Bismarck was then about fifty-five, and Von Moltke was an old man—a septuagenarian. Are we too old at forty? No. I knew a chaplain at the front who was fifty-eight years of age. In times of peace he took very little physical exercise; he was a student, a scholar, and an author. I have seen this chaplain march mile after mile in rain and mud, and under a broiling sun on dusty roads, and he was then fitter than he ever had been before, and could eat bully beef and hard biscuits like the hungriest youngster. He had the face and eyes and voice of a young man, and he laughed like a merry boy.

We left Compiègne at 3 p.m.; our horses and waggons were entrained and officers and men got into an old and evil-looking "100th" class carriage and again set off for a destination unknown. No one seemed to know where we were off to, but the entraining and route were really well carried out by the staff of the railway. At Amiens we received orders to get off at Abbeville, and after a tiring journey we reached the mouth of the Somme at 2 a.m. The waggons and horses were quickly taken out, and in the dark we trekked through Abbeville across open country to Gapennes, nine miles away. Here we met the 13th Field Ambulance, temporarily quartered in a most luxurious *château*. Our little party was dead beat for want of sleep, and some of us lay down on the floor of the village schoolhouse and slept heavily for three hours. The school was not "in" that day, otherwise I am sure the children would have been highly entertained to see three weary doctors in khaki soundly slumbering on the floor.

Still sleepy, we again had to take the road and tramp the weary miles. A large number of French ambulances passed us going back to Abbeville, and we heard that there had been some very hard fighting on the French left wing.

The 13th British Infantry Brigade caught up with us, and we pulled aside to let them pass. The officers told us that they were in a hurry—that the French had moved up a lot of troops to the south of Lille and that the whole British Army was to form up on the left of the French, and that terrific fighting was going on round Lille and Arras, and French and German cavalry screens had met farther west.

At 5 p.m. we found the headquarters of our ambulance located in a pig-sty of a farmhouse and were told that it was to move off shortly and march through the night. All the romance of night marching had gone for us, and we wanted to sleep. We were tired of walking, tired of everything, tired of the war, and vaguely wondered why we had been so foolish as to leave England.

So at nine o'clock on the same evening off we marched again into the outer darkness of a depressing, gloomy night, and we were on our feet through the whole of it. Most of the time we were standing by the roadside waiting for the congestion of the long columns in front to ease off. Sometimes we would sit in a ditch by the roadside and go off to sleep, only to be wakened a minute after by the cry, "Forward!"

About 6 a.m. we reached Croisette. The name sounds attractive, but it really was a mean-looking farmhouse at a cross-road; however, we got a very good breakfast of coffee, bread and fresh butter, and eggs. The farmer's wife was anxious to know how the war was going on. She rarely got news, but heard lots of rumours. Everybody appeared

Compiègne, showing the broken Bridge.

Ambulance crossing the Oise on a Pontoon bridge.

to be hearing rumours as well as the British Army. We told her that we had killed thousands of Germans and were on the way to slaughter those that were still left; and as this appealed to the patriotic instincts of the farm lady, she was very satisfied with our latest war bulletin.

In three nights and three days I had had only three hours' sleep, and had got to a stage when I marched, rode, and ate my food in a sort of subconscious state of reflex animation. In the late afternoon we rumbled into Thielyce, and tried fruitlessly to find some billets for our officers and men. The place was full of small cottages, and the cottagers eagerly offered each to take in one or two men; but we could not allow this, as in the event of sudden orders through the night we might not be able to get all our men together. We always lived in one large party or habitation like gipsies. One old woman of the village was extremely anxious to have some khaki soldiers stop at her house. She was curious to observe the English at close quarters, as she had never seen one before and had heard that they were such terrible fighting men. Our looks belied our reputation; we looked harmless, very dirty and dusty, but very tame.

The ambulance was parked in a field off the village street and inside a delightful clump of trees. Too tired to eat, I lay down as I was, armed *cap-à-pie*, at the foot of a tall umbrageous tree and slept a dreamless sleep.

At five o'clock next morning the sharp call of our O.C., "Field Ambulance, turn out!" aroused me again to a world of marching men and war; but I was my own man again and optimistic, and no longer wondered why I had left England.

We had a picnic breakfast sitting on the grass in the field, and at seven o'clock received orders to move off: we were to follow the 13th and 14th Brigades into Bethune and on to La Bassée, and be prepared for big casualties, as a stern battle was expected and the two brigades would probably be in action before midday. There was a feeling of expectancy in the air that morning. All the rumours about a big battle and all our quick movements and marchings by night seemed to presage a clash at arms. We hoped for old England's sake that we would do well; our pulses were stirred and we were all very much alive.

We moved off smartly down a fine old tree-lined road towards the sound of heavy guns which had been in action from daybreak. On our way we passed thousands of hurrying refugees going towards St. Pol. Without stopping, our ambulances growled their way through the ancient cobble-stoned town on to the big high road leading to Bethune.

Here again we met thousands of refugees, nearly all young men of military age. We were curious to know why these men were not in the French Army, and a French officer told us that they belonged to Lille and the surrounding districts, and had been ordered out by the French authorities to report at military depots farther south for training and active service. These "mobilisables" would have been good captures for the Germans and a considerable loss to the French Army. Amongst them I counted twenty-seven priests in black caps and cassocks; they, too, were on their way to shoulder a French rifle. One young man I noticed carrying a white rabbit in a bird-cage in one hand and a bundle of clothes and boots in the other; he was saving his rabbit from a German pie. Another fellow was walking along the road in carpet slippers and with a pair of heavy boots suspended round his neck.

The poor refugees looked tired, disappointed, and depressed, and no wonder. It is hard suddenly to have to leave your home, your friends, your wife and children, and to go away with a gnawing fear that they will be in the power of an arrogant and brutal enemy who knows no mercy. We pitied them all.

After all, there was no battle that day. We halted on the way some time, and then were rapidly marched forward towards Bethune. We were now passing through coal-mining towns and villages, and they recalled very much the villages and houses round coal areas of Scotland like Falkirk. The type of coal-miner and the coal-miner's cottage are very much the same all over the world. These people did not seem very curious or interested in our passage through their villages or towns—simply gave us a glance at passing.

That night we bivouacked in a *château* near Bethune and on the main road. We could not get any farther forward, for the road in front was blocked up by big guns and little guns, ammunition columns, engineer battalions, and infantry. We saw a number of waggons loaded up with big pontoon boats, and speculated that we must be near water. So we were. We were near the famous canal, but the boats were intended for farther west.

After tea in the kitchen of the big *château*, some of us got on our horses and rode into the city of Bethune, now full of troops, and the bustle of warlike preparations. There were all nationalities in the streets of Bethune that night. Arabs in flowing robes were on horseback in the square, looking strangely out of place in this old western city. *Spahis*, French grenadiers, French gunners, Alpine *Chasseurs* in round cloth caps, Belgian, French, and British officers, and, of course, Mr.

Thomas Atkins, quite at home, smoking a Woodbine cigarette and being petted and openly admired by the women and the girls. We heard here that Antwerp had fallen, and thought the news very serious. It was quite unexpected, as we had not known that it had been strongly besieged.

At five o'clock next morning we were on the road in a dense fog, and after going forward about half a mile were told to bivouac in a field near the road till some ammunition columns and guns got past us. This we did, but *Monsignor* wandered off alone farther down the road. We missed him for a long time, and when he did turn up he told us that he had been arrested as a spy by the French. Two or three French sentries with fixed bayonets surrounded him, and I don't know what arguments *Monsignor* used to convince them that he was an Englishman. But he came back smiling, and was evidently much tickled over the whole affair. He was the only officer in the British Army, and in fact the only member of the Expeditionary Force, who was not in khaki uniform, and it is no wonder that the French thought it odd that he should be strolling about "on his own," looking at British guns and equipment. We were all delighted, of course, at *Monsignor's* arrest, and regretted that we had not been there with our cameras. We were quite determined, if he were again arrested, to disown all knowledge of him, just to see what the French would do next.

After some hours' wait in the field we pushed on again through Bethune towards the canal. This canal was to us then simply a canal and nothing more, but along this belt of slowly flowing water was to be waged very soon one of the most terrific and sanguinary struggles recorded in history.

As we approached the canal the Norfolk Regiment came up, and we drew to the side of the road to give them the right of way. I sat on a heap of stones by the roadside and watched this fine regiment marching smartly past, and I remember thinking curiously that probably that same day, perhaps within a few hours, many of these fine fellows would have fallen and many would be maimed.

It is an impressive thing to see a regiment going into action. The Norfolks knew that they would very soon be in the thick of things, as they were marching on the sound of the heavy guns, but they looked perfectly cheerful and unconcerned. That night several of them passed under my hands on the operating table, and many more were lying very still on the wet earth not far away.

The King's Own Scottish Borderers passed us earlier in the morning, and with them was Dr. D—— as regimental surgeon. D—— was one of the first medical officers over the Aisne, and he put through some splendid service for the wounded under a heavy fire, and was mentioned in dispatches. Four days afterwards poor D—— and his stretcher-bearers were captured and sent as prisoners to Germany.

At 11 a.m. we crossed the narrow bridge spanning the now famous canal leading up towards La Bassée, and installed our ambulance headquarters in the Château Gorre on the road to Festubert. The *château* had up till that day been the headquarters of a French cavalry general, and it was a most palatially fitted-up place.

Our long journey was over. We had left the Aisne and taken up a new position near La Bassée in the north of France. We were now in a countryside destined soon to become the theatre of an intense and sanguinary struggle. It was here that our men withstood the shock of the most determined and relentless head-on attacks of the enemy. This was one of the roads to Calais, and we held the gate.

CHAPTER 14

The La Bassée Road at Château Gorre

As the fighting is still going on round this district any description of military positions or dispositions would be quite out of place.

Our headquarters at Château Gorre was a beautiful two-storied stone building, quite modern, and well arranged in every way with spacious lofty halls, dining-rooms, lounges, bedrooms, and bathrooms.

When we took up our quarters here we knew that we would soon be busy with wounded, and the central hall of the *château* was at once prepared for their reception. Two larger rooms opening to the right and to the left off the hall were covered with mattresses and blankets, hot water was prepared, operation table opened out, and towels and instruments made ready. Just when we had about finished preparations our first arrivals, four men of the Dragoon Guards, turned up. They had been wounded slightly in the arms and face while advancing along the road towards Festubert. Twenty minutes later fifty-four wounded arrived, Bedfords and Cheshires, most of whom had slight wounds of the arms and hands and scalp, and were able to walk.

Urgent orders came in to send six ambulance waggons down the Festubert road. These were sent forward with stretcher parties and six medical officers. This was the beginning of a very "bloody" night. All that evening and all night wounded were continually coming in. I was on duty in the chateau as surgeon till 4 a.m., when another medical officer relieved me. Red Cross ambulances were driven up frequently and took away all our lightly wounded and those fit to travel. These were sent to Bethune, and thus the *château* was kept from becoming too congested. These Red Cross ambulances had been provided and equipped by British residents in Paris; they were splendidly handled, and proved a godsend to us. Many of them were converted "Ford cars," and could carry six lying-down patients and one sitting up beside the driver. The stretchers were swung on trestles and chains, and fitted easily. Our ambulance waggons and stretcher-bearers were out all night and had a very dangerous time at the front. At 10.30 next morning the heavy artillery firing eased off, and at eleven o'clock occurred one of those extraordinary lulls when all the big guns and little guns cease firing and everything seems strangely silent.

A chaplain arrived at the *château* in the morning and read the service over one of our wounded who had died during the night from a broken spine. The grave was dug near the flower garden at the foot of the lawn, and many graves were dug there in the three succeeding terrible weeks of fierce, bitter fighting. On this day the Dorsets, who were in reserve and quartered near the gate of our *château*, went into action and were badly handled by the Germans, suffering severe losses, chiefly from a concealed German machine-gun opening on to them from near the canal. The Devons had to move up later to support the Dorsets, and did it in a most gallant style. About two o'clock in the afternoon we had a great number of casualties; our waggons were constantly arriving, unloading their wounded, and setting off again for the front.

The Red Cross ambulances were evacuating the light cases as speedily as possible to Bethune, but we very soon had all our rooms full of wounded men and were working at high pressure at the operation table. At three o'clock the artillery firing was tremendously heavy, and every gun was in action. The *château* shook with the explosions; every window rattled and some were broken. The concussion of the air outside and the terrible din were distinctly unpleasant. Then the cracking of the rifle-firing became audible, and reports came in that our men were retiring. Shortly after an imperative order was sent to our O.C. telling him to evacuate the *château* at once with his wounded and move off the Field Ambulance to the other side of the canal. The horses were at once put in the various supply waggons. We had only two ambulance waggons at the time, as the rest were at the front collecting wounded.

Some Red Cross ambulances, however, turned up and took away twelve of our most serious cases. All the lightly wounded were sent under charge of R.A.M.C. orderlies to walk back across the canal to Bethune. Some men with shrapnel wounds of thigh and leg also had to walk and get along somehow, and miserable and pitiable these poor fellows looked, limping and struggling along the muddy road in their bloody bandages. Things looked pretty serious at this moment, and I was ordered to mount and gallop ahead to direct the waggons on to the right road and to "round up" our poor wounded fellows who were trudging along the roads. To make matters worse, heavy rain came on. Big artillery practice always brought down the rain. I soon reached the head of our column and gave the sergeant the necessary instructions.

On the side of the road there was an old inn or *estaminet*. I pulled my horse up here and put two men on duty to stop all our walking wounded and collect them into the front room of the inn. I went inside and arranged with the woman in charge to light a big fire, make some tea, and have bread and butter and anything else she could get ready for our men, and to do it quickly. She set to work at once. I had then to gallop back to the Château Gorre to help get away the serious cases and to collect any empty lorry or waggon I could get. When I reached the *château* the O.C. told me that we had moved up some reserves, and the Germans in their turn were now retiring. He said that he would now keep his serious cases at the *château* till motor ambulances arrived.

I was ordered to gallop again to the head of our column and turn back all the supply waggons, equipment carts, and water carts, but to send the ambulance waggons with their wounded on to Bethune. It was now dark, and after incredible trouble my mission was accomplished and our drivers were already driving the carts back. I now looked in at "mine inn." All our wounded fellows were sitting round the fire having tea, bread and butter, and slices of cold boiled ham, and looked very happy. I asked the woman of the inn what the cost was, and she only charged me ten *francs*. I never parted with money so willingly. The privilege of being able to do something for these good lads, and their appreciation of the hot fire and the hot tea, was something I would not willingly forget.

The Château Gorre was once more re-established as an advanced ambulance dressing station, and continued so for over three weeks. It was situated right inside the shell zone, and had many "alarms and excursions" during this period, but none quite so dramatic and sensational as that recorded above. The work done by this ambulance at the *château* was extraordinarily good and useful, and owing to its very advanced position so close to the fighting line it was able to receive and treat the wounded very soon after they had been hit.

Towards La Bassée.
Many British dead lie here.

Low flat ground near the canal—with a trench

When the order came to evacuate at the time of the incident related above, the instructions given to our commanding officer were to get out all the lightly wounded cases and to leave the serious cases in the *château*. Our O.C. was a soldier, and he said that if he had to go he would get all the wounded out, and that he would be "damned if he would leave any seriously wounded man in the hands of the b——Germans." Strong language at times is sweet music, and our O.C. was a man of his word. The wounded men heard this story, and I heard some of them talking about it later to each other. The O.C. took a high place in their estimation.

At the *château* I was talking to a young lieutenant who had just received a commission in the D——Regiment. He had served as a private at the beginning of the war and won his sergeant's stripes for general good conduct and gallantry under fire, and was then given a commission in another regiment. He was hard put for a smoke, and could not get any cigarettes, but fortunately I was able to give him some.

Ten days later, at Bethune, he was brought in to me with a crushed arm, hanging by only a thread of muscle to the shoulder, and I had to amputate it under chloroform. He recognised me as the man who had given him the cigarettes, and said, "Hullo, doctor, you're always doing me kind things, so now take my arm off." I was very sorry that I had to do it, but such is war and the aftermath of victory.

Next day after our big alarm I was sent back by the Assistant Director of the Medical Service of this Division to take up duty at Bethune, four miles back from where we were, at the Château Gorre, and to help in the organisation for handling and treating our many wounded there. Bethune was on the other side of the canal to the *château*, and during the succeeding three or four weeks became a very big hospital centre for the British engaged in the direction of La Bassée.

The Field Ambulance headquarters, with the waggons, still remained at the *château* closer to the firing line, and evacuated their many wounded as speedily as possible in to us at Bethune. These were strenuous days of hard and obstinate fighting, and the casualties were heavy. The life of the medical officer was at this place arduous and sleepless, but the motto of the Royal Army Medical Corps is "*In arduis fidelis*," which may be freely rendered "Always do your job."

CHAPTER 15

Bethune

Bethune held a position of great importance behind our lines, for our wounded were evacuated thither from the front, and those fit to take the journey were then sent on by hospital trains to Boulogne and Rouen and then to England. This old city will be visited by many English after the war, for many English officers and men are sleeping their long sleep in the old cemetery and in various parts of the surrounding country. One day, I am sure, a monument to the memory of the brave dead will be raised in Bethune, and the mural inscription will commemorate the names of the fallen, and place on record for all time the kindness, the sympathy, and the generous hearts of the people of Bethune who helped us all so much during the hard days of the war. Owing to its many recent bombardments from guns and aeroplanes, and its proximity to the famous canal and La Bassée, Bethune has become a city of world-wide interest.

Its population was at this time a cosmopolitan one. The warriors of the East were in friendly touch with the warriors of the West. The slanting, almond-eye Gurkha, the stately bearded Sikh, the swarthy fighting men from the frontiers and central plains of India, the Turcos with their flowing robes, the dapper *Spahi*, the black-eyed Senegalese, the French Alpine *Chasseur*, and the splendid *cuirassier*, were all to be seen in its streets; and there also was Mr. Thomas Atkins, making himself, as usual, quite at home with them all, and also with the pleasant-faced smiling young women in the tobacconists and fruit shops.

Bethune, with its 14,000 inhabitants, is said to be the home of many millionaires—those manufacturing and industrial magnates who control the big industries of this thriving and populous part of France. The situation of the city is not very attractive. It is surrounded by muddy, swampy country, in some places nothing better than marshes or bogs in winter, but it is supposed to be attractive in spring and summer, when it is "a green prairie land."

The old square in the centre of the city has a very Flemish complexion, but is undoubtedly, owing to the irregularities in design and architecture of the surrounding houses and shops, a very attractive and fascinating spot. On one side are two fine old fourteenth-century Spanish houses built for some Spanish *grandees* in the days when Spain was supreme in the Netherlands. In the centre of the square is an old church and a mass of hoary buildings forming an island, and out of this island group of buildings the wonderful old Belfry of Bethune erects itself proudly skyward. The belfry was built in 1346, and behind it is the venerable church of St. Vaast, a product of the sixteenth century, with a very ornate Gothic tower,

Naturally the belfry and the tower of St. Vaast proved to be irresistibly attractive to the German gunners, and the batteries beyond La Bassée were constantly having long bowls practice at them. From the top of the belfry one could obtain a splendid view of the surrounding countryside and see the shrapnel and big shells burst miles away. Taubes were constantly flying over Bethune at this time, but later on they became very chary about visiting it.

The life of the old city during the past eight months has been rather unhappy, and it has gone through some stormy periods in the past. In 1188 a devastating plague swept the countryside, causing thousands of deaths and plunging the population into an abyss of fear and misery.

When the plague was at its height Saint Eloi appeared to two blacksmiths and recommended them to form an association of "charitables," charged to perform the last offices for the dead gratuitously and to help those in distress. This curious association exists to-day in Bethune under the name of *Confrères des Charitables*. During our stay in Bethune the charitables lived up to their old tradition and took the deepest interest in the welfare of our soldiers, made coffins for a very large number of our dead, and in their curious three-cornered "Napoleonic" hats and quaint badge and bands, solemnly followed the many dead to their last resting-place.

Bethune has passed through many sieges in its day. In 1487 it was in possession of the Germans under Philippe of Cleves, and was captured by the French under Marshal d'Erquerdes at the victory called "*Journée des Fromages*," and at a later period of its history it was fortified by the great French engineer, Vauban.

The people of Bethune opened wide their arms and welcomed

our wounded. From the mayor of the city to the humblest little shop girl these good people did all they could for our men, dead, wounded, or active. The women of the town made delicacies, soups, and special dishes, provided wines and more solid comforts, such as beds, mattresses, blankets, and sheets. Had I but lifted my little finger and asked for volunteer nurses, I could, I am sure, have obtained them in hundreds. Every day while I was there I received letters from all sorts of people offering me help and all manner of things for our men. On an afternoon at Bethune at this time it was "the thing" for ladies to visit *l'Hôpital Civil et Militaire* and see the British soldiers. Our lightly wounded men would generally be sitting about on seats outside in the courtyard of the hospital surrounded by convalescent Frenchmen and crowds of admiring ladies, who had brought cigarettes, chocolate, and cakes for the soldiers of both nations.

Although Tommy did not know a word of French and they knew no English, they seemed to thoroughly understand each other, judging by the amused faces of the elder French ladies and the screams of laughter of the younger ones. We could never quite understand how Tommy has won such an enduring place in French hearts. The French people certainly like Tommy. I was glad to see this everywhere in France, for I, too, like Tommy, although he is full of tricks.

A section of the Field Ambulance consisting of two medical officers, Royal Army Medical Corps orderlies, waggons, cooks, and equipment had already taken possession of the school called *l'École Jules Ferry*, and was getting it into some order so as to act as a Clearing Hospital, or temporary Dressing Station or temporary Clearing Hospital.

We were to hold the fort till a properly equipped Clearing Hospital with its increased personnel and supplies should arrive. This did not appear for some days, and our Field Ambulance section had the herculean task of handling all the wounded from the fighting front, where a bloody struggle was in progress round the swamps and marshy country towards La Bassée. *L'École Jules Ferry* was situated down a side street of the old city, and near the railway station. It was a very large school, with several big lofty rooms, many small side-rooms, porches and alcoves of many sorts. There was a large courtyard with latrines, and the buildings formed a hollow square with part of the courtyard in the centre. The face of the buildings looking on to the courtyard had a long sweep of verandahs. The orderlies soon got to work, cleaned and swept the rooms, and covered the floor thickly with clean straw. No beds were then available. In a small side-room off a passage-way an operating table was fixed, and the surgical instruments and dressings were laid ready. Boiling water had to be carried to the operating room in buckets from the kitchen at the end of the building. The hospital was all very crude, but it was the best that could be done under the circumstances.

We did not have to await events; the events were there at once in the guise of crowds of recently wounded men. Motor ambulance after motor ambulance dashed up with its load of wounded. These were rapidly lifted out and carried into the building; then away went the ambulance to bring in more wounded. Many and large as were the schoolrooms they were quickly filled to overflowing. The corridors and porches were then covered with straw, and this straw was soon covered with rows of wounded men. The paved courtyard under the verandahs was covered with thick straw, and again covered with wounded. Every foot, every inch of floor space in the buildings and under the verandahs was utilised. In one room we had closely packed rows four deep, with a narrow footway of straw down the centre of the room for the doctors and orderlies to pass along. So narrow was this track, that it required the agility of a mountain goat to negotiate it without bumping some poor devil's feet, and we walked along it just as a man walks across a ploughed field, stepping high and watching each step.

Those densely packed rooms during that long night were a lurid and impressive picture of the devastation of war. As more and more wounded continued to arrive we had to pack our men closer and closer together—gently push one this way, lift another one there, edge a third one closer still. So it went on. We had in our rooms a number of French wounded picked up and brought in by our ambulances, and also a fair number of German wounded. There is no nationality amongst the men in a hospital, and English, French, and German all had a little bit of floor space and a bit of straw in our schoolhouse that night. All were glad to get in out of the pouring rain, and be placed on the warm dry straw, and covered with a blanket.

All these men arrived with the first field-dressings on. Some had been put on by the surgeon with the regiment, some by bearers and orderlies, some by Field Ambulance officers, and some by the man's comrades on the field.

At first we were so busy "packing" our wounded that we could not investigate the nature of the wounds, but we were very soon un-

SLIGHTLY WOUNDED AND SICK AT BETHUNE.

ÉCOLE JULES FERRY AT BETHUNE.

der way with the professional side of our work. Every wound was examined; the slight ones were left alone, but the serious ones were re-dressed and a rough differentiation of serious and slight cases was made. Those requiring immediate surgery were brought into our operation room and anaesthetics were administered. All men in pain were given hypodermics of morphia, and our orderlies made hot drinks and soups for all those able to take nourishment. There were, of course, many men lying unconscious with severe brain wounds, and most of these men died next day. The brain injuries were amongst our most hopeless cases, but fortunately these poor fellows suffered no pain whatever, and slept stertorously till death. There was one particularly fine, strapping, young giant lieutenant of a Scotch regiment who was comfortably placed on straw and covered with a blanket, and who lay quietly sleeping, with gentle and easy respirations, all the night till the next forenoon, when he suddenly became quite still. The top of his head had been blown completely away.

The crowds of wounded behaved like brave men and took their gruelling like good sportsmen. Next day the pressure was relieved by the opportune arrival of a hospital train, and we were enabled to evacuate 250 of the cases fit for transport. More doctors and Red Cross dressers were sent to help, and the vacant places of the 250 sent away were occupied by the arrival of another 300.

As the pressure for beds showed no signs of easing off, and as the reports from the front were that the fighting was still violent and obstinate, a search was made for another building to hold more wounded. This was found at *l'Hôpital Civil et Militai*re, a permanent hospital of the city of Bethune. It was a hospital of three stories, built of brick round three sides of a big hollow square. The fourth side was occupied by the porter's lodge, the two gateways, and the residential quarters of the Reverend Mother and Sisters of the Order of St. Francis, who formed the nursing staff. The basement wards of one wing were for French military patients, and the other wings were for civilian patients; but as a matter of fact military wounded were put in all the wards except the midwifery ward, which was full of young babies and mothers. One of these young mothers, by the way, had just become the proud possessor of triplets. I had a look at them, and they seemed very fit . Their father had been away for the past three months in the trenches of the Argonne, but permission had been asked to enable him to come down and see how well his wife had done.

The top storey of the hospital had two large empty wards, each capable of holding seventy patients placed fairly closely together. I asked permission of the Reverend Mother and the hospital secretary to use these wards for the reception of our wounded.

"But yes," I was eagerly told; "you are welcome, and we shall do all we can for your English wounded." I was also offered the use of three side-rooms and part of another small ward for any wounded officers, and—greatest boon of all—the use of the two operating theatres of the hospital. These operating theatres were modern and splendidly equipped with good surgical iron operating tables, suitable for adjusting in any position, sterilisers for instruments, dressings, aprons, and operating towels, glass cases full of the latest type of instruments, and hot and cold water taps controlled by foot-pedals on the floor.

The lighting was all that one could desire. My joy knew no bounds now, for I felt that at last I would be able to do good surgery and clean surgery. Up till now the surgery I had done on the field was crude and not very clean. It was absolutely impossible to be otherwise, for we were the victims of stern military circumstances. But now things would be different, and our wounded men and officers would get the benefit of surgical cleanliness.

I asked the Reverend Mother if she would prepare one hundred straw mattresses for me, and get in some blankets. "But yes" I would get them; and also *Monsieur le Docteur* would have tables put in the centre of the wards for the dressings, and would have basins and towels. An electrician would fix up electric lights, and a kitchen stove would be put in a side-room for cooking soup, boiling water, etc. I reported all this to Surgeon-General P——, and that able officer quickly grasped the possibilities of this hospital, installed me there as operating surgeon, and directed that all serious cases requiring surgical operation should be sent to me.

A real Clearing Hospital arrived in the town next morning, and next day took in patients. It established itself in the "College for Young Ladies," and very soon the spacious quarters of this big building were filled with wounded and sick men. For besides our wounded at this time we had also a large number of sick. This hospital also sent me any case requiring surgical operation.

Work at my wards proceeded apace. The women of the city rushed eagerly to assist, and in a *clin d'œil* had made 180 straw mattresses, provided blankets, hot-water bottles, and other sick-room adjuncts. The position in Bethune was now as follows. One Clearing Hospital at the College for Young Ladies, one at the school "Jules Ferry," and my surgical wards, only for serious cases, at *l'Hôpital Civil et Militaire*. All three buildings were soon full, and over seven thousand wounded men passed through these buildings in less than three weeks.

Sir Anthony Bowlby, consulting surgeon to the army, constantly visited this hospital, and was always a welcome visitor; and his surgical opinion was as welcome as his encouragement and cheeriness of manner.

The operating theatre was presided over by Sister Ferdinande, a trained and capable nurse, with rigid antiseptic and aseptic principles. All I had to do was to tell her that I was going to amputate a limb or do a trephining operation, and ask her when she would be ready. At the agreed time everything was certain to be prepared, and I just had to scrub up, put on my sterilised apron, cap, and rubber gloves, and be ready for my part of the séance. The Reverend Mother Superior was a trained anaesthetist and administered chloroform to many of my cases during the three weeks I was there. Some days I have had her administering anaesthetics for seven hours. Seven hours' continuous administration, broken only by the taking out of one patient and the bringing in of another, is a big test of endurance for a young man; yet this old lady did it smilingly and well, and said it was "indeed nothing."

There were two Irish nuns at this hospital; one spoke French well, one was just learning, but both spoke "Irish," which is good English. These two nuns were put on nursing duty in my wards, and they were hugely delighted to get amongst the British wounded and to hear their countrymen talk. Tommy Atkins was delighted with the two Irish nuns, and told them some wonderful stories about the fighting and about the Germans. One of them asked me if I really thought that Private S—— of the Warwicks had shot two hundred Germans one afternoon. I told the sister that I did not know, but hoped he had. These two sisters were at work in the wards night and day. They told me one day that they had never heard a soldier swear. I was very glad to hear this, for it showed that Tommy was behaving himself, and I did not tell the sister that Tommy on occasion was a very past master in strange oaths.

The sisters were very concerned about the lice on our soldiers' shirts and flannels; and really this was a terrible source of anxiety to all medical officers at this time, for these cursed parasites would make the lot of our wounded men unbearable at times. One man with a fractured leg put up firmly in splints begged me to take the splints off so that he could "scratch the leg." I had really in the end to take off the splint, bathe the skin in petrol, and dust sulphur on the cotton wool, for lice had worked their way down into the warm wool next the skin, and by their "promenading" about had set up the irritation which the soldier begged to scratch. The sister once said to me that she used to think that the British soldiers were the most cleanly of men, but she found really that they were all covered with lice. I told the wondering-eyed sister that it was a regrettable fact, but nevertheless true, that the whole British Army at the front was lousy.

When our wounded arrived at the hospital they were speedily placed on the straw mattresses, quickly undressed by the sisters and other helping nuns, and covered with warm sheets and blankets and surrounded with hot bottles. Basins of hot water and soap were brought round and then the men were washed and cleaned. Their lice-infected shirts and underclothing were sterilised by dry heat.

It was the finest example of *l'entente cord*iale to see the French nuns taking off the muddy boots and *puttees*, cutting off bloodstained clothing, washing and cleaning the wounded, slipping on warm dry shirts, and tucking the blankets and pillows comfortably. Others appeared with hot soup, hot coffee, red wine, and hot gruel. These nuns were magnificent.

I wrote to Lord Grey, late Governor-General of Canada, asking him to bring to the notice of Her Majesty Queen Alexandra the splendid work performed by these ladies. Lord Grey very kindly did so, and also sent a copy of my letter to His Majesty the King, who replied through Lord Stamfordham that he had read it with much interest. Queen Alexandra sent the following letter to the Reverend Mother Superior of the Franciscan Sisters at Bethune:

> I have learned from Dr. Martin of your noble and heroic devotion for our brave and unfortunate wounded soldiers, and it is with a heart full of gratitude that I ask you to accept my most ardent and warmest thanks.
> I pray God that He will reward you for the angelic care that you have bestowed on our unfortunate soldiers, and I will never forget that it is to you, *madame*, and your sisters, that they assuredly owe their life and their recovered health.
>
> Alexandra.

This letter was published in all the leading French and British papers, including the *London Times, Tablet, Daily Mail, Figaro, Le Journal, Le Temps*, in February 1915, and excited very considerable interest and attention in France. The Abbé Bouchon d'Homme, the *Aumonier* to the hospital, wrote me later to say that the Reverend Mother and the Sisters were delighted beyond measure at Queen Alexandra's gracious message.

It may not be out of place now to describe briefly the nature of some of the wounds met with during the fighting at La Bassée. The non-medical mind is as interested in the wounds and sufferings of our men as are the doctors, and it is to the intelligent interest of the layman we owe so much of what has been done for our wounded and sick men. Compound fractures and splintered bone, septic wounds, tetanus, brain injuries, inoculations, etc., are words freely bandied about and understood by any group of ladies met together round an afternoon tea-table. Mrs. Smith-Jones will tell Mrs. Jones-Smith that her son is in hospital with a septic compound fracture and that the wound is being fully drained, and Mrs. J.-S. will reply that her sister's husband, Captain X—— of the R.F.A., is recovering from a penetrating wound of the lung, but has still some pleural effusion. So no apology is further necessary when referring to such a thing as gas gangrene.

Gas gangrene was one of the terrors of the doctors at this time. It was a new and totally unexpected complication of the wounds, and at first we did not know what to do in the face of this pressing danger. A man would get, say, a flesh wound of the arm or leg, or perhaps a fractured bone, and very soon the whole limb would become gangrenous and die. Gangrene means death of the part. It may be death of a small part or of a large part, and the worst feature of the form of gangrene met with at Bethune was its tendency to rapid spread, resulting in the speedy death of the limb and of the patient. We had many deaths from this terrible gas gangrene, and performed many amputations to save lives. A good surgeon hates to amputate a limb, and will gladly exert all his skill and knowledge to save even a toe. It was heartrending to have to perform so many amputations at Bethune, and yet these serious mutilating operations had to be performed in order to save lives.

The gangrene was caused by a group of *bacilli* called *anaerobes*, amongst which may be many organisms. About ten different organisms have been obtained from cases of gas gangrene, and these all belong to the same family of *anaerobic bacilli*. They are all spore-bearing, and grow in the absence of air. These *bacilli* are found in the soil in France and Belgium, and are always to be found in the soil of those countries which have been closely cultivated for centuries past.

If a guinea-pig is inoculated with a sample of this earth shaken up in a little water it will develop this gas gangrene and die. Imagine, then, this picture. The soil of the trenches is full of these organisms, which, if introduced into an open wound, grow and spread and cause the limb to become gangrenous. As the organism spreads up the limb it produces a gas of its own, and by pressing on the skin one can feel this gas cracking, like tissue paper, under the fingers. The treatment is to inject the parts with oxygen or peroxide of hydrogen, to make free incisions round the wound, thoroughly cleanse the wound and keep it clean, The general condition of the patients required great care, for they were all very, very ill. When a man got wounded in the trenches some dirt was bound to get into the wound, for the men's hands and clothes were usually caked with mud.

It is a natural movement to clap a hand on the wounded spot. If a man is struck on the face or limbs, he will lay down his rifle or perhaps drop it, and at once put his hand on the injured part to ascertain the extent. It is a movement which is almost involuntary. I have seen hit men do this often, and when they withdraw their hand they always look at it to see if there is any blood, and the bravest man does not like to see his own blood. The hands of the men in the trenches were infected with the *bacilli* of this gas gangrene and of tetanus, and when these infected fingers touched a recent wound, the wound itself became infected with these highly dangerous organisms.

Pieces of khaki cloth, caked in mud, were often driven into the wounds with the bullets and shrapnel, and on this cloth there were of course millions of the deadly little beasts.

If the case reached us soon after the onset of gangrene a cure could almost certainly be promised. If the case arrived late, when the limbs were dead, amputation was the only "conservative treatment" that one could adopt. Many of the cases sent to me were beyond any hope of recovery and soon died. On one day I saw in one Clearing Hospital in the town four cases dying from gas gangrene; in the other Clearing Hospital, two cases *in articulo mortis* from the same trouble; and in my own, one other case. Seven cases dying on one day from gas gangrene! None of these had been operated upon. This will give some idea of the formidable character of this complication.

None but the very serious cases were sent to me. Many cases of gas gangrene were evacuated early and sent to the Base Hospitals. Most of my cases came from one or other of the Clearing Hospitals in this town. Some arrived direct from the Field Ambulances. In every amputation for gas gangrene performed at this hospital the limb was absolutely dead and beyond the possibility of any treatment short of amputation. All the patients were in an extremely grave state, and their general condition was in every case very bad. I cannot picture any worse surgical subject than these men with gas gangrene. Numbers of them were in too low a state to admit of a general anaesthetic, and here the necessary operations were performed under conduction anaesthesia.

Dr. F——, an eminent French surgeon in charge of the French wounded in this town, saw many of my cases before, during, and after operation. I had the privilege also of seeing his gangrene cases at this time. He had amongst the French wounded the same experience as mine. Both of us had German wounded to treat, and here also we met dead limbs from gas gangrene. We were both of the opinion that the Germans at this place were also up against a very virulent "culture" here, that of the *anaerobe*. Some wounded French refugees were brought into this hospital at this period, and some of these had gas gangrene. The serious character of gas gangrene at this time could only be recognised at the front. The serious cases were retained here for operation. I am of the opinion that all cases of gangrene should be treated at the front at the nearest Clearing Hospital, and that no case should be sent to the Base till the gangrene had disappeared, subject, of course, as always, to the military situation. All the wounded admitted to this town—French, British, and German—came from the same area of the battle front.

In many of the cases of gas gangrene bones were badly shattered and pulverised, splinters of bone were lying in surrounding muscles, or had been driven out through the skin. Important nerves were injured, torn, or compressed in many of them. Important blood-vessels were frequently, but not invariably, injured. In some, big vessels had been torn through; in others, arteries and nerves were compressed by displaced fragments of bone. The wounds were dirty in most cases. The skin was black and lacerated, and muscles were extruded and covered with coagulated blood clots.—Wound full of blood clots, and containing at times pieces of khaki cloth, shrapnel fragments, nickel casing of bullets, gravel, and, in two cases, bits of rock.—So runs the record in my notes. There were, however, cases in which the bullet had drilled an apparently clean hole through a joint, like the wrist or ankle, without much apparent destruction to bone. In such cases one would not expect gas gangrene; yet it sometimes occurred.

Gas gangrene is encouraged by tight bandaging, and many of the cases had a bandage applied all too firmly. When a man is wounded in a trench his mate frequently applies the first-aid dressing, and fixes it like a tourniquet. This could perhaps be obviated by making the bandage of the first field-dressing a little wider than at present. A narrow bandage tends to become cord-like.

All the cases of gas gangrene had a very penetrating putrefactive smell, which is quite characteristic. The area of advancing gangrene is preceded by an *œdematous* zone, which fades in one direction to the area of healthy skin and in the direction towards the wound to a dullish injected area which crackles on palpation. Nearer the wound the skin is purplish and dark. Around the edges of the usually jagged wound the tissues were black or greenish-black. Extravasated blood undermined the skin all round the wound. The wound itself was full of blood clots. The limb distal to the wound was swollen, greenish-black, covered with green blebs, cold, insensitive, and pulseless in the "dead" limbs. Frequently toes and fingers were quite black. In other serious cases there might be a little warmth or a slight pulse.

If any case showed either of these two favourable signs, an attempt was made to save the limb, and was in many cases successful. The gangrene did not spread up a limb in an even circle. For example, it might reach anteriorly to the lower third of the thigh, and posteriorly be at or well above the fold of the buttock. This was due to the extravasated blood lying more towards the dependent parts and to gravity. In the upper arm the gangrene travelled rapidly up the inner side along the course of the big blood-vessels. The invasion spread upwards; very little crackling was felt below the site of the wound. The circulation below seemed to be rapidly cut off, and that portion of the limb underwent the changes associated with a complete circulatory block. Wounds of the thigh with shattering of the femur, wounds of the elbow-joint and of the metatarsus were very prone to develop this gangrene. Some of the cases were admitted within thirty-six hours after receipt of the wound, with well-marked gangrene.

In every case of amputation performed there was nothing else to be done in order to save life. The limbs were dead. In many of these cases important blood-vessels were torn, crushed, or compressed, and when the vessels were injured the gangrene developed more quickly and spread more rapidly. It is regrettable that one had to perform so many amputations at this time, but it is a matter for congratulation that so many lives were saved. One of the cases died suddenly twelve hours after a disarticulation at the shoulder-joint. Another one died three days after amputation at the hip-joint, from gangrene which progressed steadily on to the lower abdomen. There were, in addition, five deaths from gangrene following wounds of the extremities. These five were admitted in a dying condition, and passed away two to four hours after admission. One could do nothing for them surgically. Other cases died at the other Clearing Hospitals in the town. It was a sad and mournful experience seeing these fine young men die.

These cases of gas gangrene were all bad surgical subjects, for in addition to the gangrene, loss of blood, privation, and exposure subsequent to being wounded, their wounds were dangerous and mutilating, and the transportation to the hospital was, sometimes, necessarily an agonising ordeal. This will show that our Clearing Hospitals at the front should be well and thoroughly equipped with all modern appliances for the treatment of shock, and a staff fully alive to this clamant necessity. A Clearing Hospital cannot today remain as an administrative unit only.

Another complication of our wounds at this time was tetanus (or the so-called lock-jaw). When it was recognised that the *bacillus* of tetanus was also found in the soil of France and Flanders, efficient measures were at once adopted to combat its terrible effects. Accordingly anti-tetanic serum was provided at all the Base Hospitals, Clearing Hospitals, and Ambulances, and every man wounded in France or Flanders to-day gets an injection of this serum within twenty-four hours of the receipt of the wound. No deaths from tetanus have occurred since these measures have been adopted.

Tetanus caused many deaths at the beginning of the war, not only amongst our own soldiers, but also amongst the Belgians, French, and Germans. When tetanus manifests itself, when the convulsions and muscular spasms come on, it is a terrible malady to treat, and most of the cases die. At this time the injection of anti-tetanic serum does not ensure a recovery, but if this serum is given to every wounded man, then none will develop tetanus, and that is why none of the wounded men are asked if they will have the "lock-jaw injection." At the front there is no time for conscientious objectors.

Shrapnel wounds were always bad; the round bullets of lead always ripped and tore the tissues about so terribly. The Mauser bullet did not cause nearly so much damage, but it sometimes produced very lacerating wounds. The Mauser bullet "turns over" when travelling through a limb, and this turning means tearing of tissues on the path of the bullet, and often a huge jagged wound like that produced by an explosive bullet.

It has been said that we are treating wounds of an eighteenth-century character with twentieth-century technique. The eighteenth-century battle wounds were inflicted at close range, and so are many of the wounds inflicted today.

At Crecy and Agincourt both sides used arrows. The aviators of the Allies and the enemy carry steel darts which they spin down on the foe below. Bows have been used in the trenches to send inflammable arrows into the opposing lines. The Roman soldier advanced to close combat behind a shield held on his left arm, and shields have been used at certain observation spots by the Germans and in the Russian trenches; our Allies have at times used spades for a similar purpose.

Bombards were employed at Crecy, and bombards have come to their own again in the trenches from Switzerland to the sea. Hand grenades were employed in the Peninsular War, and are employed today in this War of the Nations. Our men attack the enemy and the enemy attack us with bayonets as in the days of the Crimea and the Peninsula, and our riflemen pick off the enemy by long-distance fire, and also fire at close range into solid masses of them. Even the armour of old days is represented on modern fields of battle, for the French *cuirassier* goes into action with a brass *cuirass* and helmet; and a French infantry officer of my acquaintance has worn a light shirt of chain-mail extending from his neck to beyond his hips, all through this campaign, and he said that it had saved his life on more than one occasion. In one *magasin* in Rouen shirts of beautifully made chain-mail can be purchased, and the shopkeeper told me that he had sold hundreds to French soldiers.

The hardships of the Crimean trenches—cold, rheumatism, and frostbite—have been repeated on the Yser. Gangrene was rampant amongst the wounded of Wagram, Austerlitz, and Borodino, and amongst the French and British wounded at Vittoria, Salamanca, Badajos, and other great battles of the Peninsula, and it has startlingly reappeared on the Aisne and in Flanders.

Historians of that day refer to it as hospital gangrene, or the gangrene so common after any surgical operation or wound of that time. It may, on the other hand, have been the same gas gangrene that has ominously complicated so many of our wounds in France and Flanders. The *bacillus* which produces this gangrene may belong, for all we know to the contrary, to a very old family of *bacilli*, who would look upon pedigrees dating to William the Conqueror with an aristocratic contempt when his own stretched back to the beginning of time.

There is one feature of war as carried on today which is quite new, and that is by poison gases and by poisoning wells and water supplies. In West Africa the Germans have been proved indisputably and by their own admissions to have poisoned wells and water supplies, and the whole world stands amazed and aghast at the devilish and inhuman Germans who set free poison gases to overwhelm and suffocate British, French, and Belgian soldiers in the trenches. This diabolical and ghastly method of murder is without parallel in history, and the bloodily-minded men who conceived and carried out this sinister, ferocious thing will live accursed all their days and be a name of scorn and loathing for ever.

Although the civil hospital at Bethune was such a grim place of crowded wounded, it was yet the scene of much humour. We had wounded men belonging to many different countries, and the nuns were very interested in all the odd types. Off one of the large French wards there was a small room holding eight beds, and a nun brought me in one day to see the curious occupants ranged in beds alongside each other. There were a Senegalese, an Algerian, a Zouave, an Alpine *chasseur*, a Turco, a native of Madagascar, a man of the Foreign legion, and a Frenchman. I think that the nuns always kept this ward "International." It was their little joke, and visitors were always shown this ward. The patients themselves enjoyed the *mélange*. The courtyard of the hospital was a great meeting-place for our convalescent soldiers with the French convalescents, and they used to sit about on benches surrounded by an admiring lot of French women from the town. We also had a fair number of German wounded on our hands, and one of them at this time was terribly ill, suffering from the after-effects of gas gangrene of the foot following on a bullet wound of the ankle joint. His foot was amputated, and he had a struggle for some days to keep going, but eventually pulled through. The wounded German soldiers were very tractable and easy to manage. They were obedient, gave no trouble, and seemed grateful. I cannot say the same of the two wounded German officers I had. Both were slight wounds, and ought not really to have been sent to this hospital at all. They were truculent and overbearing to the nuns and orderlies, and behaved like cads. The German has no sense of humour. He takes himself very seriously, and that amuses us. He thinks and says that we are fools, and that also amuses us. A German once said that the English would always be fools, and that the Germans would never be gentlemen. This is most obviously correct.

We asked a German sergeant-major who had been captured if the Hymn of Hate was really popular in Germany. The sergeant-major in civil life was a school teacher. He wore big spectacles and had a rough beard, and was altogether a very serious-minded man. He assured us that the German hate was a very real one, and he took the hymn very seriously. Lissauer, its author, is said to be a serious man also, and has he not been awarded the Cross of the Red Eagle by the All Highest himself? We laugh at the hymn, and this makes the German mad. Certainly we must be fools to laugh at the Hymn of Hate. The words inspire and enthral the Teuton, and the music uplifts his sentimental soul to the Empyrean.

We love as one, we hate as one.
We have one foe, and one alone—England.

The German considers this to be a purely German hymn, breathing the spirit of the Fatherland—unending hate. It is his song, and to sing it does him good. You can then understand the expression of blank amazement on the face of our captured schoolmaster—the sergeant-major with the spectacles and beard—when he was told that the Hymn of Hate was sung with gusto in the music halls of London and Paris, and was received by the audience with shrieking sounds of applause.

The Hymn of Hate sung by an Englishman in an English music hall! *Donnerwetter!* He could not understand. He had no sense of humour.

A Prussian officer was captured in November with about fifteen men, and I saw him marched in shortly after the capture. He looked arrogant, and one instinctively took a dislike to him, he was so obviously stamped "bounder."

His revolver was in its pouch on his belt. We had forgotten to take it, and he had forgotten that it was there. Our prisoner spoke English very well, and said that "he wished he had been shot. He was forever and ever disgraced at being made a prisoner. His regiment would not have him again as an officer." The impression we formed, who were standing round listening, was that this whining bounder seemed to feel it a particular disgrace to be a prisoner of the hated English. An English officer in charge at this particular place here went up to our snarling Prussian who wished "that he had been killed" and said:

"I see we have omitted to take over your revolver. It is still in your pouch and probably loaded—sure to be. You say you are sorry you were not killed. Well, go off five paces over there and blow your damned head off with your own gun. I won't interfere with you, and none of us will mourn for you."

The Prussian shut up like an oyster. We all laughed, and the soldiers round enjoyed it hugely. The eyes of the man blazed with fury, but he made no movement towards that five paces off, and handed over his revolver to our English officer, who refused to touch it, and called on a soldier to take it.

The Prussian did not see the humour of the situation, and "there's the humour on't" old Falstaff would have said.

A few days after the sinking of the *Emden*[1] the news reached the British and French in the trenches. The French were as delighted as we were. In the Argonne an advanced French trench was separated by only the width of a road from an advanced German trench. The officer in command of the French trench wrote out the news of the *Emden* fight on a piece of paper and tied this paper round a stone, which he flung into the German trench. It was received with guttural cries of annoyance. Shortly after this time from the German trench came another stone with a piece of paper inscribed, "*Monsieur*, go to Hell." The French officer, ever polite and determined to have the last word, sent back this note:

> Dear Bosches,—I have been to many places. I have been invited to visit many places in my time, but this is the first time that I have been invited to visit the German headquarters.

There is a society in London called the "Society for Lonely Soldiers." Its object is to be of some assistance to soldiers who have no relations or friends and are quite alone in the world. A young lady of this society sent a parcel of comforts to the British prison camp in Germany, and addressed the parcel to "The loneliest British soldier in Germany."

Some weeks afterwards a reply was received from the German officer in command of the camp. "Madam, your gifts have been impartially distributed amongst all the prisoners. We were unable to decide which was the *loveliest* British soldier in camp." Imagine a spectacled old German officer methodically scrutinising all the British prisoners to ascertain which was the "loveliest" one!

---

1. *The Kaiser's Raider* by Hellmuth von Mücke, two classics of war at sea is also published by Leonaur.

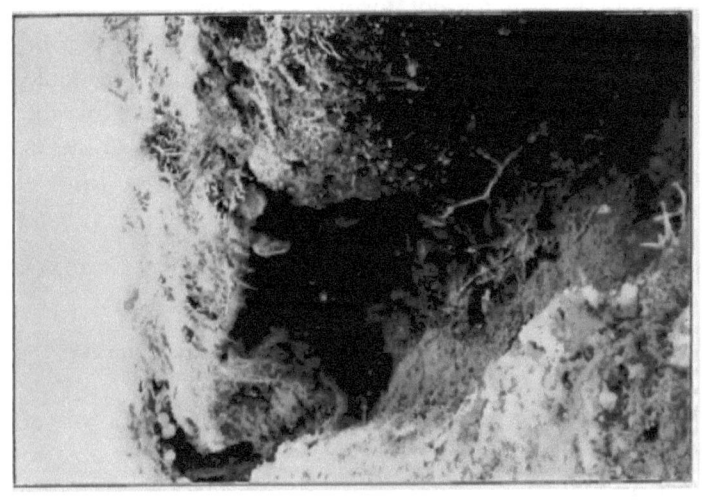
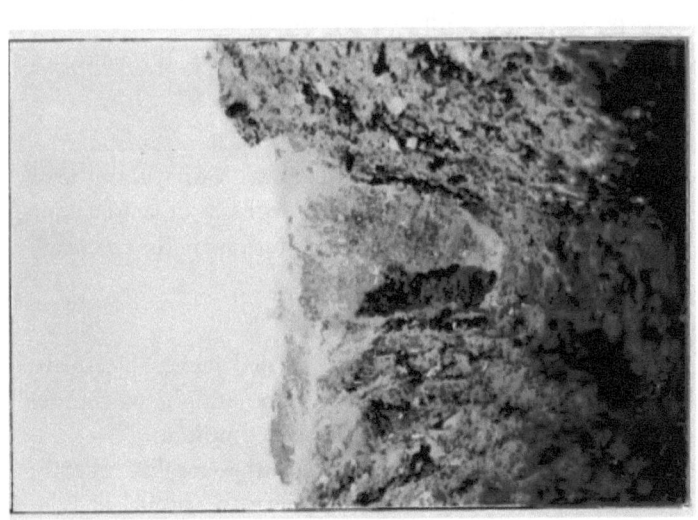

TRENCHES IN FLANDERS

Apropos of humour, read this incident reported by "Eyewitness" from the front.

> One wounded Prussian officer of a particularly offensive and truculent type, which is not uncommon, expressed the greatest contempt for our methods: 'You do not fight. You murder!' he said. 'If it had been straightforward, honest fighting we should have beaten you, but my regiment never had a chance from the first. There was a shell every ten yards. Nothing could live in such a fire.'

This from one of the apostles of frightfulness!

Now read this concluding sentence in a letter from a German lady of high social position to a Russian lady:

> We wish to carry in our hearts an undying hatred, and we utterly reject all useless verbiage on 'humanity.'
> To mothers and to German women this hate gives a sort of satisfaction without which our hearts would not be able to support,—etc. etc.

Read this order of the day, dated 26th August 1914, from General Stenger, Brigadier of the 88th Brigade, 14th Baden Army Corps. (This document is quite authentic, and is at present in the hands of the French War Office.) This is the translation:

> "The brigade on setting out today will make no prisoners; all prisoners will be killed. The wounded, with or without arms, will be put to death. Prisoners, even in large organised units, will be put to death. No living man must remain in our rear."

More will be heard of this document at the end of the war. It is a prized possession of the French just now.

Yet our wounded Prussian officer, as related above, objected to our murderous artillery fire, and said that "we do not fight, we murder." In spite of the tragic side the incident has some humour.

Dr. Ludwig Ganghofer, a Bavarian Court journalist, recently described a visit which he had paid to a German hospital in Lille. He there saw some wounded British prisoners. Two caught his eye, and thus he writes:

> As I regarded these two sulky pups of the British lion, I had a feeling as if every hair on my head stood on end. This unpleasant irritation only ceased when I had turned my German back

on the sons of civilised Albion, and looked again at suffering human beings.

"Suffering human beings" is good: our two unfortunate countrymen were not human beings. They were pups of the British lion—young lions, in fact. The German appellation for us is improving. Some weeks ago we were "Swine dogs," now we are "Young lions." Ganghofer is the Bavarian Court journalist. One wonders if that feudal power keeps a court jester.

CHAPTER 16

Some Medical Odds and Ends

FUNCTIONAL BLINDNESS.

At Bethune some of us met for the first time in this war cases of functional temporary blindness, and many other cases were met with at various points of the front.

The following example will give an idea of the condition. A young officer, nineteen years of age, was standing by a haystack in the north of France when a large Black Maria burst near him, rolled him over, and plastered him with clay, but did not kill him. The *concussion* had thrown him down. He remained unconscious for half an hour, and when he woke to consciousness he discovered he was "blind." His mental state then was terrible. He cried out, "Oh, why wasn't I killed?" "Won't someone carry me out and put me on the parapet of a trench so that I may be killed? "His grief was pathetic, and one can easily understand it. A careful examination was made of the interior of the eyes with the ophthalmoscope and nothing was found wrong. He was assured by the medical officers that he would certainly recover after perhaps a week or two of blindness. He was quiet and composed after this, but was a little bit suspicious that we were only trying to cheer him up. One medical officer then explained to him what sort of blindness it was: that it was due to concussion of the nerve of sight, and the delicate structures at the ball of the eye; that nothing was destroyed, and that a complete rest would bring back his vision. Next day he was transferred by hospital train to the base *en route* for England. This note, unknown to him, was pinned on his coat:

> Functional blindness. Any medical officer handling this officer on Hospital Train, Base Hospital, or Hospital Ship, please tell him that he will fully recover his sight.

Knowing the kind-hearted nature of the medical profession, one can be sure that he was cheered up all the way to England. I received a letter from this officer's mother some weeks after, saying that her son had completely recovered his vision, and was as well as ever.

Nerve Concussion

Nerve concussion is a pathological condition that has received more attention in this war than at any previous time. A young Fusilier at La Bassée was hit by a bullet through the fleshy part of the forearm. The wound was a purely flesh one and no important nerve could have been struck. He had paralysis of the wrist and hand, due to concussion of the important nerves of the forearm. The bullet in its course did not strike these nerves. He got completely better in eight weeks.

A Gordon Highlander was struck by a bullet in the right buttock. No important nerve was struck, yet he had paralysis of the limb owing to concussion of the sciatic nerve. He got better by rest in bed and massage of the muscles. A soldier of the Wiltshire Regiment was rolled over by the concussion of a bursting shell. He retained consciousness, but could not get up or move his right arm. The right side of his body was paralysed. He got better by rest. A Bedfordshire sergeant got a bullet wound through the upper arm, and paralysis of certain muscles supplied by nerves in the vicinity of the track of the bullet. It was thought that the nerves were divided, and after the wound had healed the nerves were exposed at an operation intending to join the severed ends. The nerves were found to be uninjured, and the incision in the skin was closed up. He made a complete recovery.

There is also the story of the soldier who suddenly recovered his voice in the presence of King George. The story is going the rounds of the hospitals, and it is said that His Majesty was extraordinarily interested in the phenomenon. This soldier was taken prisoner by the Germans during our retreat from Belgium. He was picked off the field in a dazed condition and unable to speak. He was interned later in a prison camp in Germany and was all this time quite unable to speak. When the exchange of permanently disabled prisoners of war was recently made between England and Germany, this man was sent back as permanently incapacitated on account of being dumb. He was admitted to a hospital near London. One day the king visited the hospital, and this man on getting up from his chair as the king entered the ward, inadvertently touched a heating pipe which was then very hot. He at once exclaimed "Damn," and was able to speak perfectly afterwards. The king was very much interested. Was this an hysterical loss of voice or a concussion? It was a mental shock of some kind, and the recovery was due to the other shock of touching a hot pipe.

I attended one young officer and three men who had been buried in the earth when their trench was blown up. The officer and one man were unconscious, and when the man recovered consciousness he was nervy and excitable. He had a startled, terrified expression, and when in bed he would peer round in a wild, anxious way, and then suddenly pull the blankets well over his head and curl up underneath as if anxious to shut out his surroundings, or what he thought were his surroundings. He seemed really to be living through some terrifying experiences of the past few days antecedent and up to the time when his trench was blown up and he was engulfed in the mud and debris.

The officer recovered consciousness more slowly, and spoke in a curious *staccato* speech; his nerves were completely gone, and he had fine tremors of the lips aud tongue and fingers. He told me that his memory had gone, that he had only a hazy recollection of recent things, which seemed far away and dim.

DEAF MUTISM.

Several cases of deaf mutism have occurred during the hard fighting near Ypres and La Bassée, and these are certainly very curious. The men so afflicted have written down that shells burst near them, that they were thrown down, and remembered nothing more for a time. On coming to again, they were deaf and dumb. These men also show other signs of nerve shock; they are restless, troubled with sleeplessness, and have anxious expressions. Generally all get completely well in a few weeks, but some of the cases remain mute for a much longer time.

LICE.

The medical officer at the front today has other duties besides those of attending to the sick and wounded. He is concerned with the prevention of disease, with water supplies, sanitation of billeting areas and camps, means to prevent frostbite, and so on. He has also to advise on methods of treating and avoiding vermin. Lice are, without a doubt, one of the terrors of war. These little beasts are not harmless. They take a high place in the sphere of destructive agents. I would group them in the class with shrapnel bombs and high explosives. Wherever many men are gathered closely together, and hygienic laws, owing to military needs, are in temporary abeyance, there will lice be found, constituting themselves one of the terrors of war. Officers and men get them, and once these pests gain entry to one's wardrobe they entrench themselves in their battalions and divisions, and require very drastic efforts to dislodge. In the early fighting in Flanders and in Northern France, on the Marne and Aisne, these beasts gave us great trouble. They are most active at night when one gets warm in bed. It is not the bite that counts, but, as the old French Countess once expressed it to a Minister of State, it is *"toujours le promenade."* The promenading causes irritation and insomnia. Scratching produces excoriations of the skin, and then a whole lot of sequent complications. Lice are factors in the spread of typhus fever, and when typhus visits an army in the field it carries death and desolation to thousands. To illustrate the point read this extract from a letter written from an English hospital in Serbia:

> The great scourge of this country is typhus fever. It was introduced by the Austrian prisoners at Christmas. Out of 2500 Austrian prisoners at Uskub, 1000 had died of fever and 1200 were down with it. It is a terrible disease, and is carried not by infection but by lice. One has to take tremendous precautions to avoid these creatures.

The majority of our wounded taken from the fighting line at La Bassée to the hospital at Bethune were infested with lice. Lice invaded the clothing of all who handled these poor fellows, and very drastic measures had to be taken to combat the scourge.

The following story will illustrate the vitality of these nasty little beasts. Our Field Ambulance once stopped at a small town in Northern France and was billeted in a French convent. The good sisters allowed us the use of the schoolrooms, the kitchen, and some of the bedrooms. All the officers were anxious to get their shirts and linen washed. The laundrywoman duly appeared and boiled all these articles, and the sisters ironed them for us. On the afternoon of the ironing the Mother Superior and two sisters came to us in a state of excitement, talking rapidly, and evidently overcome with amazement. They explained that our shirts had been boiled and then dried in the open air. When they began to iron the necks of our shirts the lice sprang to life and were exceedingly active. They assured us solemnly that scores sprang to active life under the comfortable warmth of the hot iron. I do not doubt the story. The heat had matured the chitinous envelope in which the young lice lay, and out they came, joyous, active, and sportive on the nice warm surface. Hence the amazement, the uplifted hands, and the consternation of the good sisters. The riddle of their extermination has not yet been completely solved, but measures are in active progress. It is an unsavoury subject, but it is a very important one for troops in camp and in the field.

Shell Fumes.

Thou shalt not kill,
But do not strive
Officiously to keep alive.

A great deal has been written on the effect of shell fumes in this war. So much is hearsay and so little really authentic, that one cannot dogmatise.

One naval surgeon said that men exposed to fumes of bursting shells develop acute pneumonia, which proves fatal as a rule. This is supposed to be due to the nitric peroxide produced by the explosion.

Artillery officers have told me that stories were going the round of the batteries that the Germans fired certain shells at our aeroplanes which, on bursting, set free certain gases which intoxicated the aviators.

A French gunner-major circumstantially related that a German trench which had been heavily shelled with turpinite shells was found full of dead Germans, standing or sitting in life-like attitudes and with faces *quite black*. He said that the look-out man was lying in his natural attitude holding field-glasses to his eyes. He was apparently alive, but was really dead, stiff, and with black face and hands. These statements have not been confirmed, but the stories of similar incidents are many. There is no doubt that lyddite and melinite fumes can, when inhaled, produce sudden poisonous changes. I have myself seen British soldiers and German prisoners, after having been exposed to these fumes, come in with deeply yellow jaundiced skin. One man, in fact, looked exactly like a man suffering from acute jaundice.

It is also said that the fumes induce drowsiness. Turpinite shells were employed at one stage of the war and are to be employed again. M. Turpin has recently been at the front with a French battery. Certainly turpinite does emit dangerous fumes. Many believe that it is some form of cyanogen gas—allied to prussic acid.

The force of these high explosives is well illustrated by an occurrence of 25th January. Previous to making an assault the Germans fired a mine under our front trench near the railway east of Cuinchy. The explosion hurled a piece of rail weighing 25 lbs. a distance of over a mile, into a field close to where some of our men were working.

It is reported that on 1st February the detonation of one of our lyddite shells in the enemy trenches on the embankment south of the canal, threw a German soldier right across the railway and the canal amongst our men on the north side of the latter.

At Fort Condé, on the Aisne, the air concussion of a bursting shell from a French 75 mm. lifted a large four-wheeled country waggon bodily out of a yard and planted it on the roof of a barn. The waggon was not injured. A bursting shell is the very incarnation of violence. Lord Fisher said that *"The Essence of War is Violence. Moderation in War is Imbecility. Hit first. Hit hard. Hit everywhere."* The big shells today do all this.

The fumes emitted by bursting charges of lyddite, melinite, or turpinite must not be confused with the poison gases sent out over our men by the Germans. The lyddite and melinite are put in the shells for a definite object which is permitted by the Hague Convention, and by the opinion of mankind generally. Their object is to burst the shell at the desired time and distance, and plaster the enemy with the iron or shrapnel. They are not intended to kill, and do not kill by poisonous fumes. The German poison gas is intended to kill, and does produce intolerable agony and lingering deaths, and for this the German stands accused before High Heaven.

Neurasthenia or "Nerves."

Many officers and some men have been sent back from the front in France and Flanders suffering from Nerves. These men are not "nervous" as the public generally understand that term. They are brave and courageous men who are anxious to do their duty. They are, moreover, men who have done their duty in the face of a determined foe, have endured great hardships and discomforts in the trenches and batteries, and have faced death in all the many hellish shapes that it assumes today. I said "many officers and some men" have been so afflicted, and it is true that the officer is much more prone to get "nerves" than is the simple soldier. The life of the officer is one of responsibility and worry, but the soldier's mental lot is simpler—he just does what he is told and has "not to reason why." The education and upbringing of the officer are different, as a rule, from that of the soldier, and heredity has an influence on a man's nervous organisation. In civil life anyone can call to mind certain boys and girls who are more "nervous" than others. I do not mean more afraid of danger or more effeminate, but more likely to be exalted or depressed by certain circumstances than their more stolid neighbours.

What is true of homes and of schools is equally true of nations. Unreal though it sounds, there is no doubt that the Germans are more emotional than the French, and German leaders know full well the emotional side of their people. The German is easily exalted and can be easily depressed. The Frenchman can be made furiously angry when he is affronted or insulted, but he is not easily depressed, and he is too cautious to be easily exalted. The German soldier and people must be strengthened and mentally sustained by stories of German victories and prowess, but the Frenchman, like the Englishman, is most formidable when he knows the worst there is to know and is "up against things."

It may be that our officers who develop neurasthenia at the front are more emotional and imaginative than those who do not, but they are no less courageous. An officer was sent to England for neurasthenia, and felt ashamed to tell his friends that he was sent back as his "nerve was gone." He was not in the list of wounded, yet his brain and nervous system had received a wound as much as the man with a bullet-hole through his shoulder, and the treatment for these "mental wounds" is like that for most other wounds, "time and rest," but the mental wound also requires quietness. The officer with the mental wound, the nerve shock, the neurasthenia, cannot be treated successfully in the general wards of a noisy hospital. He must be put in quiet and peaceful surroundings and live in an atmosphere free from noise, bustle, and commotion. His treatment must also be directed by physicians who are authorities on this subject. A successful general practitioner or a renowned obstetrician are not likely to achieve brilliant results in treating neurasthenia.

Fortunately the medical profession has already arranged special provision for these nerve cases, and the results, I am sure, will be eminently good.

At Bethune one able artillery officer was brought into the Clearing Hospital suffering from neurasthenia. He had been through the retreat, the righting on the Marne and Aisne, and at La Bassée, and had done splendid service with his battery, and had been promoted. When I saw him he was walking up and down a room like a caged animal.

I wished him good morning, and he pulled up suddenly in his stride, gazed at me with widely open eyes, and replied in a hesitating *staccato* voice, "G-g-good m-m-morning, doctor." He had never stuttered before. Then away he went up and down again. I got him to sit down on a box and told him to light his pipe and talk about himself. He filled his pipe with difficulty, stuffing the tobacco into the bowl with trembling and agitated fingers. He broke several wooden matches in trying to light them. He had lost the fine, practised discrimination necessary to rub a match on the side of the box, and he "jabbed" his match hard on it. I lit a match and gave it to him, as I was interested to see how he would light the pipe. He let that match fall. I lit another, and with this he burned his finger. I then held a lighted match over his pipe, and in a jerky way he managed to light the tobacco; but he could not smoke properly, and the pipe soon went out.

In the same jerky way he told me that he was forty-four years of age and had never been ill before. He was a good rifle shot, and had killed big game in India. He was a fair billiard player, and had been a temperate man all his life in all things. Talking in his spasmodic fashion, he had to stop for a word, and he then waved his hand about and frowned, as if angry with himself for having forgotten it. Up till a week ago he had been in perfect health, although the "strain" of the war had been tremendous; then one of his brother officers and a sergeant had been killed close beside him, and his guns had to be moved to another position under a heavy fire. He could not sleep that night, and the firing of the guns, which previously had not troubled him in the least, now worried him. Next day he could not eat. In a few days he was a physical and mental wreck. He was sent to England, and I heard that he had made a complete recovery.

One officer developed neurasthenia on the Aisne. His regiment had done brilliantly, but had suffered severe losses. The officer said that he was going to blow his brains out, so he was invalided into the hands of the doctors and later made a good recovery. He was suffering from the effects of strain and mental shock.

Another officer on the staff was standing close by his chief when a shell fell near, killing his chief outright. The staff officer had to be sent home for neurasthenia.

Our wounded often show signs of neurasthenia. I well remember at the hospital at Bethune one man who had had to have his arm off at the shoulder joint for a bad shrapnel wound. He was dangerously ill and semiconscious for several days. When he had fully roused to his surroundings and the knowledge of his weakness he was like a little child, crying and begging me to get him away from the sound of the firing. He said that he would be happy if only he could get away to some place where he would not hear the sound of the guns. On the day the German aeroplane dropped a bomb near the hospital the windows of the building shook and rattled with the concussion, and this poor devil screamed aloud with terror and tried to get out of bed and crawl away—anywhere from the sound of the firing.

The French nursing sisters told me that the wounded Frenchmen work themselves into a terrible state of excitement in hospital when the firing is very brisk. They beg and beg to be taken away to the south of France, as far away as possible from the sound of conflict.

These were all brave men with injured nervous systems.

SMALL ARM AMMUNITION.

The Germans have charged the British, French, Russians, and Belgians with using Dum-Dum bullets. The Austrians have made the same charge against the Serbians and Montenegrins. The Triple Entente and its Allies have accused the Germans and Austrians of firing Dum-Dum bullets—so there you are.

The Dum-Dum bullet was first made at Dum-Dum, near Calcutta. It was a Lee-Enfield bullet with an imperfect nickel sheath. This nickel or cupro-nickel sheath in the Dum-Dum stops at the "shoulder" of the bullet, and the point is therefore bare lead, a continuation of the core of the bullet. Some modifications of the Dum-Dum exist . By rubbing the point of a nickel-coated Lee-Enfield bullet on a rough stone the cover is rubbed off, exposing the core of lead. A saw or file can make incisions in the long axis of the bullet exposing the lead this way, but leaving the tip covered with nickel. The destiny of a Dum-Dum is to break up when it strikes a bone. If it strikes a bone at a high rate of velocity it fragments and rips and tears the bone and surrounding soft structures. It is supposed to have greater "stopping power" against an infantry charge than an undeformed bullet. This supposition is incorrect.

Certainly a Dum-Dum in traversing a limb or the chest can cause terrible and widespread destruction. In wounds inflicted by a Dum-Dum bits of the lead core and casing are scattered in various directions. But,—and this is important,—the same thing can be found in a wound inflicted by an undeformed Lee-Metford, Lebel, or Mauser bullet. The only certain proof of the employment of the Dum-Dums is to find them in the trenches captured from the enemy, or in the cartridge belts of wounded or prisoners. Again, a man may have a bullet wound with a small entrance hole and a large, gaping, jagged exit. One unaccustomed to bullet wounds would immediately say that such a wound was caused by an explosive bullet. But it can be caused by the ordinary Lee-Metford, Lebel, and Mauser bullets. I have seen these wounds frequently amongst Germans, French, and British. The explanation is that the bullet on striking a bone often carries along with it a fragment, large or small, and it is this fragment of bone that tears out a passage to the exit wound. The German bullet is easily extracted from the cartridge. It is almost impossible to extract the Lee-Metford bullet without strong instruments.

The Germans have made use of this fact to extract the bullet from the cartridge and put it back "upside down," that is, with the nickel point inside the metal cartridge case, and the base with its exposed lead core outwards. Such a bullet on striking a bone expands and fragments, and causes great damage. I am not repeating a rumour when I make this statement. I have seen these cartridges with the inverted bullets in the belts of German prisoners captured in the trenches. Other surgeons have seen them also. The French say that it is a common practice amongst the Germans, and so did our men at Ypres. One German prisoner on the Yser when confronted with these bullets taken from his own belt, admitted having used them. He said that his company officer told him that they were useful to break down barbed-wire entanglements!

There is one interesting point about the German bullet, and that is its property of spinning on its short axis when it strikes an object. The centre of gravity of the German bullet is low down on its base, owing to its long and tapering shoulder. It therefore turns over on reaching its object. I had on the Aisne one man of the Norfolk Regiment admitted with a tiny entrance wound between the great and second toes of the foot. The bullet was found lodged in the large heel bone, and its base was facing towards the entrance wound. It could not have entered the foot in that position, because the entrance wound was too small. A bullet spinning round when traversing a limb can cause considerably more damage than one that pursues a direct course, and this fact is important in brain injuries. The bullet penetrates the skull by a small punctured opening, and then whirls round and round inside the brain. It may then again strike the bone on the other side with its long axis and cause considerable shattering and bleeding. This spinning action of the Mauser was a thing that every surgeon had to remember when treating his wounded.

The Hague Convention of 1907 prohibits "the use of projectiles calculated to cause unnecessary suffering." The Hague Declarations of 1899 decide to "abstain from the use of bullets which expand or flatten easily in the human body," such as bullets with a hard envelope which does not entirely cover the core or is pierced with incisions. The St. Petersburg Declaration of 1868 agrees to abolish the use of "any projectile of a weight below 400 grams which is either explosive or charged with fulminating or inflammable substances."

The *British Medical Journal* of 21st November 1914 reports as follows on the subject of small arm ammunition:

The British service ammunition is known technically as Mark VII. .303 S.A. Ammunition. The length of the bullet is 1.28 inches; weight, 174 grains; muzzle velocity, 2440 feet per second. The bullet is a pointed one with an envelope of cupro-nickel which completely covers the core except at the base. The ordinary German service ammunition is very similar. Length of bullet, 1.105 inches; weight, 154 grains; muzzle velocity, 2970 feet per second. This bullet is pointed, with a steel envelope coated with cupro-nickel covering the cone except at the base. Both bullets carry out the provisions of the Hague Convention.

There is clear evidence that Germany has not confined herself solely to this unobjectionable ammunition. Her troops, both in Togoland and in France, have been proved to have used bullets with a soft core and hard, thin envelope not entirely covering the core, which type of bullet is expanding and therefore expressly prohibited by the Hague Convention.

Such bullets, of no less than three types, were found on the bodies of dead native soldiers serving with the German armed forces against British troops in Togoland in August, and on the persons of German, European, and native armed troops captured by us in that colony. All the British wounded treated in the British hospitals during the operations in Togoland were wounded by soft-nosed bullets of large calibre, and the injuries which these projectiles inflicted, in marked contrast to those treated by the British medical staff amongst the German wounded, were extremely severe, bones being shattered and the tissue so extensively damaged that amputation had to be performed. The use of these bullets was the subject of a written protest by the general officer commanding the British troops in Nigeria to the German acting governor of Togoland.

Again at Gundelu, in France, on 19th September 1914, soft-nosed bullets were found on the dead bodies of German soldiers of the *Landwehr*, and on the persons of soldiers of the *Landwehr* made prisoners of war by the British troops. One of these bullets has reached the War Office. It is undoubtedly expanding and directly prohibited by the Hague Convention. I am sure that Germany will be terribly upset at this, for Germany, we know, pays great respect to the articles of the Hague Convention!

CHAPTER 17

We Leave Bethune

One afternoon a German aeroplane dropped a bomb at the hospital gate, and a second one on a house near the gate. They burst with a terrific crash, shook the building and rattled the glass and startled us all. The same voyaging Taube dropped another bomb in the square of the city, and an old woman, a man, and a baby were struck. The old lady had to have her leg amputated and died on the succeeding day; the man received a shell wound in the back of the head and he died a few days afterwards; the baby was injured in the stomach and also died next day. One of our Army Service Corps men was struck by a piece of shell on the leg and received a serious wound. A corporal of the Army Service ran upstairs to me in the ward where I was busy dressing some cases and excitedly told me that his back was broken and that he thought he would soon be paralysed. We undressed him and found that a small piece of shell had made a slight wound on the muscles of the back, but that he was otherwise all right. He was reassured about the paralysis and the broken back. Two days afterwards another German aeroplane—or it may have been the same beast that had visited us before—flew over the city and dropped some more bombs, killing some unfortunate people and injuring others.

On the following morning at three o'clock I was in one of the wards admitting some wounded men just in from the trenches, when the unmistakable burst of a Black Maria was heard close at hand. The shell had burst not far from the hospital, and was followed by two more, one near the railway station, and one near the college not far away. The Germans had the range perfectly, and we expected a big bombardment. The authorities decided that Bethune was no longer a safe place for our Clearing Hospitals, and we were ordered to prepare for the evacuation of our wounded as soon as possible. This was soon done, and all were conveyed by ambulance motors to the hospital trains, with the exception of seven men. These men were all dying from severe injuries to the brain, and no good would be served by sending them down to the Base. So the seven poor fellows were put in beds alongside each other in one ward, and in three days they were dead, and buried in the now well-filled cemetery at Bethune.

The two Clearing Hospitals in the city—British and Indian—were sent to Chocques, near Lillers.

It was with a little heartache that I left Bethune and its good sisters. We had passed through days and nights of racking work and worry, and we had the satisfaction of feeling that we had all done our best. It is mournful to leave a place associated with many stirring episodes and with many warm friendships, for in times like those at Bethune firm friendships were quickly made. In saying goodbye one seems to leave them behind forever—and that is always sad.

The nuns at this hospital were simply splendid all through, and I can quite understand how the religious sisters have come to their own again in France.

From the earliest times and up till about eight years ago all the nursing in the French hospitals was done by sisters belonging to the various religious orders. Then came one of the big political upheavals for which France has been so noted in the past, and the nursing sisters gradually disappeared from the hospitals owing to the hostility of the State to the Church and all connected with it. The nursing sisters of these orders were at the time of this change well-trained medical and surgical nurses. As they were no longer able to exercise their professional skill, and no more of the younger nuns were trained in nursing, it followed that on the outbreak of war only the older nuns were capable of undertaking skilled nursing in the many hospitals. The demand for nurses was a clamant one, for from the very beginning of the war there were large casualties. It was said that the nursing by the lay sisters who succeeded the religious sisters was not of such a high order as in the old days owing to the absence of the strict and rigid discipline, the very fibre of the life of a sister in religion. I have heard this both from French surgeons and from visiting British surgeons.

When the war broke out France was as ill prepared in her military medical branch as we were, and she was suddenly confronted with the problem of handling and treating many thousands of wounded.

M. Clemenceau, an ex-Premier of France and a Doctor of Medicine, is also the editor of *L'Homme Enchaîné*. At the outbreak of war this journal was known as *L'Homme Libre*, and Clemenceau so violently attacked the medical disorganisation and lack of preparation that the paper was promptly suppressed. It, however, emerged next day under its new title, *The Man in Chains*, and under this title appears daily in Paris.

Clemenceau's efforts, however, were continued, and France soon had everything in good going order. It was at this critical phase that the Franciscan sisters, and the sisters of other religious orders, quietly took their places beside the wounded French soldiers. Just as quietly they opened up their convents, churches, and buildings, warehouses, *châteaux*, cottages, railway waiting-rooms, and turned them into hospitals for the wounded and sick men. Working tirelessly night and day, knowing no fatigue and shrinking from no task or danger, and glorying in their mission, they performed marvels. The younger sisters were put to subordinate nursing duties, and so rigorously trained by the elder ones in the principles of nursing.

These juniors are now very competent nurses, for they learn quickly amongst the ample material that war provides. The wounded French soldier loves and idolises the nursing sister. He demands her presence, and makes her his confidante. The nun is supremely happy to be back in her old place, and pets and humours the wounded soldier, soothes his ardent soul, and, by her skill, heals his wounds.

I do not think that any future government of France will ever dare to oust the religious sisters from the hospitals. These quiet-voiced, simple-robed women, carrying help and compassionate pity in the welter of blood and slaughter, have come "to their own "again.

When writing of the religious orders one naturally thinks of the priests of France, and one of the many interesting and instructive evolutions taking place during this war is that of the changing relation of the people and State towards the Catholic Church.

One has only to be a little time with the French troops in the field to recognise and be impressed by their deep attachment to the Catholic Church. I visited many churches in France and Belgium during the earlier stages of the war, and at all hours, and have always found, sometimes few, sometimes many, Belgian and French soldiers on their knees and devoutly at prayer in the sacred buildings. Women, of course, were always to be seen there, but that was not surprising. It was surprising to see so many soldiers.

The French soldier takes his religion seriously in these days, and is not ashamed, whenever the opportunity occurs, to enter a church and pray. It was rare to see a khaki soldier praying in church; one often saw them there on visits of curiosity gazing at the old windows and old scroll-work of the churches. The British, soldier will always attend a church parade, and he will be most reverent during a service, and will sing lustily and amen loudly; but a church parade is to him very often a drill, and Tommy cheerfully attends a drill parade because it is his duty to. In reading letters from British soldiers at the front and comparing them with those of French soldiers one cannot help being struck by the religious serious note pervading those of the latter, and its absence in the former. It may be that we are less emotional than the French, and as a nation are shy of writing of our inner selves.

It was my duty once to censor the letters written by wounded men in a Clearing Hospital at the front. The letters were distinctly humorous at times; only two discussed matters of faith. In one a soldier was writing to his mother, and he said:

> I pray every day as I promised you to. I pray standing up, and always time my prayer for three o'clock in the afternoon, for that is the time when the fellows over the way let off most of their big guns and rifles at us.

This man was either a wag and teasing his mother, or he really believed in the efficacy of surrounding himself with an atmosphere of prayer when the enemy fire was hottest. The other fervent letter was from a soldier who had received a slight shell wound of the scalp. His was a letter written to a clergyman near London. This warrior informed the clergyman that he prayed silently amongst his comrades, and daily read a passage out of his Testament. The letter ended up by asking the clergyman to send him some Woodbine cigarettes, as he, the writer, hadn't had a smoke for a fortnight and saw no chance of getting one. I showed this letter to our field chaplain, who visited this Christian soldier in the ward. The chaplain told me afterwards that the man was absolutely destitute of any religious beliefs, and had never read a Testament in his life; and furthermore—that he had three packets of Woodbine cigarettes, and had also smoked a considerable number during the past fortnight.

French officers have told me that before the war it was considered bad form for a military officer to attend Mass, and that an officer who attended Mass regularly need not expect promotion in the army. Attending Mass is not considered bad form today, and soldiers of all grades from general to grenadier attend the services in the field. Was the religious trait there all the time, and only held back by the conventional strictness, or has the seriousness of the war compelled a little self-analysis and a return to the faith of their fathers? My impression is that the priests and the nursing sisters of the religious orders have helped to stir up this present state amongst a people who have always been, deep down, much attached to their Church and its religious observances. Even the Reign of Terror could not stamp out the influence of the Church in France, although it turned churches into meat marts and blacksmiths' forges, and plastered their walls with "*Liberté, Egalité, Fraternité.*"

The French priest has no official status in the State. He is simply a citizen, and is liable, like all other citizens, to be mobilised for military duty. Over 20,000 French priests and brothers of various orders are serving with the French colours in this war. I have spoken to French priests about this law that compels them to serve as soldiers. They do not cavil at it, and, in fact, prefer to act the patriot's part, for the priest is every bit a good Frenchman. Be the priest a simple soldier in the trenches, with battery, commissariat, ammunition, or *brancardiers*, he is nevertheless still a priest, and is at all times ready and eager to exercise his priestly duties. He has proved himself time and time again to be a cool, intrepid, and reliable soldier, and he has also proved himself in the hour of trial a comfort and spiritual help to those about to die. One has heard of hundreds of instances in this war when the priest, serving as soldier in the ranks, has conducted Mass in some broken-down cottage or barn in the firing zone, buried his dead comrades with the rites of the Church, and carried out the last offices to the dying.

One of the ablest of the French artillery officers, now in charge of a battery, is a priest, and in times of peace is a well-known *abbé* and writer on theology. Another learned *abbé* and a great preacher was mobilised in July, and was badly wounded at Charleroi. When lying stricken on the ground he heard a mortally wounded soldier calling him. The *abbé* painfully crawled to the dying soldier and administered the last office, and while doing so was again wounded. He was later on conveyed by hospital train to Paris. President Poincaré had heard the story, and met the train on its arrival in Paris. He went into the carriage where lay the badly wounded and apparently dying *abbé*, and decorated him with the *Legion d'Honneur*. I am glad to say that the *abbé*, although now a cripple, recovered from his wounds.

The *Aumonier* to the French Hospital at Bethune was a very fine priest. He was not mobilised as a soldier owing to defective vision, but he acted as priest and as a stretcher-bearer to the hospital. His lifelong friend, another priest and lecturer on Natural History at the College at Bethune, was fighting as a private in the Argonne. One day the *abbé* told me that he had received a letter from his friend describing his life in the trenches, saying, "I live the life of a rabbit. I live in a hole in the ground. At night I come out to feed."

A few days after this the *abbé* heard that his friend was killed—shot dead through the head. When the *abbé* told me of this I murmured the usual, "Hard luck."

"No," said the *abbé*, becoming very serious. "It is not what you call the Hard Luck. It is the good luck. It is how a good priest would wish to die."

It has been asked many times during this war, "What is Christianity doing after the past 1900 years?" and many have answered, "Crucified men and women. Mutilated prisoners of war. Outraged women and slaughtered children. Cities and towns in ashes. Misery, tears, and the moaning of millions." If this is the indictment, it is not against Christianity, but against one people only, that of Lutheran Germany. But these hellish deeds of "Christian" Germany have but served to bring more clearly and brightly into view the Christian spirit of other peoples' brotherliness, help for the distressed, and that

Kindness in another's trouble,
Courage in your own.

The Belgian and French soldiers fighting at first to defend their homes, their women, and their children and old men, and fighting now for vengeance to punish the bloody invaders, are examples of a good, healthy Christianity.

The open, warm welcome of France and England to the Belgian refugees, the colossal funds for the alleviation of distress, and helping of the wounded and the sick, show that the "greatest of these," Charity, is not yet dead on the earth.

Our definition of "Christianity" depends upon the point of view. To me the Turco and the Gurkha are very good Christians and the German nation is *infidel*. Every General Order issued by the *Kaiser* ends not with an appeal to the Almighty, but with an affirmation that God is fighting for the German cause.

The Saxons and Bavarians will sack a town and inflict nameless horrors on helpless civilians, shoot old men for sport, kill children, torture women, commit sacrilege in the churches, smash altars and relics, destroy historic and beautiful windows and treasures of art, bayonet priests, violate shrieking nuns, and with hands smeared in blood they will at the word of command praise their German God.

CHAPTER 18

Over the Belgian Frontier

Our Clearing Hospital remained at Chocques for four or five days, and while here had a fair, but not a large, number of wounded. These were quickly sent off by hospital trains, which pulled on to a siding not far from us. The Indian Clearing Hospital was now also establishing itself in the small town, and the Indian hospital assistants were a source of great and wondering curiosity to the small boys and girls. Our Clearing Hospital was now ordered to a place farther north, and as I had only been temporarily attached to it during a time of great rush at Bethune, my place was now with my own Field Ambulance at the front, and somewhere near the Belgian frontier.

A motorcar going to Hazebrouck gave me a lift as far as there, and another driver brought me to Bailleul. Here, after I had reported my arrival, Surgeon-General Porter informed me of the exact location of my ambulance.

Bailleul is a town of considerable importance in the north of France, and has been the object of many visits from Taubes, a sure indication that there must be a church or a hospital in Bailleul. The church and the hospital were very close together, and the Taubes made many a gallant attempt to get them both. One evening one of them got the hospital—a bomb fell fair on the roof and into a ward full of wounded men, killing two and wounding again a man already grievously wounded. The old church has so far escaped. The square at Bailleul near the church was a busy place in those days, as the town was a Divisional Headquarters and a corps "*poste commandemen*," and where there are headquarters and "brass hats" there also are many rank and file. It was here that, some weeks later, I saw that fine battalion, the Liverpool Scottish, parade in the street and march out to the trenches. They were standing on parade in the street for about twenty minutes before moving off and the day was bitterly cold. The bare knees of the men looked blue and the kilt did not impress us as a good winter dress. Why Highlanders choose to expose their knees is quite beyond me. The knee joint is a big and complex anatomical structure, and is easily affected by sudden changes of temperature, so why cover up every other joint in the body and leave this bare?

Greatly daring though the ladies are today in their draping arrangements, they do not dare to walk about with bare knees. What prevents them must certainly be their appreciation of the delicacy of this joint—the delicate mechanism of an important articulation.

Twenty years hence, veterans of the Liverpool Scottish will tell their children how they got rheumatism in their knee joints from the cold mud of the Flanders trenches in the year of our Lord 1914.

I left Bailleul on a Red-Cross Wolseley car driven by a queer character who used to be with us on the Aisne doing transport work. He was thought to have been killed and duly buried, and I was therefore agreeably surprised to see my odd friend again. He was a wonderfully cheery pessimist. He usually had a long budget of most depressing news, of disasters by flood and field, and great disappointments, but he envisaged them all with a rosy hue and predicted a great tomorrow. He did not like the war, for although it had not changed his occupation—that of a chauffeur—it had seriously affected his emoluments. In the piping times of peace he would take small parties on touring journeys in France, Germany, and Switzerland—sometimes a honeymoon couple, sometimes an American millionaire, and he did exceedingly well in tips.

We had a rough passage up from Bailleul and were twice bogged in the mud beside the road, and had twice to be hauled out. The roads here, and right over the frontier into southern Belgium, were very bad in these days. Our men, when on the Aisne, said many hard words about the mud there, but the Aisne was an asphalt path compared with Belgium.

However, we slowly squelched and skidded our way over the Belgian frontier and reached Ouderdom, not very far from Ypres. For the last few miles we had been following Napoleon's maxim to his marshals: "*Marching on the sound of the guns.*" The heavy artillery, French, British, and German, was making a deafening roar.

This really completed the journey from the Aisne to Flanders. We were at our "farthest north," and this journey impressed one with the length of the huge battle-line, although it only embraced, after all, a part of the great whole. From Switzerland to the Channel stretched a wavy line of trenches, across plains, spanning canals, through and around swamps, in front of great cities and small villages, traversing great forests and over mountain passes and peaks. At one end submerged country flooded by Alpine snow, sand dunes at the other; and in these trenches lined with soldiers, and swept by artillery, stern fighting was going on over practically every mile.

Our ambulance headquarters was about the most God-forsaken place that one could possibly imagine. The first impression one received was a dirty pond, full of fetid water and surrounded by heaped-up straw manure. The Belgian, like the Frenchman, loves to have a manure heap at his front door. Closely abutting on this putrefactive manure was the cottage itself, with one front room, a small side-room or box off this front room, a kitchen, a bedroom, and another box at the back. From the kitchen a rickety stair led up to a windy loft full of corn and hops and bags of potatoes.

Next the living quarters and part of the house came stalls for cattle, and the *tout ensemble* was unlovely and smelly. Twelve medical officers, two chaplains, and a quartermaster lived in the tiny little front room, or crowded round a table in it. When the table was in the room there was barely space to pass between it and the wall. Six or seven officers slept on the floor of this den at night, and in the morning had to rise early, roll up their valises and pack them round the wall. The O.C. and a chaplain slept in the box off our only room, and the rest of us slept in the loft amidst the wheat and hops and the bitter cold draughts.

Our cooks lived, smoked, worked, and slept in the kitchen, and this apartment *Madame* invaded during the day to do her domestic cooking. *Madame* "with the terrible voice" gave our cooks a bad time, and frequently chased them out and took their pots and pans off the fire, utterly disorganising our meals.

Madame was not popular, and in my dreams I sometimes still hear her raucous voice.

The Flemish farmer, the proud owner of this very dirty and uninviting farm, had a family of three little children, and was besides the humble husband of the lady whose voice was more terrifying than the screech of bursting shrapnel.

Poor *Madame*, she did not look kindly on us, and we never even saw her smile—except once, and that story comes later.

At 4 a.m. her strident, penetrating tones would fill the cottage and wake us all to a world of cold and discomfort, of greasy bacon, muddy tea, and sodden mousy bread.

She was watchful and suspicious of our men, who slept with the poultry in the surrounding stables and outhouses, and openly accused them of stealing her straw.

What they could do with the straw after having stolen it *Madame* did not choose to say—perhaps she thought that they ate it!

We met many Flemish besides *Madame* and her family at this time, and although we sympathised greatly with them, we could not bring ourselves to like them. It was all so different with the French, whom we liked and who liked us. The Flemings did not seem to care for us; they certainly never made us any demonstrations of affection. Perhaps it was the difference in tongue. They spoke French with an Irish-Dutch brogue, and our accent was, of course, a pure Anglo-Parisian.

French officers told us here that they did not like the Flemings, and that the Flemings were not cordial with them. Belgian officers, it is well known, do not see eye to eye with the French officers, but pull amazingly well with the British, to whom they are warm and communicative.

Tommy Atkins as a rule likes every one, but he neither understood nor cared for the Flemings. This was quite noticeable. We found those round Ouderdom, Ypres, and Dickebusch sullen, dour, and suspicious. We were not welcomed, and their surly, heavy manner towards us was very apparent. There was no responsiveness, no *gaieté de coeur*, no cheerfulness.

Historical traditions and the likes and hates of centuries die hard. The Flemings and the English had often been friends in the past, but the French and Flemings had always been on opposite sides of the fence, and whenever the French came into the Flemish garden it was to fight, and not to play.

We wondered if *Madame* of our cottage knew her Belgian history. We were quite sure that she would have been more amiable and sweet had she known that Flanders had been England's ally in the Hundred Years' War, and that the bowmen of Mons were more than once ranged on England's side; that Baldwin II., Count of Flanders, a former ruler of the land where stood *Madame's* farm, was a son-in-law of Alfred the Great of England, and that Baldwin V., also a Count of Flanders, was father-in-law to William the Conqueror, and fitted out Flemish ships to convey Flemish men to Pevensey to kill Harold's Anglo-Saxons.

The Flemings have long memories about the French, and never

forget the "Battle of the Spurs" or the "Battle of Roosebeke," for in these two epoch-making battles the French were the enemy.

The manifesto issued by the King of the Belgians to his people at the beginning of the war in August cited the Battle of the Spurs fought at Courtrai. At this famous encounter, a band of Flemish artisans and citizens, armed with billhooks, axes, and scythes, attacked with the maddest fury a disciplined French army of steel-clad knights and men-at-arms and utterly defeated it. This battle reference was hardly quite happy when Joffre was hurrying his army corps over the frontier to Namur.

At Roosebeke, in 1382, the French met another citizen army under Philip van Artevelde, and slew him and twenty-five thousand men. It is said that Flemish fathers and mothers handed down this bitter tale to their children for three centuries, and in later years told of Cassel, Ramillies, Oudenarde, Malplaquet, Jemappes, and Waterloo—all glaring instances of French turbulence on peaceful Flanders land. So the Flemings were distrustful always of the Gallic cock, and had apparently forgotten about their connection with our Alfred the Great and our William of Normandy.

During our occupation of this mean farmhouse, situated behind its Flemish manure heap, the weather was bitingly cold. The rain of the first week was succeeded by a heavy snow and frost, and as we had no fire of any sort and were not able to take much physical exercise, we were all day and night chilled to our very marrow.

November 1914 in Flanders will be remembered by many thousands of Englishmen as a month of intense and bitter cold, when to the dangers and ever-present death of the trenches were added the miseries and tortures of frostbitten feet and legs, and a merciless cutting wind. This was the period when men, stiffened and paralysed with cold, had to be pulled out of the trenches and dragged or carried to the rear to bring back a slowing circulation to the affected limbs. This was also the period when men could not be spared from the firing line, when the Germans were making those formidable rushes in strong columns, and leaving thousands of dead to mark the place where the rush had been stayed and the column crumpled up.

The little town of Dickebusch was on the road to our left, and through it ran a highway to Ypres. Where the road turned to the right into Ypres was an advanced station of a Field Ambulance, and, as one of the medical officers of it was known to me, I walked along this highway one morning in order to hear the latest news. He was always a very safe man to call upon for news, for what he did not know authentically, he would invent. The road to this advanced station lay behind several batteries of French "seventy-fives," the pride and glory of the French gunner. The road was quite close to these guns, but they were so wonderfully concealed with straw and branches of trees that an ordinary traveller would have passed them by until their presence was indicated by their mighty roar. The gunners were hard at it this morning, pouring an unending string of bursting shells on the German positions, and the din was terrible.

Suddenly the Germans got the range of the road. One shell burst far in front of me on the road, and one far behind about the same moment, and a bolt for cover was the immediate sequence. I got into a dugout behind some French guns and then witnessed a wonderful display of artillery practice. Shell after shell fell with marvellous precision up and down the road, and one followed the other with a lightning speed. The road was excavated with volcanic craters, of flying stones and earth clouds, and mighty showers of debris were sprayed tumultuously on every side.

A French officer pointed out where the next shell would land; and he was always right—he knew the "general idea" possessing the mind of the German gunner, and correctly surmised that after the road had been systematically covered, the firing would cease. It was a big waste of ammunition, for nothing was damaged except the road, and the French gunners, as soon as the firing was over, ran to their pet "seventy-fives" and opened furiously back in order to show that their bark was as good as ever. The French batteries at this particular place did enormous damage to the Germans in their attacks south of Ypres, and as they are no longer at this roadside but somewhere farther on, no valuable information is being given away in relating the fact.

The French gunners, both at this critical phase of the war and on the Aisne, were wonderful fellows. Night and day, in rain, hail, sleet, or snow, their great guns never stopped. In the blackest night and in howling gales of sleety wind they could be heard near by and in the far distance, for ever pounding into the enemy. This policy of continuous fire is wonderfully heartening to the French troops in the trenches, and the moral effect is tremendous. On the Aisne the French guns were always busy, but the British, alas, were generally silent. I have heard men on the Aisne pathetically say, "Why don't our guns fire?" "Why don't they reply to the German fire?" and the questioning was not confined to soldiers, for it was a common topic of conversation amongst officers. On the Aisne we did not have enough artillery, and we had not enough ammunition for the artillery we did have. It was the same at this period at Ypres. England, the greatest engineering country of the world, the richest and most prosperous Empire of this or any other time, made a very poor showing on the Continent. Small as our army was, it was not equipped perfectly. Our army in France may have been the "best shooting army," but if so it was with the rifle. In artillery we were entirely outclassed by the Germans and put to eternal shame by the French. On the Aisne the Germans had big 8-inch howitzers and we had nothing to meet them. Against the guns that had battered the forts of Maubeuge and crumpled up Namur what had we to offer? Nothing. The Germans had an unlimited supply of machine-guns on the Aisne and the Yser, and we had a paltry few. We were short of ammunition, but the Germans and the French had plenty.

When we required high explosive shells to beat down entrenchments and trenches we had nothing but shrapnel, which was absolutely useless for this purpose. Because shrapnel was effective in the South African War and high explosives unnecessary there, it was concluded that the same set of circumstances would be repeated in France and Belgium.

In September 1914 I saw the four 6-inch howitzer batteries arrive on the Aisne from England, and the news of their arrival spread like wildfire amongst our men, who thought that at last "mighty England was sending mighty guns." They were mighty guns right enough, but there was not enough ammunition sent with them. As a nation we always muddle through, but it is rather pitiful to think that muddles mean the death of many brave men, and that our woeful lack of big guns and ammunition has meant many British graves in France and Flanders.

A ride through Ypres at this time was an interesting and exciting affair—interesting from the historic associations of the old Flemish capital, and exciting from the German "Black Marias" falling about. The old Cloth Hall was then still standing—only one corner and a door had been battered about, but Ypres itself was very mournful and desolate. A bombarded town, empty of all its people and with ruins all round where once was industry, wealth, and moving crowds, presents a very sad spectacle. I suppose Ypres, stormy as her history has been in the past, had never been so empty before. At one time 200,000 people were said to have lived in Ypres. That was in the days of her splendour as the ancient capital of Flanders, when the wonderful Cloth Hall was built by the clothworkers of the thirteenth century, in that turbulent epoch when citizens and workpeople were fighting down and curbing the old feudal tyranny—for it was in Belgium that the common people established the first free city north of the Alps.

On the ride through this famous old city to our positions beyond, the terrible evidences of the German bombardment surrounded one in monumental impressiveness. Dead horses were lying in coagulated pools of blood in every street. Whole rows of old, closely-built Spanish and Flemish houses and shops were crumbled and shattered. The fane was ripped, torn, and covered with window glass shattered into millions of fine fragments; roofs had disappeared from some houses, and walls blown out of others. Tumbled masonry, smoking ashes, and excavated, torn-up roadways—all bore witness to the terrible character of the first German bombardment.

In one tobacconist's shop in the square, just opposite the Cloth Hall, the large plate-glass window had been completely destroyed, but the shop stood otherwise uninjured and intact. One could easily have taken boxes of cigars and pipes by simply putting a hand through the window-frame in passing, but although the temptation was there, not one cigar was touched by a British soldier. Imagine the genial Saxon or the crucifying Bavarian letting such a chance slip!

I got off my horse and led it through the street, as it clearly did not like passing the dead horses on the roadway. After having tied it to a street-post in front of a fair-sized hotel or *estaminet*, I walked into the front bar-parlour, which was open to the street. The evidences of a hasty exit were ludicrously patent. A half-emptied glass of beer and a full one stood close together on the bar counter, and near them lay a good pipe full of tobacco which had not been lighted. On a small table in a corner of the *café* was a tray with two large empty clean glasses; on the same table stood a bottle of red wine, and close beside it a corkscrew, holding the impaled extracted cork. One light chair near this table lay overturned on the floor; the other had been hastily drawn back, as was shown by the tracks on the sawdust floor.

I thought of Pompeii when old Vesuvius belched ashes and molten lava and buried the gay Roman pleasure-city as it stood. The Pompeian wine-bibbers and "mine host" could not escape from that engulfing darkness and the fiery cinders, and perforce died nobly standing by their bottles. But in that drinking-room at Ypres there was no dying the death beside the beer and the good red wine. No Sherlock

Holmes was necessary to reconstruct the picture—the two cronies drinking their morning ale at the bar, and the two comfortable Yprian *burghers* waiting for the filling of their glasses from the bottle just uncorked, the burly "mine host" in white apron and with bottle in hand—all suddenly electrified by a sinister whistling overhead, and then the mighty explosion, the roar of falling masonry, the smashing of hundreds of window-panes, the concussion of air; then another earthquake smash, and then another, till the house and street were rocking with the shocks. This was no time to light a pipe, to drink amber beer and ruddy wine. It was time to get out of Ypres. So down went the forgotten pipe and bottle, back went the chairs, and out streamed our terrified quintet to the tormented street, leaving the room and its contents as I saw it.

On approaching the bridge on the far side of the town I saw the only remaining inhabitant. This was a middle-aged woman with a grey shawl over her head and shoulders, and she was looking out of a window of a partly shattered house. I felt sorry for her, she looked so very lonely in that broken house.

That afternoon she was arrested by the Belgians as a spy. My compassion had been utterly thrown away.

Near this same bridge on another occasion my arrival was providential. An army service corps driver was speeding his motor towards the city when he was struck by enemy shrapnel. He had just sufficient strength to stop his lorry before fainting from the shock and the rush of blood from a grievous wound of the right thigh. Blood was pumping out of the wound, and it appeared as if the femoral artery had been torn. Fortunately it was not, and we were soon able to control the haemorrhage, put the wounded man on his lorry, and drive him back to one of the ambulance stations in a cottage near the roadside.

The road from Ypres to our trenches was a busy but pathetic highway—busy with marching men, waggons, gallopers, generals, and staff officers, and pathetic from the many graves and small graveyards near the roadside and the many full ambulance waggons rumbling along on the uneven, jolty *pavé*.

The road was frequently visited with enemy shells, and no one travelled along it unless on business. "Trespassers will be prosecuted" was an unnecessary injunction on the Ypres roads, The headquarter staff of the 15th Brigade beyond Ypres had a narrow escape one morning. A big shell burst in the grounds of the *château* occupied by the brigadier and his staff. The staff, who were in the building at the time, went out to look at the hole it had made. Whilst looking at the pit, another shell landed on the *château* itself and burst into the room just vacated by them. A soldier servant was killed and one staff officer was wounded.

An advanced ambulance station, with wounded men and medical officers in it, was struck fairly by another shell and badly holed, causing loss of life. No place was safe from these long bowls of the enemy, and though artillery practice of this sort may not be of much military importance, it yet produces an air of uncertainty and caution and jumpiness.

The country surrounding Ypres and Ypres itself were very dismal. The old elm trees on the roads, and the silent, deserted streets were shrouded in a ghostly veil of melancholy.

On a subsequent visit to the site of the old Cloth Hall one saw little more than ruins, for the famous building had in the interval been correctly ranged by the enemy guns and duly shattered. Later on more destruction took place, and visitors of the year 2015 will be shown some stones and broken pillars, all that was left of a famous hall which had stood for seven centuries and had been destroyed "one hundred years ago."

When peace comes again to Belgium, Ypres and its roads, its Hill 60 and its graves will be a place of holy pilgrimage to thousands of English, French, and Germans, for here fell and are buried their bravest dead.

But the curious tripper and the Cook's tourist had better keep away from Ypres. Let the friends of the dead and the quiet country folk have the land in their possession for a season.

The railway station at Vlamertinge, near Ypres, frequently had a very fine armoured train in its sidings. The train was manned by Jack Tars with naval guns, and the engine and car looked very attractive in a wonderful coat of futurist colours—splashes of green and khaki and brown. This *H.M.S Chameleon* was a very good cruiser and very nippy in moving across country. The sailors were very cheerful and seemed to like their ship amazingly.

On the roads near our headquarters running from Renninghelst to Vlamertinge, and hence along the main highway to Ypres, a large number of Belgian soldiers were at work repairing the *pavé* and widening the road surface by laying prepared trunks of trees laid closely together in the mud at the sides. They were fine sturdy men and full of life and cheerfulness, a different type altogether from the countryfolk we met in the farms. These were the men who had fought from Liége to the Yser, and were still on Belgian soil. They were very bitter about the Germans. They said that they asked for no quarter and would give none in the fighting.

These Belgians on the roads were men who had been temporarily sent back to "recuperate," and while at this work they enjoyed good food, warm quarters, and sleep. At eleven o'clock every morning a very fine motor kitchen would pass along the road. Each man had his canteen ready, the cook ladled out to him a good helping of mashed potatoes, boiled mutton, and thick gravy, and another cook handed him a big chunk of white bread. It was all done very expeditiously and in good order. After getting his share each man would sit on his rolled-up overcoat on the roadside and spoon the mutton and potatoes into his mouth with the bread. Knives and forks and spoons, after all, are really only luxuries.

The roads were in a frightful state during these November weeks. The narrow pave was full of ruts, deep and dangerous, and skirted on either side by a slope of boggy quagmire churned up by the wheels of hundreds of heavy motor transports, and beyond this again on either side was a deep ditch.

Any skidding motor would land in the ditch, and the righting of these embedded cars was at times a titanic task, productive of much loss of temper and bad language.

The narrow *pavé* would not permit of two vehicles crossing abreast, and when two met, neither wished to surrender the "crown of the causeway." It was a point of honour not to budge and to wear down the other side by abusive epithets. Uncle Toby used to say that our army swore horribly in Flanders, but the swearing in Toby's day was not a patch on the rich vocabulary and full-blooded oaths of our London taxi-drivers in Flanders in 1914.

The London taxi-driver, always eloquent, reached his highest nights when addressing the quivering blancmange-like mud of a Belgian road.

I have seen old French non-commissioned officers who probably did not know a single word of what was said on these occasions, but who envisaged the situation perfectly, stand by with approving and admiring faces while the driver was embracing in his comprehensive abuse all things living and dead, the heavens above, the earth beneath, and the waters under the earth.

At Ouderdom we met Alphonse, soldier of France. Two medical

officers were one morning sipping some red wine in an *estaminet* in the village when in swaggered a very small French soldier.

He had a boy's face and figure and voice, but bore the assured manner of a man of the world. He was small even for a French boy. A carbine was swung across his back, and his belt carried a bayonet and cartridges. He wore the French blue overcoat with the ends tucked up in the approved style and with the buttons polished and bright. His little legs were encased in the familiar red trousers tucked into heavy boots several sizes too large for him, and his *képi* was placed on his small, closely cropped head at a jaunty angle. Such was Alphonse, the complete soldier of France, full private in a famous Parisian rifle battalion.

Alphonse swaggered into the *café*, ordered his glass of red wine with the *sang-froid* and assurance of a veteran grenadier, and tossed it off as easily as a Falstaff.

"How old are you, Alphonse?"

"But fourteen years, *mon officier*."

"Have you killed many Germans?"

"But yes, perhaps thirteen, perhaps fifteen; who can tell when one is fighting every day? But certainly I kill many Bosches."

"And with what did you kill them, Alphonse?"

"*Avec mon carabine*"—this with a smack of his hand on the barrel of the gun. A smart soldierly salute, and our gallant killer of thirteen, perhaps fifteen, peaceful, amiable German soldiers strode out of the *café*.

A corporal of Alphonse's regiment told us that at the beginning of the war Alphonse was a young devil of a gamin in Paris. In his leisure moments he sold newspapers in the streets, and in his working hours he was up to some devilry.

When this regiment marched out of Paris towards the frontier Alphonse marched alongside it, a bright-eyed, hopeful, cheerful youth clad in ragged clothes and down-at-heel boots. He was told to go home, but said that he had no home and was going instead to kill Germans. So in the good French way the regiment adopted Alphonse, gave him a uniform and a gun, and a new pair of boots, and took him on the strength.

The little gamin turned out a very cunning soldier. He was a dead shot, and the corporal assured us that he had accounted for a good many of the enemy. At night Alphonse would crawl out of the trenches and scout well into the enemy lines. Frequently he brought back valuable information of preparations for a German surprise attack. He was so small and so cute that he escaped observation.

In December Alphonse was presented to President Poincaré on one of his many visits to the French front, and the president promised him a commission and the *Legion d'Honneur* when he should reach the age of twenty-one years. I have grave fears for the gallant, snub-nosed, blue-eyed Alphonse, young in years but old in sin. He is already too fond of the rich red wine of France, and scouting at night inside the enemy lines is a duty full of peril. But Alphonse can teach a lesson in patriotism that many a flower-socked, straw-hatted knut on a London promenade would do well to learn.

The Flemings are very devout Catholics, perhaps the most Catholic of all peoples today; so our ambulance was given the hall-mark of respectability because we had with it a *Monsignor*, The presence of a Catholic prelate with our ambulance, distinguished it in a notable degree from all other ambulances, and we tried to live up to our presumed reputation.

Whenever *Monsignor* appeared on the roads near Ouderdom the Belgian soldiers would immediately stop work and, carrying their pickaxes and shovels, crowd round him for a talk and the latest news. *Monsignor* was a good linguist and a cheerful optimist, and never handed on any bad news to the soldiers. One morning he was asked for news, and appealed to me what to say. We told them that the Russians had another victory, and that the German dead could be counted by thousands. This was very palatable and thoroughly appreciated. We were not asked to give any details of the victory, which was perhaps fortunate.

Monsignor would sometimes walk along this road with his hands behind his back and with two or three cigarettes sticking out prominently from between his fingers. The Belgian soldiers would then stalk after him, with broad grins on their faces, and pull away a cigarette. *Monsignor* never looked behind. That would not be playing the game at all, but his eyes would twinkle, and I have no doubt whatever that he hugely enjoyed the fun.

There were days when *Monsignor* had a wardrobe consisting of but one shirt and one pair of trousers—the other articles of apparel had all been given away. Then he would begin again to collect mufflers and socks when supplies came in, and hand them out almost immediately to some poor devils who had nothing. If our chaplain appeared any day to be more cheerful than usual, one could make quite sure that he had just given away his boots or his shirt or his towel to some poor

French, Belgian, or British Tommy. The only thing he kept a tight hold on was his toothbrush.

One day *Monsignor* appeared with a cardboard box in his hand and told us that he was going to Renninghelst, a small town about two miles from our headquarters. Lieutenant X—— and myself asked leave to accompany him. We had to ask permission, for *Monsignor* was a senior chaplain and a lieutenant-colonel in rank, although he never said anything about that. We discovered it accidentally. Being a colonel interested him only in a vague impersonal sort of way. He told us once that a soldier is diffident and shy before a colonel, but is natural and communicative to his minister or priest who is not flagged and starred.

On this lovely winter morning, when the whole countryside was white with frozen snow, we had a sharp bracing walk to the curious old town, then the headquarters of General B—— and his staff of a French Division. The village streets were packed full of French and Belgian soldiery, from *Spahis* to Alpine *Chasseurs*. We worked our way round the carts and through the jostling men to a little shop opposite the church. *Monsignor* was hailed joyfully by many of his old friends, who on this particular morning were not working on the roads.

The mystery of the cardboard box was then unravelled, for after cutting the string and throwing away the cover we saw that it was full of small religious medals and scapularies. There was a big rush for the medals, and we were all squeezed up together by the pressing soldiers, hundreds of whom were holding their grimy paws out for the metal discs. As *Monsignor* was hard at work I took a hand also and helped in the distribution. At last all were gone. Hundreds more men had come up with hands out, but had to leave unsatisfied. I asked *Monsignor* if the medals lost any virtue by having been handed out by me, a Protestant. He assured me that it was all right, as the Belgians and French must have thought I was a good Catholic.

Every Field Ambulance has two chaplains attached to it. Ours had a Church of England one and a Roman Catholic. Another ambulance would have perhaps a Wesleyan and a Catholic, or a Presbyterian and an Anglican. These chaplains were not designed for the spiritual needs of the ambulance men, but as each ambulance kept in touch with a brigade consisting of four battalions, the chaplain could also, by being with the ambulance headquarters, keep in touch with the brigade, and could also meet the wounded brought in from that brigade, administer the rites of the Church to those requiring it, and bury the

Monsignor distributing medals to Belgian soldiers at the roadside

dead. The chaplains did not restrict themselves to the men of their own faith, but helped and worked all they knew for all. After all, an ambulance station full of wounded men is not the place for religious exercises, and a wise chaplain helped in making the men as comfortable as possible, bringing round soup, taking off boots, distributing cigarettes and tobacco, writing letters and "gossiping"—the wounded like someone to talk to them and to talk to, and the chaplains could make a "cheery atmosphere" even in such a gloomy place as a barn full of recently wounded men.

Most of the chaplains had a good sense of proportion. Some had not. One bleak, miserable day, I saw a well-meaning but mournful chaplain go up to a lorry full of wounded men packed close together on the straw, uncomfortable and shivering and miserable. He handed to each of them a small religious tract exhorting him to read it. The men took them with a polite "Thank you, sir," but their faces displayed no enthusiasm. This was not the time for tracts. Shortly afterwards another chaplain, a man of the world, came up to the lorry with a "Cheer up, boys. You'll soon be in warm comfortable quarters. Have you any smokes?" The men had none, and out came a dozen packets of Woodbine cigarettes from the chaplain's pockets and two boxes of matches. The expression on the men's faces altered at once. The atmosphere had altered, the sense of proportion had been restored.

Men in hospital like to hear good news. I knew one chaplain who managed never to go into a room full of wounded and sick men without bringing some cheery report for everybody. He never actually fabricated news, but he had a wonderful gift of exaggeration. If we were in the same position, we had "held the line against incredible odds." If the French had taken an enemy trench, "they had driven a wedge into the German position and produced consternation." If Russian cavalry had made a reconnaissance in the Masurian Lakes, "they were sweeping like locusts all over East Prussia, and had set fire to the *Kaiser's* favourite hunting-lodge."

The men never inquired about details, general statements were quite good enough.

This was better than telling men that the "war would be a terribly long one; that we would have to make great sacrifices; but, please God, we would win in the end." I have heard a chaplain talk like this to wounded men, and I knew that he "wasn't delivering the right goods."

Renninghelst is a large village, or rather a very small town. It is situated close to the Franco-Belgian frontier, and at this period was of importance as an ambulance centre for wounded French and Belgians who were occupying the line of trenches in the front. The country all round is real Flanders land—flat, low-lying, damp, and uninviting. The renowned *Mont de Cats* can be seen from it, and round this *mont* some hard fighting was taking place. The old village has a queer Dutch-looking church with a closely packed graveyard around it, planted thickly with stone and iron crosses to the memory of ancient departed *burghers*, whose Flemish-Dutch names are inscribed there to commemorate their ages and their virtues. Eighty, eighty-five, and ninety seemed to be the usual age of these old *burghers* for slipping off this mortal coil in this quiet sleepy old place in Southern Belgium. There are many new graves now round the Renninghelst countryside, and they are for men who have died young, suddenly, and in the springtime of their days. The interior of this old Flemish church is lofty, and has little in the way of adornment, for there are no millionaires in its congregation to give great stained-glass windows or carved pulpits.

On my first visit to the church it was full of French soldiers, some sleeping and others lolling round on the straw that thickly covered the stone floor. A big group were crowded round a charcoal brazier warming themselves and watching the progress of a savoury stew. The French soldiers are wonderful cooks, and the stew this day was to be a good one, for the *pièce de résistance* was a fine fat hare which had been caught that morning near the front. The two cooks were exercising great care to make the stew a success, and the air of the place was a cheerful, expectant one.

Some days after this visit I was again at Renninghelst, and the church was now a temporary hospital. The floor was still covered with straw, but wounded men were lying close together on it. The charcoal brazier was still there and giving out a welcome heat on this cold wintry day. Ambulance waggons were in the street next the church full of wounded soldiers, and more were coming up the road.

French army surgeons were busy amongst the red-breeched men in the church, and three of them were engaged round an improvised operating table near the altar, where a man deeply under chloroform was having his jaw wired with silver wire for a bad fracture from a piece of shell.

The old white-haired, weary-looking priest of the parish was leaning over a dying man and bending his head low to catch the last faint whispers. Some women of the village were carrying round cups of hot broth to the men propped along the wall, and others were hurrying in with blankets and pillows.

One soldier I observed to be very blanched and tossing restlessly on his straw. Restlessness is always an important sign in wounded men, and on going up to this poor devil and turning down his rough blanket the cause of the trouble was apparent. He was bleeding freely through a bandaged wound of the leg. The dressings were soaked with blood, and as the French surgeons were occupied I broke a professional rule and treated this patient without asking his doctor's permission. The bleeding was soon controlled, and the threatened death from haemorrhage averted.

As I was completing the last turns of the bandage a voice murmured over my shoulder, "*Vive l'entente cordiale.*" The speaker was the chief surgeon, just released from his work on the operating table. He thanked me for helping, and said that he and his two assistants had been up all night, and had been very busy. Most of the men had been wounded by shrapnel. Shrapnel makes very bad wounds; it rips, tears, and lacerates the tissues, and repair is often impossible in face of the anatomical devastation. The French were having a great deal of trouble with their wounds, as we were also. All the wounds became septic. There is very little clean surgery in this war. The wounds rarely heal by first intention, and a fractured, splintered bone meant months of rest and painful dressings in hospital and a tardy convalescence.

The fighting all along this front had been extraordinarily severe. The French hospitals and the French medical staff were taxed to the utmost. Every available fighting man was in the trenches or waiting as supports. The German hammer was making mighty swings on the Allied anvil, and nowhere were the blows so heavy and so long sustained as on that famous Ypres salient. It was bent and dented, but not broken. The character of the fighting can be grasped from two incidents. One famous infantry regiment left England at full strength. All of its original officers were killed, wounded, or missing. Of the second lot of officers, all were killed, wounded, or missing. Its third supply of officers were now grimly up against the same chain of events.

One of the first British Divisions left England with 12,000 men and 400 officers. When it was withdrawn from the front to rest and refit, it could only muster 2336 men and 44 officers!

A famous French regiment with a long roll of battle honours went into action one frosty morning near Reims. It went forward a gleaming column of more than a thousand bayonets. Two days afterwards forty-nine men, led by an old bearded sergeant, marched back. These were all that were left. The sergeant had a bloody bandage across his forehead—he had lost an eye—but the French brigadier-general embraced and kissed him on the cheek. The French officers standing near stood rigidly at the salute, and tears were running down their cheeks.

The losses on our side were heavy indeed, but on the German side I am glad to know that they were colossal. The annihilation of German battalions and brigades is an argument that the Germans fully understand, and the only thing that will convince the German that the game is up is heavy and continuous loss of fighting men and difficulty in filling their ranks. This sounds very brutal, but we are living in a hard age.

I was much struck by the splendid way the women of this small Belgian town rallied round to help the wounded. We found the same thing in France; no trouble was too great, and all was done so cheerfully and sympathetically. This is the "women's day" in France. One cannot help admiring their courage and ability in France's hour of trial. Husbands, sons, brothers, fathers—all are on the frontier, and the women carry on the business of France. They make the most stupendous sacrifices and exhibit a sublime patience. None are so joyful as the women when a French victory is announced, and none so pitiful as they when the wounded, the corollary to every victory, arrive at the towns and villages.

This war, which the German has carried on with an animal ferocity and a degenerate lust unequalled in history, has demonstrated to the world the unfaltering nobility of character of the French woman, and that her fervent soul can rise serene and cool in the midst of the most appalling troubles.

When our troops landed at Le Havre in August, it was noticed at once what a big part the women were taking in the business life of the place. There were women conductors on the trams, women in the tobacconist shops, women in the *cafés* as attendants, in the streets selling newspapers, and in all the big *magasins*.

In Rouen, women conducted coal and timber yards, vegetable and produce businesses, bakeries, butcheries, fishmongeries, grocers' and ironmongers' stores. Women drove carts and waggons, acted as tally clerks on wharves, did everything, in fact—and did it all soberly, quietly, and well. They were always tidy, smart, and cheerful, and did not stop work at eleven o'clock for a glass of beer, or spend many quarters of hours filling and lighting pipes of tobacco.

One woman I know—a rosy-cheeked, blue-eyed Norman dame—did the catering for a large officers' mess in one of the camps at Rouen. At 5 a.m. she was at the mess tent with her pony-cart laden with wine, vegetables, preserves, and fruit. I have passed her shop at nine o'clock at night and have seen her then busily selling dried fish, pickles, and vinegar to her customers. She told me that she was too busy to sleep. This was in 1915, and she had been running the business with no other help than that of two small daughters since July 1914.

Her husband was on the Argonne front, and she was keeping the flag flying till his return. Incidentally, she was making money. Catering for an officers' mess is fairly lucrative.

On the march from the Marne to the Aisne, and on the Aisne itself, women were to be seen doing ordinary farm work—building stacks, carting in the wheat, driving waggon-loads of hay and peas, milking the cows, making cider and butter, tilling the soil,—and tending the children into the bargain.

The most amazing thing of all was to see women working in the fields behind our batteries only a mile away.

At Venizel, on the Aisne bank, our engineers were throwing a pontoon bridge across the river under a heavy shrapnel fire. Shells were bursting up and down the river's bank and on the waters of the river, yet about a quarter of a mile behind three women were busily engaged cutting turnips for the cows.

On the march from the Aisne to La Bassée, our Field Ambulance bivouacked at the Château of Longpont. The Comte and Comtesse de M—— were in residence at the *château*, and we were told by the *comtesse* that General von Kluck, commanding the right wing of the invading army, had in August stopped for a day and a night at the *château* with his *état-major*. We asked how Von Kluck had behaved, and the *comtesse* said that he had been *très agréable*. When he arrived, she interviewed him and begged him to respect the old *château* and its old abbey, the pictures and the tapestries. The general promised that he would do so, and that he would give orders that the villagers in the hamlet near the *château* gates were not to be molested. It was the apple season, and the apple trees of Longpont were laden with delicious fruit. Von Kluck "asked permission" of the *comtesse* for his soldiers to take some apples off the trees. This the *comtesse* graciously permitted, and the dusty German soldiery helped themselves to the apples and did not break a branch off a single tree.

The *comtesse* provided new eggs and butter and bread for the general's breakfast, and he invited her to honour the meal with her presence. But the *comtesse* sent a note that she would not break bread with her country's enemy. This was one of the few *châteaux* and one of the few villages that the German Saligoth did not destroy or outrage before leaving.

Some German generals approved of outrages and atrocities, to wit, Rupprecht of Bavaria. Some disapproved, and Von Kluck, it is said, was one of these—but I "hae ma doots."

This leads to one of the blackest pictures of this war—a picture grim and loathsome. It is a subject which the women of France will discuss freely and openly and with a concentrated bitterness that one can readily understand. I have spoken to many educated French women on this subject, and have heard many curious and amazing tales and incidents. The subject is that of the women who have been ravished and outraged by the German soldiery.

Many of these victims, married women and young girls, are to-day pregnant to German fathers, and the burning question with the women of France is how best to help their unfortunate sisters, and what is to be done for the offspring.

In the French Chamber of Deputies the subject has been debated with equal freedom and openness. Leading French newspapers too, such as the *Figaro, Le Temps, Echo de Paris,* and others, have envisaged the position in powerful and appealing articles.

One journal advocated that in the exceptional circumstances it was perfectly justifiable to carry out abortion and interrupt the period of gestation. Opinions were sought from leading French physicians and from the Academy of Medicine. These unhesitatingly condemned such a course, pointing out that the mission of the medical profession was to save life; and also that the induction of premature labour was at all times a dangerous and risky operation to the mother, and in certain circumstances would be fatal.

The Catholic Church in France spoke strongly and certainly in the same direction, and condemned as utterly wrong and sinful any measure that had for its object the death of the unborn child.

The women of France, however, do not share these latter views.

Arrangements have now been completed for the reception of these pitiful expectant mothers into certain maternity homes, where they will be attended by skilled doctors and nurses at the State expense. After birth the child is to be brought up by the State at some place undeclared. The mother will not see the child at any time, and will know nothing of its future.

The clergy all over Northern France are attending to this matter, and everything will be done as secretly as possible in the unusual circumstances.

No wonder that the French woman speaks of the German soldier as a loathly thing.

CHAPTER 19

We Leave Belgium

At the end of November our ambulance was ordered to St. Jans Capelle. We were not sorry to leave our house, with its evil pond and manure heap, and the voice of *Madame*.

Madame, by the way, was very amiable when we told her that we were to leave. She did not say that she was sorry, but she no longer screeched at our cooks or railed at our men for eating her straw. Just as our ambulance was about to move off, and *Madame* stood at the door with the first approach to a frosty smile that we had ever seen on her face, a French sergeant and ten men of a balloon section arrived. The sergeant had a lump of chalk in his hand and scrawled on the door, "*Ballon. 3 sous Officiers. Hommes x.*" He brusquely informed *Madame* that the quarters just vacated by us were to be at once taken by his balloon section.

Madame raged and raved, but the sergeant was imperturbable, and suddenly quietened *Madame* by saying that if she objected very much he would begin to think that she was a German spy. The sergeant told us that as a matter of fact they were not satisfied about *Madame's* husband's patriotism. We knew that *Madame* and her sulky husband would now have a much worse time than when we occupied the house, for at least we tried to give little trouble, and lavishly paid for any vegetables, milk, or food that we got from the farmer. The French insist on the "articles of war," and when they occupy a house they really do occupy it and make themselves very much at home.

This mention of *Madame's* husband being of doubtful honesty, reminded us of a curious incident that occurred early in our stay at this place. There was another farm close to the one we occupied, and this farm was owned by a man who, we were told, was a cousin of "*Monsieur* our farmer." At this house a man was stopping who said that he was a refugee from Ypres. He told us that he was a baker from Boston, United States of America, and that he and his wife, who were Belgians, had been visiting their native country when war broke out. He said that his wife and two children were in Brussels when the Germans occupied the city, and that he himself was stopping with a friend in Ypres when the Germans first bombarded it; he then left Ypres and came to stop at this farmer's house. This man used to walk every day along a road which passed behind some French batteries of 75 mm., but one day he did not come back. We asked his farmer friend what had become of him, and he said that he had left to go to America. We thought the circumstance odd at the time, and when our sergeant told us about *Madame's* husband being under suspicion we asked him if he knew anything about this other man, the Boston baker. He said that he did, for he had seen the fellow arrested and sent back to be tried for spying. That perhaps explained why *Madame* did not like us, and why her vituperation and objections were suddenly silenced when the French balloon sergeant talked about German spies.

After leaving the inhospitable cottage-headquarters, our ambulance had a long day's trek over the Belgian frontier to St. Jans Capelle. This place was close to Bailleul. We put our men into billets near at hand and got quarters for ourselves in the convent, where the sisters gave us a big dormitory full of clean white beds with blankets and sheets. This was indeed luxury after all our roughing times from the Marne till now. We were always perfectly willing to undergo inconvenience and hardships, but none of us ever missed an opportunity of availing himself of the luxuries and amenities of civilisation whenever they presented themselves. We had the fine front room of the convent for a dining- and sitting-room, and, greatest boon of all, a fire to sit round. The cold was intense at this time, and the whole country was frozen hard in snow and ice. This was the period when frostbite was so terrible to our men in the trenches, and the Clearing Hospitals and Ambulance Stations were so busy treating the frozen men.

It was found necessary to relieve frequently the freezing soldiers in the advanced trenches, and every three days they were allowed out from the terrible mud ditches, with death on the parapet and frostbite at the bottom.

Braziers of burning charcoal were put into the trenches, but were found to be ineffective and harmful to the feet. The people of England did magnificent work in sending out gum boots, skin overcoats, and protectives of all sort, but in spite of all that was done the frostbite incapacitated many men. The recoveries were always slow, and could not be effected at the front, so all these limping men were sent back to England for rest and change. Many methods of treatment were tried for the frostbite, but time alone seemed to be the chief curative factor. In some cases the feet were swollen, and small bloody exudates could be seen under the big toe and the outer side of the foot where the boot pressed. Sometimes the skin was broken and ulcers formed at the site. In other cases toes became completely gangrenous or dead. The feet were rubbed and massaged with various oils and swathed in cotton wool, but wrapping in wool aggravated the suffering, and the men felt much more relief when the feet were left exposed.

The worst time for the cold-feet men was from one o'clock to three in the morning. They would often go off to sleep peacefully, but would wake up at these hours suffering excruciating pain in their feet and calves and up the spine. Nothing would relieve this pain but hypodermic injections of morphia. One officer described his state to me, and said that he had been standing in a trench in mud over his boot-tops. At first his feet felt very cold, and he tried to warm them by stamping, but this method of exercise was too sloppy. Then sensation seemed to go and he felt quite comfortable, because although his feet felt very heavy they did not feel cold, only dead. On the fifth day he could hardly walk and had to be helped out of the trenches. He was unable to walk to the ambulance, a short way back, and the feet were found to be so swollen in hospital that the boots had to be cut off. Then the worst time of all came on, for as the circulation gradually returned he suffered diabolical pain in his feet and calves, and this pain was always worst in the early mornings. Eight weeks after having been lifted out of the trench he was still limping about with two sticks, and was making a normal but very slow recovery.

This officer told me that one night the men in his trenches were ordered out to make a bayonet attack, but half of them were in such a condition that they could not crawl out of the trench. Fortunately the Germans were pushed back by those who could, otherwise the poor devils left behind would have been captured or killed.

The Indians round the Bethune district suffered very severely from the frostbite, and these poor men deserved our greatest sympathy during this period, trying and terrible enough to men reared in a fairly rigorous climate like that of England or Scotland. The misery of the life to men who had never lived out of tropical India was enough to wear down any but the stoutest hearts. History will give due credit

GOING TOWARDS THE TRENCHES AT YPRES.

FRENCH SOLDIERS GOING TO THE TRENCHES.

and praise to these Indians, that they rose superior to their environment and soon proved what sterling good soldiers they are. I visited at an Indian Clearing Hospital the first lot of casualties from the M—— Division. This Clearing Hospital took over the École Jules Ferry at Bethune, and occupied it for a few weeks after our Clearing Hospital had vacated it. The doctors belonged to the Indian Medical Service, and the native Indian doctors belonging to the subordinate medical service acted under the white doctors. Some temporary lieutenants of the Royal Army Medical Corps were also on the staff.

The dusky warriors were arriving in scores, brought in on motor ambulances, and very woeful they looked, covered with mud and bloody bandages. They had not been long at the front, and their first experience of modern war was a very desperate ordeal.

The night was dark and gloomy and a heavy rain was soaking the countryside. The mud-splashed cars dashed into the dripping courtyard, fitfully lit up by the sombre gleams of smoky lanterns tied to posts. Round about were the dark-faced bearers ready to help out the wounded. Those who could walk got out of the ambulances themselves and the stretcher cases were taken out by the bearers. The scene on this night impressed one with the far-reaching character of this war, for here were men from the central plains of India, the far-off frontiers and the slopes of the Himalayas, gathered together in a muddy, marshy region of France, and wounded in trying to hold a line of ditches against the most determined and scientific fighting men of Europe.

> *Rulers alike and subject, splendid the roll-call rings,*
> *Rajahs and Maharajahs, Kings and the sons of Kings,*
> *From the land where the skies are molten*
> *And the suns strike down and parch:*
> *Out of the East they are marching,*
> *Into the West they march.*

One swarthy Sikh with a fine beard was asked what he thought of the war.

"*Sahib*, it is a very good war. It is a man's war. The old men, the women, and the children are in the villages. The warriors are out fighting. It is very good." This optimist had got through with a slight wound of the right hand, and perhaps that accounted for his cheery outlook. Most of the wounded on that night looked as if they would have been better pleased to be with "the old men, the women, and the children in the villages."

There is no doubt that the Indians are pleased to be fighting alongside us in this "good war," but they have a respect for the German because he is a fierce fighter, and perhaps also because of his ruthlessness, an attitude which appeals to the Oriental mind.

The Gurkha is a funny little man and a swashbuckler. His small sturdy frame, his slanting, watchful eyes with the glint of the devil in them, his bandolier, rifle, and deadly *kukri*, with its broad razor-edged blade, make up a picture of force and fighting cunning.

Plaster this man with thick mud, put a bloody bandage round his head, and place him in a dimly lit corner of a dripping court on a dark, rainy night, then indeed he looks a breathing symbol of murder and imminent destruction. When the Gurkha is out "on the job" at night, prowling far from his trenches and within the enemy lines, with no weapon but his broad, sharp knife and with a mind intent on slaying, he is a formidable and fearsome adversary.

At first our Indian troops found it difficult to accustom themselves to the novel form of war in wet, cold trenches, a bad climate, and with every surrounding strange and inhospitable. The loss of their British officers and native non-commissioned officers was at first very heavy, and this discouraged the men, who look so much to their officers who know their language and understand them. But these brave fellows soon "found themselves," and have since those dark October days proved again and again that when the call comes they can be relied upon to fight with as much determination as ever they have done in the past. An experienced British officer of a native regiment told me that what the Indians missed very much in France was opium. He said that the Indian had always been accustomed to his opium in India, that he did not take much, but really was the better for a little. He took it in small quantity as a soporific stimulant, just as our grandfathers took snuff, and he assured me that when the Indians had to meet the hellish conditions of modern war at the front last winter a little opium to each man would have meant a great deal. In this I cordially agree with him, for the medicinal and stimulant effects of small doses of opium are undoubted.

The question of feeding our Indian soldiers was a difficult one, and required very careful handling. An old Sikh was wounded near Bethune and was taken to the British Clearing Hospital. He refused to take anything but biscuits and water. Fortunately we were able to remove the old ritualist to the native Clearing Hospital, otherwise we would have been at an *impasse*.

Amongst both Hindoos and Mohammedans the caste prejudices and ritualistic ceremonies must be remembered and observed in the providing and killing of animals for consumption. The French also have native troops with them and have the same difficulties to overcome, and this helps us considerably in arranging a joint commissariat scheme. A Sikh soldier will not eat a sheep killed in the Mohammedan method by cutting its throat, and the Mohammedan soldier will not eat a sheep killed in the Sikh method by a slashing stroke on the back of the neck. So there you are. These things do not seem to be very important, but they are important all the same. Ask the Jew who refuses the unclean pork, and the good Churchman who refuses meat on Fridays.

The following story, which I heard at the front, illustrates the accommodating nature of the Gurkha. When his regiments were embarking on the transports at an Indian port, the point arose whether he would eat frozen mutton. The British officers agreed to let the matter be solved by the men. So they called up the *subadar*, who, after a little wrinkling of the eyebrow, said, "I think, *Sahib*, the regiment will be willing to eat the iced sheep provided one of them is always present to see the animal frozen to death."

In Rouen there is an encampment for goats for the Indians, and we were told that these goats were good mountain fellows from the Pyrenees. Four Indians, under the charge of an old, venerable, long-bearded native, used to drive them from their encampment to the Indian convalescent depot about two miles outside the city.

The goats, in spite of the shouting and rushing about of the drivers, would not keep their ranks and dress by the right in marching through Normandy's capital city. The delight of the French people, who always turned up in crowds to see the goats march past, passed all bounds when one would make a wild dash up a side street, hotly pursued by an irate turbaned Indian. Another source of great joy was to see the goats march slowly along the train line and hold up the train traffic.

The Indians were always of absorbing interest to the French, and crowds of men and women would walk on a fine afternoon from the city to the Indian depot camp for convalescents to see our brown-faced fighting men.

On one winter day in Rouen, just after a heavy fall of snow, a company of French soldiers under a non-commissioned officer was marching past the Indian encampment. The Indians lined up the fence alongside the road and bombarded the French with a rapid fire of snowballs. The French looked surprised, and, forgetting discipline but still keeping their ranks, poured a heavy fusillade of snowballs on the men of India. The incident is illustrative of the good feeling that exists between the French and their Indian allies.

The Abbé Bouchon d'Homme of our hospital at Bethune told me with great glee one morning that the mayor of the town had had a "poser" put to him by the Indians. One of these had just died from wounds, and he had evidently been a fire-worshipper. The dead man's comrades asked the mayor of Bethune to provide them with timber, as they wished to burn the deceased in the cemetery of the city. The mayor was staggered at the request, and although he had, so the *abbé* said, some curiosity to see the ceremony of fire carried out, he had to "turn down" the proposition. So the man was buried in the usual way.

Goodbye to the Front.

The Army Headquarters, now that our line had been firmly established and locked firmly on our right with the French and on our left with the Belgians and French, decided to allow a short leave, at intervals, and in rotation, to officers and as many men as possible. The leave was specially designed for those who had been through the retreat, the Marne, and the Aisne. New troops were arriving at the front and gradually taking the place of the veterans temporarily retired to recuperate.

The 5th Division had been amongst the hard knocks from the beginning and we got off early.

I left the front by a motor bus, which conveyed a group of seven officers from Bailleul to Boulogne, and from thence we reached England by the ferry steamer.

It felt uncanny to be away from the sound of the guns. Ever since August our lives had been punctuated with incessant gun-fire; we had roused each morning to the sound of heavy artillery, we had gone to sleep with cannonades for a lullaby, and during the long day had listened to the Devil's Orchestra of lyddite, melinite, shrapnel, and rifle fire; and now away from it all we seemed to live in a curiously still and silent world.

London was a very inviting place to return to. The hot bath, the good bed, the morning newspaper at breakfast had never been so much appreciated before. The rough knocking about and the strain had left its effects on the health of many of us, and these four days' rest and recuperation, mental and physical, were a godsend.

At the end of the holiday I was appointed Surgical Specialist to a Base Hospital in Rouen, and for a time my lines were cast in quieter waters. But the allurement of the front—the call of the wild with its excitements and uncertainties—lasted for some time longer. It is a curious fact, but true, that the men at the front would like to get to the Base, and when they get there they want to return to the front. "Those behind say forward, and those in front say back."

The memories of days spent at the front can never be quite forgotten. Time may blunt the clearness of outline of some of the incidents in a hazy mist, but there are others that will stand out clear and undimmed to the last.

The surgeon sees the very seamy side of war. He comes close to the men stricken down in the field, helpless and bleeding and in pain. He stands by them in their dark hours in hospital and by their bedsides when they die.

While the world is hearing the earthquake voice of Victory, he is perhaps kneeling on the straw easing the path to death of a dying man, one of the victors in the fight, or perhaps operating in a mean cottage, surrounded by wounded men waiting their turn on the table.

The gallant charge, the brave defence, the storming of the enemy's position are heralded in dispatches and in song and story, but translated into the notebook of the "Surgeon in Khaki" they represent many dead, many wounded, much crippling and mutilation, tears, distress, and broken hearts.

I have seen brave men die the death in battle—changed in a second of time from forceful, vital, volcanic energy to still, inanimate rest. I have seen mortally wounded men pass uncomplainingly and composedly to the valley of the shadow, and I have seen faces become anxious and troubled at the thought of those dear and loving ones left behind and of the aching hearts and tears.

I have written letters of farewell from dying men and officers to wives and sweethearts and children, and have felt the horror and misery of it all. It is a sad and mournful sight to see brave young men die.

Yet, though the life of the "Surgeon in Khaki" is amidst this aftermath of battle, he has the infinite satisfaction of knowing that he can, and does, hold out a hand of help to the hurt and maimed soldier crawling out of the welter of blood and destruction, and that he is doing the work of the Compassionate and Pitying One.

Affliction's sons are brothers in distress,
A brother to relieve! How exquisite the Bliss.

This war has brought out many faults in our national life, but it has also brought out many shining virtues, and to the Faith and Hope of the people in the prowess of the soldiers, we must add the Charity shown by the people of this Empire to our sick and wounded. By subscriptions to ambulance funds, Red Cross funds, and hospitals, and by doing all that was humanly possible to help those hurt in battle, the people of today have made a name that posterity will honour and strive in vain to equal. They have also helped the Belgian and Serbian Red Gross movements and have shown that

Kindness in another's trouble,
Courage in your own,

—which is always so admirable a trait.

Our fighting men are magnificent, and the hardihood and patient endurance of our wounded are beyond all praise. I have seen our men in actual fight, I have watched the French gunners at work and seen the French infantry charge with the bayonet and throw back a German rush, and I feel a complete confidence of the ultimate final success of the Allied arms—for to such men is given the Victory.

A Surgeon in Belgium

The Nursing Staff, Furnes

Contents

Preface	203
To Antwerp	205
The Hospital	210
The Day's Work	215
Antwerp	223
Termonde	229
The Château	235
Malines	241
Lierre	245
A Pause	252
The Siege	255
Contich	259
The Bombardment—Night	266
The Bombardment—Day	270
The Night Journey	277
Furnes	281
Poperinghe	288
Furnes Again	294
Work at Furnes	300

Furnes—The Town	306
A Journey	312
The Ambulance Corps	316
Pervyse—The Trenches	321
Ypres	327
Some Conclusions	334

Preface

To write the true story of three months' work in a hospital is a task before which the boldest man might quail. Let my very dear friends of the Belgian Field Hospital breathe again, for I have attempted nothing of the sort. I would sooner throw aside my last claim to self-respect, and write my autobiography. It would at least be safer. But there were events which happened around us, there was an atmosphere in which we lived, so different from those of our lives at home that one felt compelled to try to picture them before they merged into the shadowy memories of the past. And this is all that I have attempted. To all who worked with me through those months I owe a deep debt of gratitude. That they would do everything in their power to make the hospital a success went without saying, but it was quite another matter that they should all have conspired to make the time for me one of the happiest upon which I shall ever look back.

Where all have been so kind, it is almost invidious to mention names, and yet there are two which must stand by themselves. To the genius and the invincible resource of Madame Sindici the hospital owes an incalculable debt. Her friendship is one of my most delightful memories. The sterling powers of Dr. Beavis brought us safely many a time through deep water, and but for his enterprise the hospital would have come to an abrupt conclusion with Antwerp. There could have been no more delightful colleague, and without his aid much of this book would never have been written.

For the Belgian Field Hospital I can wish nothing better than that its star may continue to shine in the future as it has always done in the past, and that a sensible British public may generously support the most enterprising hospital in the war.

H. S. S.

Chapter 1

To Antwerp

When, one Saturday afternoon in September, we stepped on board the boat for Ostend, it was with a thrill of expectation. For weeks we had read and spoken of one thing only—the War—and now we were to see it for ourselves, we were even in some way to be a part of it. The curtain was rising for us upon the greatest drama in all the lurid history of strife. We should see the armies as they went out to fight, and we should care for the wounded when their work was done. We might hear the roar of the guns and the scream of the shells. To us, that was war.

And, indeed, we have seen more of war in these few weeks than has fallen to the lot of many an old campaigner. We have been through the siege of Antwerp, we have lived and worked always close to the firing-line, and I have seen a great cruiser roll over and sink, the victim of a submarine. But these are not the things which will live in our minds. These things are the mere framing of the grim picture. The cruiser has been blotted out by the weary faces of an endless stream of fugitives, and the scream of the shells has been drowned by the cry of a child. For, though the soldiers may fight, it is the people who suffer, and the toll of war is not the life which it takes, but the life which it destroys.

I suppose, and I hope, that there is not a man amongst us who has not in his heart wished to go to the front, and to do what he could. The thought may have been only transitory, and may soon have been blotted out by self-interest; and there is many a strong man who has thrust it from him because he knew that his duty lay at home. But to everyone the wish must have come, though only to a few can come the opportunity. We all want to do our share, but it is only human that we should at the same time long to be there in the great business of the hour, to see war as it really is, to feel the thrill of its supreme moments, perhaps in our heart of hearts to make quite certain that we are not cowards. And when we return, what do we bring with us? We all bring a few bits of shell, pictures of ruined churches, perhaps a German helmet—and our friends are full of envy. And some of us return with scenes burnt into our brain of horror and of pathos such as no human pen can describe. Yet it is only when we sit down in the quiet of our homes that we realise the deeper meaning of all that we have seen, that we grasp the secret of the strange aspects of humanity which have passed before us.

What we have seen is a world in which the social conventions under which we live, and which form a great part or the whole of most of our lives, have been torn down. Men and women are no longer limited by the close barriers of convention. They must think and act for themselves, and for once it is the men and women that we see, and not the mere symbols which pass as coin in a world at peace. To the student of men and women, the field of war is the greatest opportunity in the world. It is a veritable dissecting-room, where all the queer machinery that goes to the making of us lies open to our view. On the whole, I am very glad that I am a mere surgeon, and that I can limit my dissections to men's bodies. Human Anatomy is bad enough, but after the last three months the mere thought of an analysis of Human Motives fills me with terror.

Our boat was one of the older paddle steamers. We were so fortunate as to have a friend at court, and the best cabins on the ship were placed at our disposal. I was very grateful to that friend, for it was very rough, and our paddle-boxes were often under water. We consoled ourselves by the thought that at least in a rough sea we were safe from submarines, but the consolation became somewhat threadbare as time went on. Gradually the tall white cliffs of Dover sank behind us, splendid symbols of the quiet power which guards them. But for those great white cliffs, and the waves which wash their base, how different the history of England would have been! They broke the power of Spain in her proudest days, Napoleon gazed at them in vain as at the walls of a fortress beyond his grasp, and against them Germany will fling herself to her own destruction. Germany has yet to learn the strength which lies concealed behind those cliffs, the energy and resource which have earned for England the command of the sea. It was a bad day for Germany when she ventured to question that command. She will receive a convincing answer to her question.

We reached Ostend, and put up for the night at the Hôtel Terminus. Ostend was empty, and many of the hotels were closed. A few bombs had been dropped upon the town some days before, and caused considerable excitement—about all that most bombs ever succeed in doing, as we afterwards discovered. But it had been enough to cause an exodus. No one dreamt that in less than three weeks' time the town would be packed with refugees, and that to get either a bed or a meal would be for many of them almost impossible. Everywhere we found an absolute confidence as to the course of the war, and the general opinion was that the Germans would be driven out of Belgium in less than six weeks.

Two of our friends in Antwerp had come down to meet us by motor, and we decided to go back with them by road, as trains, though still running, were slow and uncertain. It was a terrible day, pouring in torrents and blowing a hurricane. Our route lay through Bruges and Ghent, but the direct road to Bruges was in a bad condition, and we chose the indirect road through Blankenberghe. We left Ostend by the magnificent bridge, with its four tall columns, which opens the way towards the north-east, and as we crossed it I met the first symbol of war. A soldier stepped forward, and held his rifle across our path. My companion leaned forward and murmured, "Namur," the soldier saluted, and we passed on. It was all very simple, and, but for the one word, silent; but it was the first time I had heard a password, and it made an immense impression on my mind. We had crossed the threshold of war. I very soon had other things to think about.

The road from Ostend to Blankenberghe is about the one good motor road in Belgium, and my companion evidently intended to demonstrate the fact to me beyond all possibility of doubt. We were driving into the teeth of a squall, but there seemed to be no limits to the power of his engine. I watched the hand of his speedometer rise till it touched sixty miles per hour. On the splendid asphalt surface of the road there was no vibration, but a north-east wind across the sand-dunes is no trifle, and I was grateful when we turned south-eastwards at Blankenberghe, and I could breathe again.

As I said, that road by the dunes is unique. The roads of Belgium, for the most part, conform to one regular pattern. In the centre is a paved causeway, set with small stone blocks, whilst on each side is a couple of yards of loose sand, or in wet weather of deep mud. The causeway is usually only just wide enough for the passing of two motors, and on the smaller roads it is not sufficient even for this. As there is no speed limit, and everyone drives at the top power of his engine, the skill required to drive without mishap is considerable. After a little rain the stone is covered with a layer of greasy mud, and to keep a car upon it at a high speed is positively a gymnastic feat. In spite of every precaution, an occasional descent into the mud at the roadside is inevitable, and from that only a very powerful car can extricate itself with any ease. A small car will often have to slowly push its way out backwards.

In dry weather the conditions are almost as bad, for often the roadside is merely loose sand, which gives no hold for a wheel. For a country so damp and low-lying as Belgium, there is probably nothing to equal a paved road, but it is a pity that the paving was not made a little wider. Every now and then we met one of the huge, unwieldy carts which seem to be relics of a prehistoric age—rough plank affairs of enormous strength and a design so primitive as to be a constant source of wonder. They could only be pulled along at a slow walk and with vast effort by a couple of huge horses, and the load the cart was carrying never seemed to bear any proportion to the mechanism of its transport.

The roads are bad, but they will not account for those carts. The little front wheels are a stroke of mechanical ineptitude positively amounting to genius, and when they are replaced by a single wheel, and the whole affair resembles a huge tricycle, one instinctively looks round for a dinosaur. Time after time we met them stuck in the mud or partially overturned, but the drivers seemed in no way disconcerted; it was evidently all part of the regular business of the day. When one thinks of the Brussels coachwork which adorns our most expensive motors, and of the great engineering works of Liege, those carts are a really wonderful example of persistence of type.

We passed through Bruges at a pace positively disrespectful to that fine old town. There is no town in Belgium so uniform in the magnificence of its antiquity, and it is good to think that—so far, at any rate—it has escaped destruction. As we crossed the square, the clock in the belfry struck the hour, and began to play its chimes. It is a wonderful old clock, and every quarter of an hour it plays a tune—a very attractive performance, unless you happen to live opposite. I remember once thinking very hard things about the maker of that clock, but perhaps it was not his fault that one of the bells was a quarter of a tone flat. At the gates our passports were examined, and we travelled on to Ghent by the Ecloo Road, one of the main thoroughfares of

Belgium.

Beyond an occasional sentry, there was nothing to indicate that we were passing through a country at war, except that we rarely saw a man of military age. All were women, old men, or children. Certainly the men of Belgium had risen to the occasion. The women were doing everything—working in the fields, tending the cattle, driving the market-carts and the milk-carts with their polished brass cans. After leaving Ghent, the men came into view, for at Lokeren and St. Nicholas were important military stations, whilst nearer to Antwerp very extensive entrenchments and wire entanglements were being constructed. The trenches were most elaborate, carefully constructed and covered in; and I believe that all the main approaches to the city were defended in the same way. Antwerp could never have been taken by assault, but with modern artillery it would have been quite easy to destroy it over the heads of its defenders. The Germans have probably by now rendered it impregnable, for though in modern war it is impossible to defend one's own cities, the same does not apply to the enemy. In future, forts will presumably be placed at points of strategic importance only, and as far as possible from towns.

Passing through the western fortifications, we came upon the long bridge of boats which had been thrown across the Scheldt. The river is here more than a quarter of a mile wide, and the long row of sailing barges was most picturesque. The roadway was of wooden planks, and only just wide enough to allow one vehicle to pass at a time, the tall spars of the barges rising on each side. It is strange that a city of such wealth as Antwerp should not have bridged a river which, after all, is not wider than the Thames. We were told that a tunnel was in contemplation. The bridge of boats was only a tribute to the necessities of war. We did not dream that a fortnight later it would be our one hope of escape.

CHAPTER 2

The Hospital

Antwerp is one of the richest cities in Europe, and our hospital was placed in its wealthiest quarter. The Boulevard Leopold is a magnificent avenue, with a wide roadway in the centre flanked by broad paths planted with trees. Beyond these, again, on each side is a paved road with a tram-line, whilst a wide pavement runs along the houses. There are many such boulevards in Antwerp, and they give to the city an air of spaciousness and opulence in striking contrast to the more utilitarian plan of London or of most of our large towns. We talk a great deal about fresh air, but we are not always ready to pay for it.

Our hospital occupied one of the largest houses on the south-east side. A huge doorway led into an outer hall through which the garden was directly reached behind the house. On the right-hand side of this outer hall a wide flight of steps led to inner glass doors and the great central hall of the building. As a private house it must have been magnificent; as a hospital it was as spacious and airy as one could desire. The hall was paved with marble, and on either side opened lofty reception rooms, whilst in front wide marble staircases led to the first floor. This first floor and another above it were occupied entirely by wards, each containing from six to twelve beds.

On the ground floor on the right-hand side were two large wards, really magnificent rooms, and one smaller, all these overlooking the Boulevard. On the left were the office, the common room, and the operating theatre. Behind the house was a large paved courtyard, flanked on the right by a garden border and on the left by a wide glass-roofed corridor. The house had previously been used as a school, and on the opposite side of the courtyard was the gymnasium, with dormitories above. The gymnasium furnished our dining-hall, whilst several of the staff slept in the rooms above.

A WARD AT ANTWERP

It will be seen that the building was in many ways well adapted to the needs of a hospital and to the accommodation of the large staff required. We had in all 150 beds, and a staff of about 50. The latter included 8 doctors, 20 nurses, 5 dressers, lay assistants, and motor drivers. In addition to these there was a kitchen staff of Belgians, so that the management of the whole was quite a large undertaking, especially in a town where ordinary provisions were becoming more and more difficult to obtain. In the later days of the siege, when milk was not to be had and the only available water was salt, the lot of our housekeeper was anything but happy. Providing meals for over 200 people in a besieged town is no small matter. But it was managed somehow, and our cuisine was positively astonishing, to which I think we largely owe the fact that none of the staff was ever ill. Soldiers are not the only people who fight on their stomachs.

The management of the hospital centred in the office, and it was so typical of Belgium as to be really worth a few words of description. It was quite a small room, and it was always crowded. Four of us had seats round a table in the centre, and at another table in the window sat our Belgian secretary, Monsieur Herman, and his two clerks. But that was only the beginning of it. All day long there was a constant stream of men, women, and children pouring into that room, bringing letters, asking questions, always talking volubly to us and amongst themselves. At first we thought that this extraordinary turmoil was due to our want of space, but we soon found that it was one of the institutions of the country.

In England an official's room is the very home of silence, and is by no means easy of access. If he is a high official, a series of ante-rooms is interposed between his sacred person and an inquisitive world. But in Belgium everyone walks straight in without removing his cigar. The great man sits at his desk surrounded by a perfect Babel, but he is always polite, always ready to hear what you have to say and to do what he can to help. He appears to be able to deal with half a dozen different problems at the same time without ever being ruffled or confused. There is an immense amount of talking and shaking of hands, and at first the brain of a mere Englishman is apt to whirl; but the business is done rapidly and completely. Belgium is above all things democratic, and our office was a good introduction to it.

The common room was large and airy, overlooking the courtyard, and a few rugs and armchairs made it a very comfortable place when the work of the day was done. Anyone who has worked in a hospital will know what a difference such a room makes to the work—work that must be carried on at all hours of the day or night; nor will he need to be told of the constant supply of tea and coffee that will be found there. We go about telling our patients of the evils of excessive tea- drinking, and we set them an example they would find it hard to follow. We do not mention how often tea and a hot bath have been our substitute for a night's sleep.' A good common room and an unlimited supply of tea will do much to oil the wheels of hospital life.

But to myself the all-important room was the operating theatre, for upon its resources depended entirely our opportunities for surgical work. It was in every way admirable, and I know plenty of hospitals in London whose theatres would not bear comparison with ours. Three long windows faced the courtyard; there was a great bunch of electric lights in the ceiling, and there was a constant supply of boiling water. What more could the heart of surgeon desire? There were two operating tables and an equipment of instruments to vie with any in a London hospital. Somebody must have been very extravagant over those instruments, I thought as I looked at them; but he was right and I was wrong, for there were very few of those instruments for which I was not grateful before long. The surgery of war is a very different thing from the surgery of home.

The wards were full when we arrived, and I had a wonderful opportunity of studying the effects of rifle and shell fire. Most of the wounds were fortunately slight, but some of them were terrible, and, indeed, in some cases it seemed little short of miraculous that the men had survived. But on every side one saw nothing but cheerful faces, and one would never have dreamt what some of those men had gone through. They were all smoking cigarettes, laughing, and chatting, as cheery a set of fellows as one could meet. You would never have suspected that a few days before those same men had been carried into the hospital in most cases at their last gasp from loss of blood and exposure, for none but serious cases were admitted. The cheeriest man in the place was De Rasquinet, a wounded officer who had been christened "Ragtime" for short, and for affection. A week before he had been struck by a shell in the left side, and a large piece of the shell had gone clean through, wounding the kidney behind and the bowel in front. That man crawled across several fields, a distance of nearly a mile, on his hands and knees, dragging with him to a place of safety a wounded companion.

When from loss of blood he could drag him along no longer, he left him under a hedge, and dragged himself another half-mile till he could get help. When he was brought into the hospital, he was so exhausted from pain and loss of blood that no one thought that he could live for more than a few hours, but by sheer pluck he had pulled through. Even now he was desperately ill with as horrible a wound as a man could have, but nothing was going to depress him. I am glad to say that what is known in surgery as a short circuit was an immediate success, and when we left him three weeks later in Ghent he was to all intents perfectly well.

There were plenty of other serious cases, some of them with ghastly injuries, and many of them must have suffered agonising pain; but they were all doing their best to make light of their troubles, whilst their gratitude for what was done for them was extraordinary. The Belgians are by nature a cheerful race, but these were brave men, and we felt glad that we had come out to do what we could for them.

But if we give them credit for their courage and cheerfulness, we must not forget how largely they owed it to the devoted attention—yes, and to the courage and cheerfulness—of the nurses. I wonder how many of us realise what Britain owes to her nurses. We take them as a matter of course, we regard nursing as a very suitable profession for a woman to take up—if she can find nothing better to do; perhaps we may have been ill, and we were grateful for a nurse's kindness. But how many of us realise all the long years of drudgery that have given the skill we appreciated, the devotion to her work that has made the British nurse what she is? And how many of us realise that we English-speaking nations alone in the world have such nurses?

Except in small groups, they are unknown in France, Belgium, Germany, Russia, or any other country in the world. In no other land will women leave homes of ease and often of luxury to do work that no servant would touch, for wages that no servant would take—work for which there will be very little reward but the unmeasured gratitude of the very few. They stand today as an unanswerable proof that as nations we have risen higher in the level of civilization than any of our neighbours. To their influence on medicine and surgery I shall refer again. Here I only wish to acknowledge our debt. As a mere patient I would rather have a good nurse than a good physician, if I were so unfortunate as to have to make the choice. A surgeon is a dangerous fellow, and must be treated with respect. But as a rule the physician gives his blessing, the surgeon does his operation, but it is the nurse who does the work.

CHAPTER 3

The Day's Work

In any hospital at home or abroad there is a large amount of routine work, which must be carried on in an orderly and systematic manner, and upon the thoroughness with which this is done will largely depend the effectiveness of the hospital. Patients must be fed and washed, beds must be made and the wards swept and tidied, wounds must be dressed and splints adjusted. In an English hospital everything is arranged to facilitate this routine work. Close to every ward is a sink-room with an adequate supply of hot and cold water, dinner arrives in hot tins from the kitchens as if by magic, whilst each ward has its own arrangements for preparing the smaller meals. The beds are of a convenient height, and there is an ample supply of sheets and pillow-cases, and of dressing materials of all kinds arranged on tables which run noiselessly up and down the wards.

At home all these things are a matter of course; abroad they simply did not exist. Four or five gas- rings represented our hot-water supply and our ward-kitchens for our 150 patients, and the dinners had to be carried up from the large kitchens in the basement. The beds were so low as to break one's back, and had iron sides which were always in the way; and when we came to the end of our sheets—well, we came to the end of them, and that was all. In every way the work was heavier and more difficult than at home, for all our patients were heavy men, and every wound was septic, and had, in many cases, to be dressed several times a day. Everyone had to work hard, sometimes very hard; but as a rule we got through the drudgery in the morning, and in the afternoon everything was in order, and we should, I think, have compared very favourably in appearance with most hospitals at home.

But we had to meet one set of conditions which would, I think, baffle many hospitals at home. Every now and then, without any warning, from 50 to 100, even in one case 150, wounded would be brought to our door. There was no use in putting up a notice "House Full"; the men were wounded and they must be attended to. In such a case our arrangement was a simple one: all who could walk went straight upstairs, the gravest cases went straight to the theatre or waited their turn in the great hall, the others were accommodated on the ground floor. We had a number of folding beds for emergency, and we had no rules as to overcrowding. In the morning the authorities would clear out as many patients as we wished. Sometimes we were hard put to it to find room for them all, but we always managed somehow, and we never refused admission to a single patient on the score of want of room. The authorities soon discovered the capacity of the hospital for dealing with really serious cases, and as a result our beds were crowded with injuries of the gravest kind. What appealed to us far more was the appreciation of the men themselves. We felt that we had not worked in vain when we heard that the soldiers in the trenches begged to be taken "*à l'Hôpital Anglais.*"

The condition of the men when they reached us was often pitiable in the extreme. Most of them had been living in the trenches for weeks exposed to all kinds of weather, their clothes were often sodden and caked with dirt, and the men themselves showed clear traces of exposure and insecure sleep. In most cases they had lain in the trenches for hours after being wounded, for as a rule it is impossible to remove the wounded at once with any degree of safety. Indeed, when the fighting is at all severe they must lie till dark before it is safe for the stretcher-bearers to go for them. This was so at Furnes, but at Antwerp we were usually able to get them in within a few hours. Even a few hours' delay with a bad wound may be a serious matter, and in every serious case our attention was first directed to the condition of the patient himself and not to his wound. Probably he had lost blood, his injury had produced more or less shock, he had certainly been lying for hours in pain. He had to be got warm, his circulation had to be restored, he had to be saved from pain and protected from further shock. Hot bottles, blankets, brandy, and morphia worked wonders in a very short time, and one could then proceed to deal with wounds. Our patients were young and vigorous, and their rate of recovery was extraordinary.

When a rush came we all had to work our hardest, and the scenes in any part of the hospital required steady nerves; but perhaps the cen-

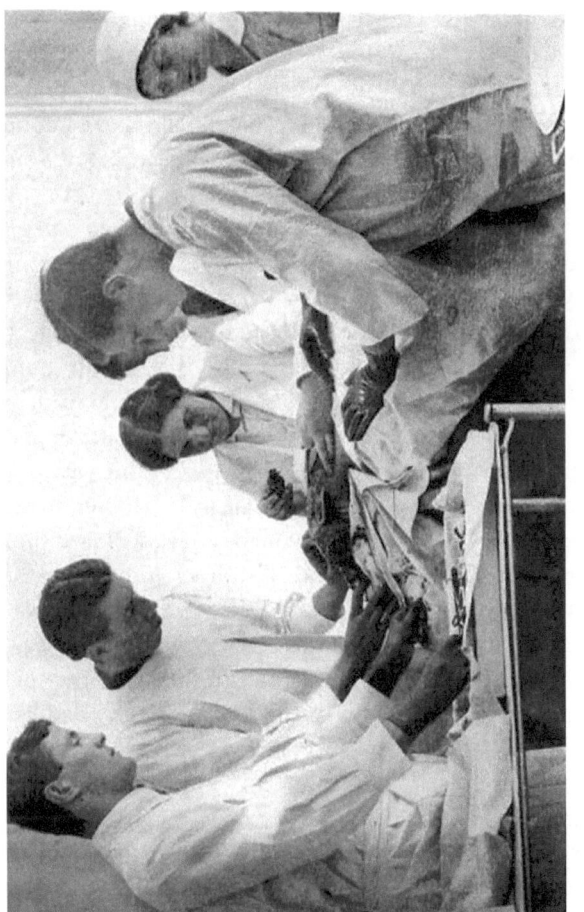

An operation at Antwerp

tre of interest was the theatre. Here all the worst cases were brought—men with ghastly injuries from which the most hardened might well turn away in horror; men almost dead from loss of blood, or, worst of all, with a tiny puncture in the wall of the abdomen which looks so innocent, but which, in this war at least, means, apart from a difficult and dangerous operation, a terrible death. With all these we had to deal as rapidly and completely as possible, reducing each case to a form which it would be practicable to nurse, where the patient would be free from unnecessary pain, and where he would have the greatest possible chance of ultimate recovery. Of course, all this was done under anaesthesia. What a field hospital must have been before the days of anaesthesia is too horrible to contemplate.

Even in civil hospitals the surgeons must have reached a degree of "*Kultur*" beside which its present exponents are mere children. It is not so many years since a famous surgeon, who was fond of walking back from his work at the London Hospital along the Whitechapel Road, used to be pointed to with horror by the Aldgate butchers, whose opinion on such a subject was probably worth consideration. But now all that is changed. The surgeon can be a human being again, and indeed, except when he goes round his wards, his patients may never know, of his existence. They go to sleep in a quiet anteroom, and they waken up in the ward. Of the operation and all its difficulties they know no more than their friends at home. Perhaps even more wonderful is the newer method of spinal anaesthesia, which we used largely for the difficult abdominal cases.

With the injection of a minute quantity of fluid into the spine all sensation disappears up to the level of the arms, and, provided he cannot see what is going on, any operation below that level can be carried out without the patient knowing anything about it at all. It is rather uncanny at first to see a patient lying smoking a cigarette and reading the paper whilst on the other side of a screen a big operation is in progress. But for many cases this method is unsuitable, and without chloroform we should indeed have been at a loss. The Belgians are an abstemious race, and they took it beautifully. I am afraid they were a striking contrast to their brothers on this side of the water. Chloroform does not mix well with alcohol in the human body, and the British working man is rather fond of demonstrating the fact.

With surgery on rather bold lines it was extraordinary how much could be done, especially in the way of saving limbs. During the whole of our stay in Antwerp we never once had to resort to an amputation.

We were dealing with healthy and vigorous men, and once they had got over the shock of injury they had wonderful powers of recovery. We very soon found that we were dealing with cases to which the ordinary rules of surgery did not apply. The fundamental principles of the art must always be the same, but here the conditions of their application were essentially different from those of civil practice. Two of these conditions were of general interest: the great destruction of the tissues in most wounds, and the infection of the wounds, which was almost universal.

Where a wound has been produced by a large fragment of shell, one expects to see considerable damage; in fact, a whole limb may be torn off, or death may be instant from some terrible injury to the body. But where the object of the enemy is the injury of individuals, and not the destruction of buildings, they often use shrapnel, and the resulting wounds resemble those from the old smooth-bore guns of our ancestors. Shrapnel consists of a large number of bullets about half an inch in diameter packed together in a case, which carries also a charge of explosive timed to burst at the moment when it reaches its object. The balls are small and round, and if they go straight through soft tissues they do not do much damage. If, however, they strike a bone, they are so soft that their shape becomes irregular, and the injury they can produce in their further course is almost without limit. On the whole, they do not as a rule produce great damage, for in many cases they are nearly spent when they reach their mark. Pieces of the case will, of course, have much the same effect as an ordinary shell.

The effects of rifle-fire, particularly at short ranges, have led to a great deal of discussion, and each side has accused the other of using dum-dum bullets. The ordinary bullet consists of a lead core with a casing of nickel, since the soft lead would soon choke rifling. Such a bullet under ordinary circumstances makes a clean perforation, piercing the soft tissues, and sometimes the bones, with very little damage. In a dum-dum bullet the casing at the tip is cut or removed, with the result that, on striking, the casing spreads out and forms a rough, irregular missile, which does terrific damage. Such bullets were forbidden by the Geneva Convention.

But the German bullet is much more subtle than this. It is short and pointed, and when it strikes it turns completely over and goes through backwards. The base of the bullet has no cover, and consequently spreads in a manner precisely similar to that in a dum-dum, with equally deadly results. There could be no greater contrast than that between the wounds with which we had to deal in South Africa, produced by ordinary bullets, and those which our soldiers are now receiving from German rifles. The former were often so slight that it was quite a common occurrence for a soldier to discover accidentally that he had been wounded some time previously. In the present war rifle wounds have been amongst the most deadly with which we have had to deal.

It will thus be seen that in most cases the wounds were anything but clean-cut; with very few exceptions, they were never surgically clean. By surgically clean we mean that no bacteria are present which can interfere with the healing of the tissues, and only those who are familiar with surgical work can realise the importance of this condition. Its maintenance is implied in the term "aseptic surgery," and upon this depends the whole distinction between the surgery of the present and the surgery of the past. Without it the great advances of modern surgery would be entirely impossible. When we say, then, that every wound with which we had to deal was infected with bacteria, it will be realised how different were the problems which we had to face compared with those of work at home. But the difference was even more striking, for the bacteria which had infected the wounds were not those commonly met with in England. These wounds were for the most part received in the open country, and they were soiled by earth, manure, fragments of cloth covered with mud. They were therefore infected by the organisms which flourish on such soil, and not by the far more deadly denizens of our great cities. It is true that in soil one may meet with tetanus and other virulent bacteria, but in our experience these were rare.

Now, there is one way in which all such infections may be defeated—by plenty of fresh air, or, better still, by oxygen. We had some very striking proofs of this, for in several cases the wounds were so horribly foul that it was impossible to tolerate their presence in the wards; and in these cases we made it a practice to put the patient in the open air, of course suitably protected, and to leave the wound exposed to the winds of heaven, with only a thin piece of gauze to protect it. The results were almost magical, for in two or three days the wounds lost their odour and began to look clean, whilst the patients lost all signs of the poisoning which had been so marked before. It may be partly to this that we owe the fact that we never had a case of tetanus. In all cases we treated our wounds with solutions of oxygen, and we avoided covering them up with heavy dressings; and we found that this plan was successful as well as economical.

Though any detailed description of surgical treatment would be out of place, there was one which in these surroundings was novel, and which was perhaps of general interest. Amongst all the cases which came to us, certainly the most awkward were the fractured thighs. It was not a question of a broken leg in the ordinary sense of the term. In every case there was a large infected wound to deal with, and as a rule several inches of the bone had been blown clean away. At first we regarded these cases with horror, for anything more hopeless than a thigh with 6 inches missing it is difficult to imagine. Splints presented almost insuperable difficulties, for the wounds had to be dressed two or three times, and however skilfully the splint was arranged, the least movement meant for the patient unendurable agony. After some hesitation we attempted the method of fixation by means of steel plates, which was introduced with such success by Sir Arbuthnot Lane in the case of simple fractures. The missing portion of the bone is replaced by a long steel plate, screwed by means of small steel screws to the portions which remain, "demonstrating," as a colleague put it, "*the triumph of mind over the absence of matter.*"

The result was a brilliant success, for not only could the limb now be handled as if there were no fracture at all, to the infinite comfort of the patient, but the wounds themselves cleared up with great rapidity. We were told that the plates would break loose, that the screws would come out, that the patient would come to a bad end through the violent sepsis induced by the presence of a "foreign body" in the shape of the steel plate. But none of these disasters happened, the cases did extremely well, and one of our most indignant critics returned to his own hospital after seeing them with his pockets full of plates. The only difficulty with some of them was to induce them to stop in bed, and it is a fact that on the night of our bombardment I met one of them walking downstairs, leaning on a dresser's arm, ten days after the operation.

And this brings me to a subject on which I feel very strongly, the folly of removing bullets. If a bullet is doing any harm, pressing on some nerve, interfering with a joint, or in any way causing pain or inconvenience, by all means let it be removed, though even then it should in most cases never be touched until the wound is completely healed. But the mere presence of a bullet inside the body will of itself do no harm at all. The old idea that it will cause infection died long ago. It may have brought infection with it; but the removal of the bullet will not remove the infection, but rather in most cases make it fire up. We now know that, provided they are clean, we can introduce steel plates, silver wires, silver nets, into the body without causing any trouble at all, and a bullet is no worse than any of these. It is a matter in which the public are very largely to blame, for they consider that unless the bullet has been removed the surgeon has not done his job. Unless he has some specific reason for it, I know that the surgeon who removes a bullet does not know his work. It may be the mark of a Scotch ancestry, but if I ever get a bullet in my own anatomy, I shall keep it.

CHAPTER 4

Antwerp

There is no port in Europe which holds such a dominant position as Antwerp, and there is none whose history has involved such amazing changes of fortune. In the middle of the sixteenth century she was the foremost city in Europe, at its close she was ruined. For two hundred years she lay prostrate under the blighting influence of Spain and Austria, and throttled by the commercial jealousy of England and Holland. A few weeks ago she was the foremost port on the Continent, the third in the world; now her wharves stand idle, and she herself is a prisoner in the hands of the enemy. Who can tell what the next turn of the wheel will bring?

Placed centrally between north and south, on a deep and wide river, Antwerp is the natural outlet of Central Europe towards the West, and it is no wonder that four hundred years ago she gathered to herself the commerce of the Netherlands, in which Ypres, Bruges, and Ghent had been her forerunners. For fifty years she was the Queen of the North, and the centre of a vast ocean trade with England, France, Spain, Portugal, and Italy, till the religious bigotry of Philip II of Spain and the awful scenes of the Spanish Fury reduced her to ruin. For two hundred years the Scheldt was blocked by Holland, and the ocean trade of Antwerp obliterated. Her population disappeared, her wharves rotted, and her canals were choked with mud. It is hard to apportion the share of wickedness between a monarch who destroys men and women to satisfy his own religious lust, and a nation which drains the life-blood of another to satisfy its lust for gold. One wonders in what category the instigator of the present war should appear.

At the very beginning of last century Napoleon visited Antwerp, and asserted that it was "little better than a heap of ruins." He recognised its incomparable position as a port and as a fortress, and he determined to raise it to its former prosperity, and to make it the strongest fortress in Europe. He spent large sums of money upon it, and his refusal to part with Antwerp is said to have broken off the negotiations of Chatillon, and to have been the chief cause of his exile to St. Helena. Alas his enemies did not profit by his genius. We are the allies of his armies now, but we have lost Antwerp. Germany will be utterly and completely crushed before she parts with that incomparable prize. A mere glance at the map of Europe is sufficient to convince anyone that in a war between England and Germany it is a point of the first strategical importance. That our access to it should be hampered by the control of Holland over the Scheldt is one of the eccentricities of diplomacy which are unintelligible to the plain man. The blame for its loss must rest equally between Britain and Belgium, for Belgium, the richest country in Europe for her size, attempted to defend her greatest stronghold with obsolete guns; whilst we, who claim the mastery of the seas, sacrificed the greatest seaport in Europe to the arrangements of an obsolete diplomacy. If we are to retain our great position on the seas, Antwerp must be regained. She is the European outpost of Britain, and, as has so often been pointed out, the mouth of the Scheldt is opposite to the mouth of the Thames.

In Antwerp, as we saw her, it was almost impossible to realise the vicissitudes through which she had passed, or to remember that her present prosperity was of little more than fifty years' growth. On all sides we were surrounded by wide boulevards, lined by magnificent houses and public buildings. There are few streets in Europe to eclipse the great Avenue des Arts, which, with its continuations, extends the whole length of the city from north to south. The theatres, the Central Station, the banks, would adorn any city, and the shops everywhere spoke of a wealth not restricted to the few. The wide streets, the trees, the roomy white houses, many of them great palaces, made a deep impression upon us after the darkness and dirt of London.

Even in the poorer quarters there was plenty of light and air, and on no occasion did we find the slums which surround the wealthiest streets all over London. In the older parts of the city the streets were, of course, narrower; but even here one had the compensation of wonderful bits of architecture at unexpected corners, splendid relics of an illustrious past. They are only remnants, but they speak of a time when men worked for love rather than for wages, and when an artisan took a pride in the labour of his hands. If it had not been for the hand of the destroyer, what a marvellous city Antwerp would have been! One likes to think that the great creations of the past are not all lost, and that in the land to which the souls of the Masters have passed we may find still living the mighty thoughts to which their love gave birth. Are our cathedrals only stones and mortar, and are our paintings only dust and oil?

The inhabitants of Antwerp were as delightful as their city. On all sides we were welcomed with a kindness and a consideration not always accorded to those who are so bold as to wish to help their fellow-men. Everywhere we met with a courtesy and a generosity by which, in the tragedy of their country, we were deeply touched. They all seemed genuinely delighted to see us, from the queen herself to the children in the streets. Our medical confreres treated us royally, and the mere thought of professional jealousy with such men is simply ludicrous. They constantly visited our hospital, and they always showed the keenest interest in our work and in any novelties in treatment we were able to show them; and when we went to see them, we were shown all the best that they had, and we brought away many an ingenious idea which it was worth while going far to obtain. Wherever we moved amongst the Belgians, we always found the same simplicity of purpose, the same generosity of impulse. Everywhere we met the same gratitude for what England was doing for Belgium; no one ever referred to the sacrifices which Belgium has made for England.

The one thing which so impressed us in the character of the Belgians whom we met was its simplicity, and the men who had risen to high rank did not seem to have lost it in their climb to fame. But it was just this, the most delightful of their characteristics, which must have made war for them supremely difficult. For strict discipline and simplicity are almost incompatible. None of us tower so far above our fellows that we can command instant obedience for our own sakes. We have to cover ourselves with gold lace, to entrench ourselves in rank, and to provide ourselves with all sorts of artificial aids before we can rely on being obeyed. These things are foreign to the Belgian mind, and as a result one noticed in their soldiers a certain lack of the stern discipline which war demands. Individually they are brave men and magnificent fighters. They only lacked the organisation which has made the little British Army the envy of the world.

The fact is that they are in no sense a warlike nation, in spite of their turbulent history of the past, and, indeed, few things could be more incompatible than turbulence and modern warfare. It demands on the part of the masses of combatants an obedience and a disre-

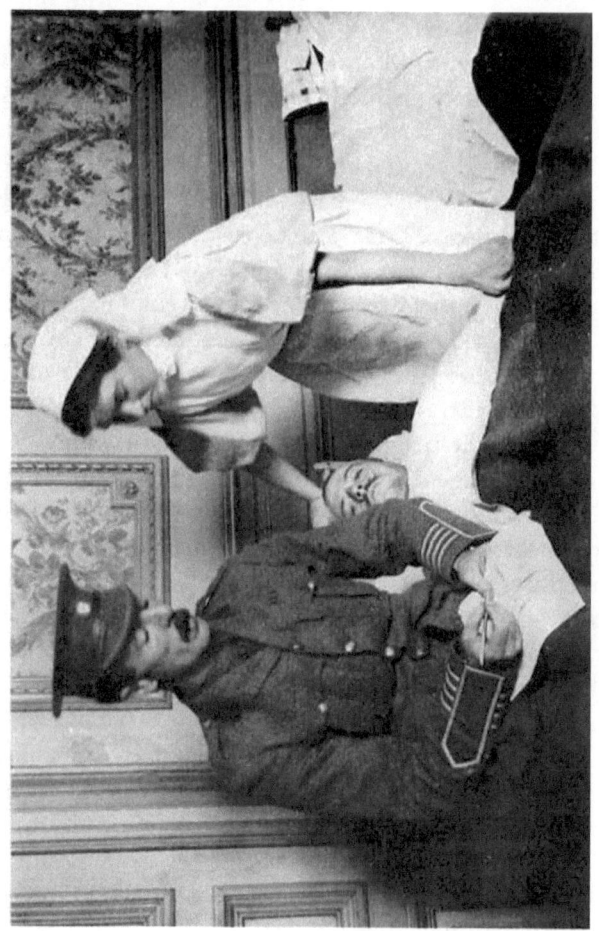

The Director, Dr. Beavis, at Antwerp

gard of life which are repellent to human nature, and the Belgians are above all things human. Germany is governed by soldiers, and France by officials. Unlike the frogs in the fable, the Belgians are content to govern themselves.

It was our great regret that we had so little time in which to see the work of the Antwerp hospitals, but we made use of what opportunities we had. There are many of them, and those we saw were magnificent buildings, equipped in a way which filled us with envy. The great city hospital, the Stuivenberg, was a model of what a modern hospital ought to be. The wards were large and airy and spotlessly clean, and the nurses seemed to be extremely competent. The kitchens were equipped with all the latest appliances, steam boilers, and gas and electric cookers. But the show part of the hospital was the suite of operating theatres. I have always felt the pardonable pride of a son in the theatres of the London Hospital, but they were certainly eclipsed here. Each theatre was equipped with its own anaesthetising room, its own surgeon's room, and its own sterilizing rooms and stores, all furnished with a lavishness beyond the financial capacity of any hospital in London. Perhaps some of the equipment was unnecessary, but it was abundantly evident that the State appreciated the value of first-class surgery, and that it was prepared to pay for it. I have never heard the same accusation levelled at Great Britain.

At St. Camille we had the good fortune to see M. Lambotte at work. His reputation as a surgeon is worldwide, and it was pleasant to find that his dexterity as an operator was equal to his reputation. It is not always the case. He is an expert mechanic, and himself makes most of the very ingenious instruments which he uses. He was fixing a fractured femur with silver wires, and one could see the skilled workman in all that he did. There is no training-ground for one's hands like a carpenter's bench, and the embryo surgeon might do much worse with his time than spend six months of it in a workshop. When medical training emerges from its medieval traditions, manual training will certainly form a part, and no one will be allowed to attempt to mend a bone till he has shown his capacity to mend a chair-leg. Here, again, the surgeon was surrounded by all the appliances, and even the luxuries, that he could desire. The lot of the great surgeon abroad is indeed a happy one.

But there is one thing in which we in England are far better off— in our nursing staffs. In most of the hospitals we visited the nursing was carried on by Sisterhoods, and though some of them were evidently good nurses, most of them had no idea whatever of nursing as it is practised in our country. Fresh air, for example, is to them full of dangers. One would almost think that it savoured of the powers of evil. We went into one huge hospital of the most modern type, and equipped lavishly, and such was the atmosphere that in ten minutes I had to make a rush for the door. One large ward was full of wounded soldiers, many of them with terrible wounds, gangrenous and horrible, and every window was tightly shut. How they could live in such an atmosphere is beyond my comprehension, but the Sisters did not seem to notice it at all.

Some of the surgeons have their specially trained nurses, but nursing as a profession for the classes who are alone competent to undertake it is a conception which has yet to dawn upon the Continent, for only a woman of education and refinement can really be a nurse.

The absence on the Continent of a nursing profession such as ours is not without its influence on medicine and surgery abroad. The individual patient meets with far less consideration than would be the case in this country, and is apt to be regarded as so much raw material. In Belgium this tendency is counteracted by the natural kindliness of the Belgian, but in other countries patients are often treated with a callousness which is amazing. There is in many of the great clinics a disregard of the patient's feelings, of his sufferings, and even of his life, which would be impossible in an English hospital. The contact of a surgeon with his hospital patients as individuals is largely through the nursing staff, and his point of view will be largely influenced by them. There is no one in our profession, from the youngest dresser to the oldest physician, who does not owe a great part of his education to Sister.

Chapter 5

Termonde

Anyone who has worked in hospitals will realise how important it is for the health of the staff, nurses and doctors, that they should get out into the fresh air for at least some part of every day. It is still more necessary in a war hospital, for not only is the work more exacting, but the cases themselves involve certain risks which can only be safely taken in perfect health. Practically everyone is septic, and to anyone in the least run down the danger of infection is considerable; and infection with some of the organisms with which one meets in war is a very serious thing indeed. We had four large motors in Antwerp belonging to the members of our hospital, and always at its service, and every afternoon parties were made up to drive out into the country. As a rule calls were made at various *Croix Rouge* posts on the way, and in that way we kept in contact with the medical service of the army in the field, and gave them what help we could.

We were always provided with the password, and the whole country was open to us—a privilege we very greatly appreciated; for after a hard morning's work in the wards there are few things more delightful than a motor drive. And it gave us an opportunity of seeing war as very few but staff officers ever can see it. We learnt more about the condition of the country and of the results of German methods in one afternoon than all the literature in the world could ever teach. If only it were possible to bring home to the people of Britain one-hundredth part of what we saw with our own eyes, stringent laws would have to be passed to stop men and women from enlisting. No man who deserved the name of man, and no woman who deserved to be the mother of a child, would rest day or night till the earth had been freed from the fiends who have ravaged Belgium and made the name of German vile.

One afternoon towards the end of September we visited Termonde.

We heard that the Germans, having burnt the town, had retired, leaving it in the hands of the Belgian troops. It was a rare opportunity to see the handiwork of the enemy at close quarters, and we did not wish to miss it. Termonde is about twenty-two miles from Antwerp, and a powerful car made short work of the distance. Starting directly southwards through Boom, we reached Willebroeck and the road which runs east and west from Malines through Termonde to Ghent, and along it we turned to the right. We were now running parallel to the German lines, which at some points were only a couple of miles away on the other side of the Termonde-Malines railway.

We passed numerous Belgian outposts along the road, and for a few miles between Lippeloo and Baesrode they begged us to travel as fast as possible, as at this point we came within a mile of the railway. We did travel, and it would have taken a smart marksman to hit us at fifty miles an hour; but we felt much happier when we passed under the railway bridge of a loop line at Briel and placed it between ourselves and the enemy. The entrance to Termonde was blocked by a rough barricade of bricks and branches guarded by a squad of soldiers. They told us that no one was allowed to pass, and we were about to return disappointed, when one of us happened to mention the password. As without it we could not possibly have got so far, it had never occurred to us that they might think we had not got it; and as we had no possible business in the town, we had no arguments to oppose to their refusal to let us in. However, all was now open to us, and the cheery fellows ran forward to remove the barrier they had put up.

Termonde is, or rather was, a well-to-do town of 10,000 inhabitants lying on the Scheldt at the point where the Dendre, coming up from the south, runs into it. A river in Belgium means a route for traffic, and the town must have derived some advantage from its position as a trade junction. But it possesses an even greater one in the bridge which here crosses the Scheldt, the first road bridge above the mouth of the river, for there is none at Antwerp. At least six main roads converge upon this bridge, and they must have brought a great deal of traffic through the town. When we mention that a corresponding number of railways meet at the same spot, it will be seen Termonde was an important centre, and that it must have been a wealthy town. The Dendre runs right through the centre of the town to the point where it joins the Scheldt, and on each side runs a long stone quay planted with trees, with old-fashioned houses facing the river. With the little wooden bridges and the barges on the river it must have been a very pretty picture. Now it was little better than a heap of ruins.

The destruction of the town was extraordinarily complete, and evidently carefully organised. The whole thing had been arranged beforehand at headquarters, and these particular troops supplied with special incendiary apparatus. There is strong evidence to show that the destruction of Louvain, Termonde, and of several smaller towns, was all part of a definite plan of "frightfulness," the real object being to terrorize Holland and Denmark, and to prevent any possibility of their joining with the Allies. It is strictly scientific warfare, it produces a strictly scientific hell upon this world, and I think that one may have every reasonable hope that it leads to a strictly scientific hell in the next.

After a town has been shelled, its occupants driven out, and its buildings to a large extent broken down, the soldiers enter, each provided with a number of incendiary bombs, filled with a very inflammable compound. They set light to these and throw them into the houses, and in a very few minutes each house is blazing. In half an hour the town is a roaring furnace, and by the next day nothing is left but the bare walls. And that is almost all that there was left of Termonde. We walked along the quay beside a row of charred and blackened ruins, a twisted iron bedstead or a battered lamp being all there was to tell of the homes which these had been. A few houses were still standing untouched, and on the door of each of these was scrawled in chalk the inscription:

Gute Leute,
Nicht Anzunden,
Breitfuss, Lt.

One wondered at what cost the approval of Lieutenant Breitfuss had been obtained. His request to the soldiers not to set fire to the houses of these "good people" had been respected, but I think that if the Belgians ever return to Termonde those houses are likely to be empty. There are things worse than having your house burnt down, and one would be to win the approval of Lieutenant Breitfuss.

We crossed the Dendre and wandered up the town towards the Square. For a few moments I stood alone in a long curving street with not a soul in sight, and the utter desolation of the whole thing made me shiver. Houses, shops, banks, churches, all gutted by the flames and destroyed. The smell of burning from the smouldering ruins was sickening. Every now and then the silence was broken by the fall of bricks

TERMONDE

or plaster. Except a very few houses with that ominous inscription on their doors, there was nothing left; everything was destroyed. A little farther on I went into the remains of a large factory equipped with elaborate machinery, but so complete was the destruction that I could not discover what had been made there. There was a large gas engine and extensive shafting, all hanging in dismal chaos, and I recognised the remains of machines for making tin boxes, in which the products of the factory had, I suppose, been packed. A large pile of glass stoppers in one corner was fused up into a solid mass, and I chipped a bit off as a memento.

In the Square in front of the church of Notre Dame the German soldiers had evidently celebrated their achievement by a revel. In the centre were the remains of a bonfire, and all around were broken bottles and packs of cheap cards in confusion. Think of the scene. A blazing town around them, and every now and then the crash of falling buildings; behind them Notre Dame in flames towering up to heaven; the ancient Town Hall and the Guard House burning across the Square; and in the centre a crowd of drunken soldiers round a bonfire, playing cards. And miles away across the fields ten thousand homeless wanderers watching the destruction of all for which they had spent their lives in toil.

Of the ancient church of Notre Dame only the walls remained. The roof had fallen, all the woodwork had perished in the flames, and the stonework was calcined by the heat. Above the arch of a door was a little row of angels' heads carved in stone, but when we touched them they fell to powder. The heat inside must have been terrific, for all the features of the church had disappeared, and we were surrounded by merely a mass of debris. In the apse a few fragments of old gold brocade buried beneath masses of brick and mortar were all that remained to show where the altar had been.

The Town Hall was once a beautiful gabled building with a tall square tower ending in four little turrets. I have a drawing of it, and it must have formed quite a pleasing picture, the entrance reached by the double flight of steps of which Belgium is so fond, and from which public proclamations were read. It had been only recently restored, and it was now to all intents and purposes a heap of smoking bricks. The upper part of the tower had fallen into the roof, and the whole place was burnt out.

But no words can ever convey any idea of the utter destruction of the whole town, or of the awful loneliness by which one was surrounded. One felt that one was in the presence of wickedness such as the world has rarely seen, that the powers of darkness were very near, and that behind those blackened walls there lurked evil forms. Twilight was coming on as we turned back to our car, and a cold mist was slowly rising from the river. I am not superstitious, and in broad daylight I will scoff at ghosts with anyone, but I should not care to spend a night alone in Termonde. One could almost hear the Devil laughing at the handiwork of his children.

CHAPTER 6

The Château

One of the most astounding features of the war is the way in which the Germans, from the highest to the lowest, have given themselves up to loot. In all previous wars between civilized countries anything in the nature of loot has been checked with a stern hand, and there are cases on record when a soldier has been shot for stealing a pair of boots. But now the crown prince of the German Empire sends back to his palaces all the loot that he can collect, on innumerable transport waggons, amid the applause of his proud father's subjects. He is of course carrying out the new gospel of the Fatherland that everyone has a perfect right to whatever he is strong enough to take. But some day that doctrine may spread from the exalted and sacred circle in which it is now the guiding star to the "cannon fodder." Some day the common people will have learnt the lesson which is being so sedulously taught to them both by example and by precept, and then the day of reckoning will have come.

Loot and destruction have always gone hand in hand. The private soldier cannot carry loot, and it is one of the most primitive instincts of animal nature to destroy rather than to leave that by which others may profit. Even the pavement artist will destroy his work rather than allow some poor wretch to sit beside his pictures and collect an alms. And there is great joy in destroying that which men are too coarse to appreciate, in feeling that they have in their power that which, something tells them, belongs to a refinement they cannot attain. That was the keynote of the excesses of the French Revolution, for nothing arouses the fury of the unclean so much as cleanliness, and a man has been killed before now for daring to wash his hands. And it is this elemental love of destroying that has raged through Belgium in the last few months, for though destruction has been the policy of their commanders, the German soldier has done it for love. No order could ever comprehend the ingenious detail of much that we saw, for it bore at every turn the marks of individuality. It is interesting to ponder on a future Germany of which these men, or rather these wild beasts, will be the sons. Germany has destroyed more than the cities of Belgium; she has destroyed her own soul.

It is not in the ruined towns or the battered cathedrals of Belgium that one sees most clearly the wholehearted way in which the German soldiers have carried out the commands of their lord and made his desires their own. Louvain, Termonde, Dinant, and a hundred other towns have been uprooted by order. If you wish to see what the German soldier can do for love, you have to visit the *châteaux* which are dotted so thickly all over the Belgian countryside. Here he has had a free hand, and the destruction he wrought had no political object and served no mere utilitarian purpose. It was the work of pure affection, and it showed Germany at her best. One would like to have brought one of those *châteaux* over to England, to be kept for all time as an example of German culture, that our children might turn from it in horror, and that our country might be saved from the hypocrisy and the selfishness of which this is the fruit.

Among our many good friends in Antwerp there were few whom we valued more than the Baron d'O. He was always ready to undertake any service for us, from the most difficult to the most trivial. A man of birth and of fortune, he stood high in the service of the Belgian Government, and he was often able to do much to facilitate our arrangements with them. So when he asked us to take him out in one of our cars to see the *château* of one of his greatest friends, we were glad to be in a position to repay him in a small way for his kindness. The *château* had been occupied by the Germans, who had now retired—though only temporarily, alas!—and he was anxious to see what damage had been done and to make arrangements for putting it in order again if it should be possible.

A perfect autumn afternoon found us tearing southwards on the road to Boom in Mrs. W.'s powerful Minerva. We were going to a point rather close to the German lines, and our safety might depend on a fast car and a cool hand on the wheel. We had both, for though the hand was a lady's, its owner had earned the reputation of being the most dangerous and the safest driver in Antwerp, and that is no mean achievement. We called, as was our custom, at the *Croix Rouge* stations we passed, and at one of them we were told that there were some wounded in Termonde, and that, as the Germans were attacking it, they were in great danger. So we turned off to the right, and jolted for the next twenty minutes over a deplorable paved road.

The roar of artillery fire gradually grew louder and louder, and we were soon watching an interesting little duel between the forts of Termonde, under whose shelter we were creeping along, on the one side, and the Germans on the other. The latter were endeavouring to destroy one of the bridges which span the Scheldt at this point, one for the railway and one for the road; but so far they had not succeeded in hitting either. It was a week since our last visit to Termonde, and it seemed even more desolate and forsaken than before. The Germans had shelled it again, and most of the remaining walls had been knocked down, so that the streets were blocked at many points and the whole town was little more than a heap of bricks and mortar. There was not a living creature to be seen, and even the birds had gone. The only sound that broke the utter silence was the shriek of the shells and the crash of their explosion.

We were constantly checked by piles of fallen debris, and from one street we had to back the car out and go round by another way. At the end of a long street of ruined houses, many bearing the inscription of some braggart, "I did this," we found our wounded men. They were in a monastery near the bridge at which the Germans were directing their shells, several of which had already fallen into the building. There had been four wounded men there, but two of them, badly hurt, were so terrified at the bombardment that they had crawled away in the night. The priest thought that they were probably dead. Think of the poor wounded wretches, unable to stand, crawling away in the darkness to find some spot where they could die in peace. Two remained, and these we took with us on the car. The priest and the two nuns, the sole occupants of the monastery, absolutely refused to leave. They wished to protect the monastery from sacrilege, and in that cause they held their lives of small account. I have often thought of those gentle nuns and the fearless priest standing in the doorway as our car moved away. I hope that it went well with them, and that they did not stay at their post in vain.

By the bridge stood a company of Belgian soldiers, on guard in case, under cover of the fire of their artillery, the Germans might attempt to capture it. There was very little shelter for them, and it was positively raining shells; but they had been told to hold the bridge, and they did so until there was no longer a bridge to hold. It was as fine a piece of quiet heroism as I shall ever see, and it was typical of the Belgian soldier wherever we saw him. They never made any fuss about it, they were always quiet and self-contained, and always cheerful. But if they were given a position to hold, they held it. And that is the secret of the wonderful losing battle they have fought across Belgium. Some day they will advance and not retreat, and then I think that the Belgian Army will astonish their opponents, and perhaps their friends too.

We were soon out of Termonde and on the open road again, to our very great relief, and at the nearest dressing-station we handed over our patients, who were not badly wounded, to the surgeon, who was hard at work in a little cottage about a mile back along the road. We drove on due east, and forty minutes later found ourselves at the entrance of the lodge of our friend's house. It lay on the very edge of the Belgian front, and would have been unapproachable had there been any activity in this section of the line. Fortunately for us, the Germans were concentrating their energies around Termonde, and the *mitrailleuse* standing on the path amongst the trees at the end of the garden seemed to have gone asleep. We turned the car in the drive, and, in case things should happen, pointed its nose homewards. That is always a wise precaution, for turning a car under fire in a narrow road is one of the most trying experiences imaginable. The coolest hand may fumble with the gears at such a moment, and it is surprising how difficult it is to work them neatly when every second may be a matter of life or death, when a stopped engine may settle the fate of everyone in the car. It is foolish to take unnecessary risks, and we left the car pointing the right way, with its engine running, ready to start on the instant, while we went to have a look at the house.

It was a large country-house standing in well-timbered grounds, evidently the home of a man of wealth and taste. The front-door stood wide open, as if inviting us to enter, and as we passed into the large hall I could not help glancing at our friend's face to see what he was thinking as the obvious destruction met us on the very threshold. So thorough was it that it was impossible to believe that it had not been carried out under definite orders. Chairs, sofas, settees lay scattered about in every conceivable attitude, and in every case as far as I can recollect minus legs and backs. In a small room at the end of the hall a table had been overturned, and on the floor and around lay broken glass, crockery, knives and forks, mixed up in utter confusion, while the wall was freely splashed with ink. One fact was very striking and very suggestive: none of the pictures had been defaced, and there were many fine oil-paintings and engravings hanging on the walls of the reception-rooms.

After the destruction of the treasures of Louvain, it is absurd to imagine that the controlling motive could have been any reverence for works of art. The explanation was obvious enough. The pictures were of value, and were the loot of some superior officer. A large cabinet had evidently been smashed with the butt-end of a musket, but the beautiful china it contained was intact. The grand piano stood uninjured, presumably because it afforded entertainment. The floor was thick with playing cards.

But it was upstairs that real chaos reigned. Every wardrobe and receptacle had been burst open and the contents dragged out. Piles of dresses and clothing of every kind lay heaped upon the floor, many of them torn, as though the harsh note produced by the mere act of tearing appealed to the passion for destruction which seemed to animate these fighting men. In the housekeeper's room a sewing-machine stood on the table, its needle threaded, and a strip of cloth in position, waiting for the stitch it was destined never to receive. There were many other things to which one cannot refer, but it would have been better to have had one's house occupied by a crowd of wild beasts than by these apostles of culture.

Our friend had said very little while we walked through the deserted rooms in this splendid country-house in which he had so often stayed. Inside the house he could not speak, and it was not until we got out into the sunshine that he could relieve his overwrought feelings. Deep and bitter were the curses which he poured upon those vandals; but I stood beside him, and I did not hear half that he said, for my eyes were fixed on the *mitrailleuse* standing on the garden path under the trees. My fingers itched to pull the lever and to scatter withering death among them. It slowly came into my mind how good it would be to kill these defilers. I suppose that somewhere deep down in us there remains an elemental lust for blood, and though in the protected lives we live it rarely sees the light, when the bonds of civilization are broken it rises up and dominates. And who shall say that it is not right? There are things in Belgium for which blood alone can atone. Woe to us if when our interests are satisfied we sheath the sword, and forget the ruined homes, the murdered children of Belgium, the desecrated altars of the God in whose name we fight! He has placed the sword in our hands for vengeance, and not for peace.

I no longer wonder at the dogged courage of the Belgian soldiers, at their steady disregard of their lives, when I think of the many such pictures of wanton outrage which are burned into their memories, and which can never be effaced so long as a single German remains in their beloved land. I no longer wonder, but I do not cease to admire. Let anyone who from the depths of an armchair at home thinks that I have spoken too strongly, stimulate his imagination to the pitch of visualizing the town in which he lives destroyed, his own house a smoking heap, his wife profaned, his children murdered, and himself ruined, for these are the things of which we know. Then, and then only, will he be able to judge the bravery of the nation which, preferring death to dishonour, has in all likelihood saved both France and ourselves from sharing its terrible but glorious fate.

Chapter 7

Malines

We were frequently requested by the Belgian doctors to assist them in the various Red Cross dressing-stations around Antwerp, and it was our custom to visit several of these stations each day to give what assistance we could. One of the most important of the stations was at Malines, and one of our cars called there every day. I went out there myself on an afternoon late in September. It was a glorious day, and after a heavy morning in the wards the fresh breeze and the brilliant sunshine were delightful. Our road led almost straight south through Vieux Dieu and Contich, crossing the little River Nethe at Waelhem. The Nethe encircles Antwerp on the south and south-east, and it was here that the Belgians, and in the end the British, made their chief stand against the Germans. We crossed the bridge, and passed on to Malines under the guns of Fort Waelhem, with the great fortress of Wavre St. Catharine standing away to the left, impregnable to anything but the huge guns of today.

Malines is a large town of 60,000 inhabitants, and is the cathedral city of the Archbishop of Belgium, the brave Cardinal Mercier. Today it is important as a railway centre, and for its extensive railway workshops, but the interest of the town lies in the past. It was of importance as early as the eighth century, and since then it has changed hands on an amazing number of occasions. Yet it is said that few of the cities of Europe contain so many fine old houses in such good preservation. The cathedral church of St. Rombold dates back to the thirteenth century, and in the fifteenth century was begun the huge tower which can be seen for many miles around. It was intended that it should be 550 feet high—the highest in the world—and though it has reached little more than half that height, it is a very conspicuous landmark.

The Germans evidently found it a very tempting mark, for they began shelling it at an early stage. When we were there the tower had not been damaged, but a large hole in the roof of the church showed where a shell had entered. Inside everything was in chaos. Every window was broken, and of the fine stained glass hardly a fragment was left. A large portion of the roof was destroyed, and the floor was a confusion of chairs and debris. The wonderful carved wooden pulpit, with its almost life-size figures, was damaged. When the shell entered, the preacher's notes from the previous Sunday lay on the desk, and they were perforated by a fragment.

The *Croix Rouge* was established in a large school on the south side of the town. We drove into the large courtyard, and went in to see if there was anything for us to do. The doctor in charge, a distinguished oculist, was an old friend and was very cordial, but he said there was no fighting near, and that no cases had come in. We stood talking for a few minutes, and were just going, when one of our other cars came in with a man very badly wounded. He was a cyclist scout, and had been shot while crossing a field a few miles away. He had been picked up at considerable risk by our people:—for the Germans rarely respected a Red Cross—and brought in on the ambulance. He was wounded in the abdomen, and his right arm was shattered. He was in a desperate state, but the doctor begged me to do what I could for him, and, indeed, the power of recovery of these fellows was so remarkable that it was always worth a trial.

As rapidly as possible we got ready stimulants and hot saline solution to inject into his veins. We had not come prepared for actual operating, and the local equipment was meagre, but we succeeded in improvising a transfusion apparatus out of various odds and ends. It did not take long to get it to work, and in a few minutes he began to respond to the hot salt and water running into his vessels. Alas it was only for a moment. He was bleeding internally, and nothing could be done. I went over to the priest, who had just come, and said: "*C'est à vous, monsieur.*" He bowed, and came forward holding in his hands the holy oil. A few murmured words were spoken, the priest's finger traced the sign of the Cross, a few moments of silence, and all was over. Death is always impressive, but I shall never forget that scene. The large schoolroom, with its improvised equipment, ourselves, a crowd of nurses and doctors standing round, in the centre the sandalled priest bending downwards in his brown mantle, and the dying man, his lips moving to frame the last words he would speak on earth. It was in silence that we stole out into the sunlight of the courtyard.

We went on to Sempst, a small village at the extreme limit of the Belgian lines. A little stream ran under the road beside a farm, and a rough breastwork had been thrown across the road to defend the bridge. German soldiers could be seen a mile down the road moving behind the trees. It was only a small Belgian outpost, but it was a good enough position to hold, so long as the enemy did not bring up artillery. A machine gun was hidden beside the bridge, and would have made short work of anyone advancing up the road. My friends were talking to the men, whom we knew quite well; and for a moment I was standing alone, when one of the soldiers came up and asked about the man whom we had just left, and who had come from near by. I told him what had happened, and for a moment he did not speak. At last he looked up at me with tears in his eyes, and said simply: "He was my brother, and this morning we were laughing together." I held his hand for a moment, and then he turned away and went back to his post.

Our way home led past a villa where an encounter had taken place three days before between the Belgians and an advanced detachment of German troops, and we stopped to see the scene of the fighting. It was a large country-house standing back in its own grounds, and during the night a party of Germans had succeeded in concealing themselves inside. In the morning, by a ruse, they induced a Belgian detachment to come up the drive towards the house, never suspecting that it was not empty. Suddenly the Germans opened fire, and I believe that scarcely a single Belgian escaped. Next day, however, having surrounded the villa, the Belgians opened fire upon it with their 3-inch guns. The Germans made a bolt for it, and the whole of them were killed. As we walked up the drive we saw on the left-hand side a little row of graves with fresh flowers laid on them. They were the graves of the Belgian soldiers who had been entrapped. An officer was standing by them with bared head, and, seeing us, he came over and walked on with us to the house, which he was then occupying with his soldiers.

It was a fine house, with polished parquet floors and wide staircases. The dining-room was ornamented with delicate frescoes in gilt frames. In the drawing-room stood a new grand pianoforte, and light gilt chairs and sofas, looking strangely out of place on the field of war. By the front-door, sticking in the wall, was a shell which had failed to burst. I wonder if it is still there, or if anyone has ventured to shift it. It was half inside and half outside, and if it had exploded there would not have been much of the entrance of the house left. Upstairs the rooms were in glorious confusion. Apparently the Germans had opened all the drawers, and flung their contents on the floor, with the idea, I suppose, of taking anything they wanted. One room was plainly the nursery, for the floor was covered with children's toys of all descriptions, all broken. It may be very unreasonable, but that room made me more angry than all the rest of the house. There is something so utterly wanton in trampling on a child's toys. They may be of no value, but I have a small opinion of a man who does not treat them with respect. They are the symbols of an innocence that once was ours, the tokens of a contact with the unseen world for which we in our blindness grope longingly in vain.

CHAPTER 8

Lierre

When, years hence, some historian looks back upon the present war, and from the confusion of its battles tries to frame before his mind a picture of the whole, one grim conclusion will be forced upon his mind. He will note, perhaps, vast alterations in the map of Europe; he will lament a loss of life such as only the hand of Heaven has dealt before; he will point to the folly of the wealth destroyed. But beneath all these he will hear one insistent note from which he cannot escape, the deep keynote of the whole, the note on which the war was based, the secret of its ghastly chords, and the foundation of its dark conclusion. And he will write that in the year 1914 one of the great nations of civilized Europe relapsed into barbarism.

In the large sense a nation becomes civilized as its members recognise the advantages of sinking their personal desires and gain in the general good of the State. The fact that an individual can read and write and play the piano has nothing at all to do with the degree of his civilization, an elementary axiom of which some of our rulers seem strangely ignorant. To be of use to the State, and to train others to be of use to the State (and not only of use to themselves), should be, and indeed is, the aim of every truly civilized man. Unless it be so, his civilization is a mere veneer, ready to wear off at the first rub, and he himself a parasite upon the civilized world.

As time has gone on, the State has laid down certain rules by means of which the men who formed it could serve it better, and these are our laws which we obey not for our own good directly, but for the good of the State. From the point of view of the plain man in the street, it is all utterly illogical, for it would be logical to go and take from your neighbour whatever you wished, so long as you were strong enough to hold it. But, let us thank Heaven, no sane man is logical, and only a professor would dare to make the claim. It is one of the prerogatives of his office, and should be treated with tolerance.

And as our views of life are small and limited by our surroundings, when States grew large they took from the shoulders of the individual his responsibilities in the great State which the world has now become; and the States of which the world was composed agreed together on certain rules which should control their relations to one another, not for the good of each, but for the good of the greater State of which they were members. They are not so accurately laid down as the laws of our separate States, but they are broad, general principles for the use of statesmen and not of legalists. They are the Charter of Civilization among the nations of the world, and the nation which disregards them does so at her peril, and has handed in the abnegation of her position as a civilized State. Like the laws of each State, they are utterly illogical—at least, to those who have made up their minds that they are strong enough to hold what they can take from their neighbours.

I am often told, in half-defence of what they have done, that the Germans are conducting the war in a strictly logical manner. At first, I must admit, I was rather taken with the idea, and, indeed, one felt almost sorry for a noble nation sacrificing its feelings on the uncompromising altar of Logic. For the object of war is obviously to defeat your enemy, and it may be argued that anything which will accelerate that result is not only justifiable, but almost humane, for it will shorten the unavoidable horrors of war. I should like to mention a few of the features of logical warfare, all of which have at one time or another been adopted by our opponents, and I shall then describe as far as I can an example which I myself saw.

When an army wishes to pass through a country, the civil population is in the way. To get rid of them, the best plan, and the quickest, is to annihilate the first town of a suitable size to which the army comes. If the town is wiped out, and men, women, and children slaughtered indiscriminately, it will make such an impression in the rest of the country that the whole population will clear out and there will be no further trouble. The country will then be free for the passage of troops, and there will be no troublesome civil population to feed or govern. The conduct of the war will be greatly facilitated. Of course, it will be necessary at intervals to repeat the process, but this presents the further advantage that it advertises to other nations what they may expect if war enters their borders.

This, one of the most elementary rules of logical warfare, has been strictly observed by Germany. The sack of Louvain and the slaughter of its inhabitants met with an immediate success. Wherever the German Army arrived, they entered with few exceptions empty towns. Termonde, Malines, Antwerp, had everything swept and garnished for their reception. It would, of course, be absurdly illogical to confine one's attack to persons capable of defence. To kill a hundred women and children makes far more impression than to kill a thousand men, and it is far safer, unless, of course, it is preferred to use them as a screen to protect your own advancing troops from the enemy's fire.

It is a mistake to burden your transport with the enemy's wounded, or, indeed—low be it spoken—with your own. The former should always be killed, and the latter so far as the degree of culture of your country will allow. It is one of the regrettable points, logically, of Germany's warfare that she appears to pay some attention to her wounded, but our information on this point is deficient, and it is possible that she limits it to those who may again be useful.

To kill the medical staff of the enemy is obviously most desirable. Without them a large number of the wounded would die. If, therefore, it is possible to kill both the doctors and the wounded together, it is a great advantage, and of all possible objectives for artillery a hospital is the most valuable. So complete was our confidence in the German observance of this rule that when we heard that they were likely to bombard Antwerp, we were strongly advised to remove our Red Cross from the sight of prying aeroplanes, and we took the advice. Several other hospitals were hit, but we escaped.

There are many other rules of logical warfare, such as ignoring treaties, engagements, and, indeed, the truth in any form. But these are those with which I myself came in contact, and which therefore interested me the most. There is only one unfortunate objection to logical warfare, and that is that it is the duty of the whole civilized world, as it values its eternal salvation, to blot out from the face of the earth they have defiled the nation which practises it.

I do not wish to be unfair to those with whom we are fighting, or to arouse against them an unjust resentment. I am merely attempting to express succinctly the doctrines which have been proclaimed throughout Germany for years, of which this war is the logical outcome, and in the light of which alone its incidents can be understood. She is the home of logic, the temple where material progress is worshipped as a god. For her there is no meaning in those dim yearnings of the human mind, in which logic has no part, since their foundations are hidden in depths beneath our ken, but which alone separate us from the beasts that perish. And, above all things, I would not be thought to include in such a sweeping statement all those who call themselves German. There are many in Germany who are not of this Germany, and in the end it may be for them as much as for ourselves that we shall have fought this war.

It is only when viewed in this setting that a scene such as that we saw at Lierre can be understood. By itself it would stand naked, meaningless, and merely horrible. Clothed in these thoughts, it is pregnant with meaning, and forms a real epitome of the whole German conception of war; for horror is their dearest ally, and that scene has left on my mind a feeling of horror which I do not think that time will ever eradicate.

Lierre is an old-world town on the River Nethe, nine miles south of Antwerp, prosperous, and thoroughly Flemish. Its 20,000 inhabitants weave silk and brew beer, as they did when London was a village. Without the physical advantages of Antwerp, and without the turbulence of Ghent, Lierre has escaped their strange vicissitudes, and for hundreds of years has enjoyed the prosperity of a quiet and industrious town. Its church of St. Gommarius is renowned for its magnificent proportions, its superb window tracery, and its wonderful rood-loft—features in which it has eclipsed in glory even the great cathedrals of Belgium, and which place it alone as a unique achievement of the art of the fifteenth century. It is in no sense a military town, and has no defences, though there is a fort of the same name at no great distance from it.

Into this town, without warning of any kind, the Germans one morning dropped two of their largest shells. One fell near the church, but fortunately did no harm. One fell in the Hospital of St. Elizabeth. We heard in Antwerp that several people had been wounded, and in the afternoon two of us went out in one of our cars to see if we could be of any service. We found the town in the greatest excitement, and the streets crowded with families preparing to leave, for they rightly regarded these shells as the prelude of others. In the square was drawn up a large body of recruits just called up—rather late in the day, it seemed to us. We slowly made our way through the crowds, and, turning to the right along the Malines road, we drew up in front of the hospital on our right-hand side. The shell had fallen almost vertically on to a large wing, and as we walked across the garden we could see

Lierre

that all the windows had been broken, and that most of the roof had been blown off. The nuns met us, and took us down into the cellars to see the patients.

It was an infirmary, and crowded together in those cellars lay a strange medley of people. There were bedridden old women huddled up on mattresses, almost dead with terror. Wounded soldiers lay propped up against the walls; and women and little children, wounded in the fighting around, lay on straw and sacking. Apparently it is not enough to wound women and children; it is even necessary to destroy the harbour of refuge into which they have crept. The nuns were doing for them everything that was possible, under conditions of indescribable difficulty. They may not be trained nurses, but in the records of this war the names of the nuns of Belgium ought to be written in gold. Utterly careless of their own lives, absolutely without fear, they have cared for the sick, the wounded, and the dying, and they have faced any hardship and any danger rather than abandon those who turned to them for help.

The nuns led us upstairs to the wards where the shell had burst. The dead had been removed, but the scene that morning must have been horrible beyond description. In the upper ward six wounded soldiers had been killed, and in the lower two old women. As we stood in the upper ward, it was difficult to believe that so much damage could have been caused by a single shell. It had struck almost vertically on the tiled roof, and, exploding in the attic, had blown in the ceiling into the upper ward. I had not realised before the explosion of a large shell is not absolutely instantaneous, but, in consequence of the speed of the shell, is spread over a certain distance. Here the shell had continued to explode as it passed down through the building, blowing the floor of the upper ward down into the ward below.

A great oak beam, a foot square, was cut clean in two, the walls of both wards were pitted and pierced by fragments, and the tiled floor of the lower ward was broken up. The beds lay as they were when the dead were taken from them, the mattresses riddled with fragments and soaked with blood. Obviously no living thing could have survived in that awful hail. When the shell came the soldiers were eating walnuts, and on the bed of one lay a walnut half opened and the little penknife he was using, and both were stained. We turned away sickened at the sight, and retraced the passage with the nuns.

As we walked along, they pointed out to us marks we had not noticed before—red finger-marks and splashes of blood on the pale blue distemper of the wall. All down the passage and the staircase we could trace them, and even in the hall below. Four men had been standing in the doorway of the upper ward. Two were killed; the others, bleeding and blinded by the explosion, had groped their way along that wall and down the stair. I have seen many terrible sights, but for utter and concentrated horror I have never seen anything to equal those finger-marks, the very sign-manual of Death. When I think of them, I see, in the dim light of the early autumn morning, the four men talking; I hear the wild shriek of the shell and the deafening crash of its explosion; and then silence, and two bleeding men groping in darkness and terror for the air.

Chapter 9

A Pause

The life of a hospital at the front is a curious mixture of excitement and dullness. One week cases will be pouring in, the operating theatre will be working day and night, and everyone will have to do their utmost to keep abreast of the rush; next week there will be nothing to do, and everyone will mope about the building, and wonder why they were ever so foolish as to embark on such a futile undertaking. For it is all emergency work, and there is none of the dull routine of the ordinary hospital waiting list, which we are always trying to clear off, but which is in reality the backbone of the hospital's work.

When we first started in Antwerp, the rush of cases was so great as to be positively overwhelming. For more than twenty-four hours the surgeons in the theatre were doing double work, two tables being kept going at the same time. During that time a hundred and fifty wounded were admitted, all of them serious cases, and the hospital was full to overflowing. For the next ten days we were kept busy, but then our patients began to recover, and many of them had to go away to military convalescent hospitals. The wards began to look deserted, and yet no more patients arrived. We began to think that it was all a mistake that we had come, that there would be no more fighting round Antwerp, and that we were not wanted. Indeed, we canvassed the possibilities of work in other directions, and in the meantime we drew up elaborate arrangements to occupy our time. There were to be courses of lectures and demonstrations in the wards, and supplies of books and papers were to be obtained. Alas for the vanity of human schemes, the wounded began to pour in again, and not a lecture was given.

During that slack week we took the opportunity to see a certain amount of Antwerp, and to call on many officials and the many friends who did so much to make our work there a success and our stay a pleasure. To one lady we can never be sufficiently grateful. She placed at our disposal her magnificent house, a perfect palace in the finest quarter of the city. Several of our nurses lived there, we had a standing invitation to dinner, and, what we valued still more, there were five bathrooms ready for our use at any hour of the day. Their drawing-room had been converted into a ward for wounded officers, and held about twenty beds. One of the daughters had trained as a nurse, and under her charge it was being run in thoroughly up-to-date style. The superb tapestries with which the walls were decorated had been covered with linen, and but for the gilded panelling it might have been a ward in a particularly finished hospital. I often wonder what has happened to that house. The family had to fly to England, and unless it was destroyed by the shells, it is occupied by the Germans.

Calling in Antwerp on our professional brethren was very delightful for one's mind, but not a little trying for one's body. Their ideas of entertainment were so lavish, and it was so difficult to refuse their generosity, that it was a decided mistake to attempt two calls in the same afternoon. To be greeted at one house with claret of a rare vintage, and at the next with sweet champagne, especially when it is plain that your host will be deeply pained if a drop is left, is rather trying to a tea-drinking Briton. They were very good to us, and we owed a great deal to their help. Most of all we owed to Dr. Morlet, for he had taken radiographs of all our fractures, and of many others of our cases. We went to see him one Sunday afternoon at his beautiful house in the Avenue Plantin. He also had partly converted his house into a hospital for the wounded, and we saw twenty or thirty of them in a large drawing-room. The rest of the house was given up to the most magnificent electro-therapeutical equipment I have ever seen or heard of.

We wandered through room after room filled with superb apparatus for X-ray examinations, X-ray treatment, diathermy, and electrical treatment of every known kind. It was not merely that apparatus for all these methods was there. Whole rooms full of apparatus were given up to each subject. It was the home of a genius and an enthusiast, who thought no sum too great if it were to advance his science. Little did we think that ten days later we should pick its owner up upon the road from Antwerp, a homeless wanderer, struggling along with his wife and his family, leaving behind everything he possessed in the world, in the hope that he might save them from the Germans. We heard from him not long ago that they had carried off to Germany all the wonderful machinery on which he had spent his life.

The very next morning, while we were still at breakfast, the wounded began to arrive, and we never had another day in Antwerp that was not crowded with incident. The wounded almost always came in large batches, and the reason of this was the method of distribution adopted by the authorities. All the injured out at the front were collected as far as possible to one centre, where a train was waiting to receive them. There they remained until the train was sufficiently filled, when it brought them into the Central Station of Antwerp. At this point was established the distributing station, with a staff of medical officers, who arranged the destination of each man. Antwerp has a very complete system of electric trams, scarcely a street being without one, and of these full use was made for the transport of the wounded. Those who could sit went in ordinary cars, but for the stretcher cases there were cars specially fitted to take ordinary stretchers. A car was filled up with cases for one hospital, and in most cases it could deposit them at the door.

It was an admirable method of dealing with them, simple and expeditious, and it involved far less pain and injury to the men than a long journey on an ambulance. In fact, we were only allowed in exceptional circumstances to bring in wounded on our cars, and it is obvious that it was a wise plan, for endless confusion would have been the result if anyone could have picked up the wounded and carried them off where they liked. Our cars were limited for the most part to carrying the injured to the various dressing- stations and to the train, and for these purposes they were always welcomed. They were soon well known at the trenches, and wherever the fighting was heaviest you might be sure to find one of them. Many were the hairbreadth escapes of which they had to tell, for if there were wounded they brought them out of danger, shells or no shells. And it says as much for the coolness of the drivers as for their good luck that no one was ever injured; for danger is halved by cool judgment, and a bold driver will come safely through where timidity would fail.

CHAPTER 10

The Siege

It is difficult to say exactly when the Siege of Antwerp began. For weeks we heard the distant boom of the guns steadily drawing nearer day by day, and all night the sky was lit up by distant flashes. But so peculiar was the position of Antwerp that it was not till the last ten days that our life was seriously affected, and not till the very end that communication with our friends and the getting of supplies became difficult. Our first real domestic tragedy was the destruction of the waterworks on the 30th of September. They lay just behind Waelhem, some six miles south of Antwerp, and into them the Germans poured from the other side of Malines a stream of 28-centimetre shells, with the result that the great reservoir burst. Until one has had to do without a water-supply in a large city it is impossible to realise to what a degree we are dependent upon it. In Antwerp, fortunately, a water-supply has been regarded as somewhat of an innovation, and almost every house, in the better class quarters at least, has its own wells and pumps.

It was, however, the end of the summer, and the wells were low; our own pumps would give us barely enough water for drinking purposes. The authorities did all they could, and pumped up water from the Scheldt for a few hours each day, enabling us, with considerable difficulty, to keep the drainage system clear. But this water was tidal and brackish, whilst as to the number of bacteria it contained it was better not to inquire. We boiled and drank it when we could get nothing else, but of all the nauseous draughts I have ever consumed, not excluding certain hospital mixtures of high repute, tea made with really salt water is the worst. Coffee was a little better, though not much, and upon that we chiefly relied. But I really think that that was one of the most unpleasant of our experiences. A more serious matter from the point of view of our work was the absence of water in the operating theatre. We stored it as well as we could in jugs, but in a rush that was inadequate, and we began to realise what the difficulties were with which surgeons had to contend in South Africa.

We were really driven out of Antwerp at a very fortunate moment, and I have often wondered what we should have done if we had stopped there for another week. Such a very large proportion of the inhabitants of Antwerp had already disappeared that there was never any great shortage of supplies. Milk and butter were the first things to go, and fresh vegetables followed soon after. It was always a mystery to me that with the country in such a condition they went on for as long as they did. The peasants must have worked their farms until they were absolutely driven out, and indeed in our expeditions into the country we often saw fields being ploughed and cattle being fed when shells were falling only a few fields away. However, margarine and condensed milk are not bad substitutes for the real articles, and the supply of bread held out to the very end.

A greater difficulty was with our kitchen staff of Belgian women, for a good many of them took fright and left us, and it was not at all easy to get their places filled. As the week went on the pressure of the enemy became steadily greater. On Tuesday, the 29th of September, the great fortress of Wavre St. Catherine fell, blown up, it is believed, by the accidental explosion of a shell inside the galleries. It had been seriously battered by the big German howitzers, and it could not in any case have held out for another day. But the results of the explosion were terrible. Many of the wounded came to us, and they were the worst cases we had so far seen.

On Thursday Fort Waelhem succumbed after a magnificent resistance. The garrison held it until it was a mere heap of ruins, and, indeed, they had the greatest difficulty in making their way out. I think that there is very little doubt that the Germans were using against these forts their largest guns, the great 42-centimetre howitzers. It is known that two of these were brought northwards past Brussels after the fall of Maubeuge, and a fragment which was given to us was almost conclusive. It was brought to us one morning as an offering by a grateful patient, and it came from the neighbourhood of Fort Waelhem. It was a mass of polished steel two feet long, a foot wide, and three inches thick, and it weighed about fifty pounds. It was very irregular in shape, with edges sharp as razors, without a particle of rust upon it. It had been picked up where it fell still hot, and it was by far the finest fragment of shell I have ever seen. Alas we had to leave it behind, and it lies buried in a back-garden beside our hospital. Some day it will be dug up, and will be exhibited as conclusive evidence that the Germans did use their big guns in shelling the town.

The destruction produced by such a shell is almost past belief. I have seen a large house struck by a single shell of a much smaller size than this, and it simply crumpled up like a pack of cards. As a house it disappeared, and all that was left was a heap of bricks and mortar. When one considers that these guns have a range of some ten miles, giving Mont Blanc considerable clearance on the way, and that one of them out at Harrow could drop shells neatly into Charing Cross, some idea of their power can be obtained.

Every day we had visits from the enemy's aeroplanes, dropping bombs or literature, or merely giving the range of hospitals and other suitable objectives to the German gunners. From the roof of the hospital one could get a magnificent view of their evolutions, and a few kindred spirits always made a rush for a door on to the roof, the secret of which was carefully preserved, as the accommodation was limited. It was a very pretty sight to watch the Taube soaring overhead, followed by the puffs of smoke from the explosion of shells fired from the forts. The puffs would come nearer and nearer as the gunners found the range, until one felt that the next must bring the Taube down. Then suddenly the airman would turn his machine off in another direction, and the shells would fall wider than ever. One's feelings were torn between admiration for the airman's daring and an unholy desire to see him fall.

It was evident that Antwerp could not withstand much longer the pressure of the enemy's guns, and we were not surprised when on Friday we received an official notice from the British Consul-General, Sir Cecil Herstlet, that the government were about to leave for Ostend, and advising all British subjects to leave by a boat which had been provided for them on Saturday. On Saturday morning came an order from the Belgian Army Medical Service instructing us to place on tramcars all our wounded, and to send them to the railway station. It appeared evident that Antwerp was to be evacuated, and we took the order to clear out our wounded as an intimation that our services would be no longer required. We got all our men ready for transport, and proceeded to pack up the hospital. The tramcars arrived, and we bade goodbye to our patients, and saw them off, some in ordinary trams and some in specially equipped stretcher-cars. It was a dismal scene.

The hall of the hospital was still covered with stretchers on which lay patients waiting their turn for the cars to take them, and the whole hospital was in process of being dismantled, when tramcars began to arrive back from the station with the patients we had just packed off. They told us that the whole of Antwerp was covered with tramloads of wounded soldiers, that there were five thousand in the square in front of the railway station, and that two trains had been provided to take them away! It was evident that some extraordinary blunder had been made; and while we were in doubt as to what to do, a second order came to us cancelling entirely the evacuation order which we and all the other hospitals in Antwerp had received a few hours before. It was all so perplexing that we felt that the only satisfactory plan was to go round to the British Consul and find out what it all meant. We came back with the great news that British Marines were coming to hold Antwerp. That was good enough for us. In less than an hour the hospital was in working order again, and the patients were back in their beds, and a more jubilant set of patients I have never seen. It was the most joyful day in the history of the hospital, and if we had had a case of champagne, it should have been opened. As it was, we had to be content with salt coffee.

But there was one dreadful tragedy. Some of our patients had not returned. In the confusion at the station one tramcar loaded with our patients had been sent off to another hospital by mistake. And the worst of it was that some of these were our favourite patients. There was nothing for it but to start next morning and make a tour of the hospitals in search of them. We were not long in finding them, for most of them were in a large hospital close by. I do not think we shall ever forget the reception we got when we found them. They had left us on stretchers, but they tried to get out of bed to come away with us, and one of them was a septic fractured thigh with a hole in his leg into which you could put your fist, and another had recently had a serious abdominal operation.

They seized our hands and would scarcely let us go until we had promised that as soon as we had arranged with the authorities they should come back to our hospital. It was managed after a little diplomacy, and they all came back next day, and we were again a united family.

Chapter 11

Contich

Sunday, the 4th of October, dawned with an extraordinary feeling of relief and expectancy in the air. The invincible British had arrived, huge guns were on their way, a vast body of French and British troops was advancing by forced marches, and would attack our besiegers in the rear, and beyond all possibility of doubt crush them utterly. But perhaps the most convincing proof of all was the round head of the First Lord of the Admiralty calmly having his lunch in the Hôtel St. Antoine. Surely nothing can inspire such confidence as the sight of an Englishman eating. It is one of the most substantial phenomena in nature, and certainly on this occasion I found the sight more convincing than a political speech. Obviously we were saved, and one felt a momentary pang of pity for the misguided Germans who had taken on such an impossible task. The sight of British troops in the streets and of three armoured cars carrying machine guns settled the question, and we went home to spread the good news and to follow the noble example of the First Lord.

In the afternoon three of us went off in one of the motors for a short run, partly to see if we could be of any use at the front with the wounded, and partly to see, if possible, the British troops. We took a stretcher with us, in case there should be any wounded to bring in from outlying posts. Everywhere we found signs of the confidence which the British had brought. It was visible in the face of every Belgian soldier, and even the children cheered our khaki uniforms as we passed. Everywhere there were signs of a new activity and of a new hope. The trenches and wire entanglements around the town, already very extensive, were being perfected, and to our eyes they looked impregnable. We did not then realise how useless it is to attempt to defend a town, and, unfortunately, our ignorance was not limited to civilians. It is a curious freak of modern war that a ploughed field should be stronger than any citadel. But, as I say, these things were hidden from us, and our allies gave the finishing touches to their trenches, to the high entertainment of the Angels, as Stevenson would have told us. If only those miles of trench and acres of barbed wire had been placed ten miles away, and backed by British guns, the story of Antwerp might have been a very different one.

The road to Boom is like all the main roads of Belgium. The central causeway was becoming worn by the constant passage of heavy motor lorries tearing backwards and forwards at racing speed. The sides were deep in dust, for there had been little rain. On each side rose poplars in ordered succession, and the long, straight stretches of the road were framed in the endless vista of their tall trunks. And in that frame moved a picture too utterly piteous for any words to describe—a whole country fleeing before the Huns. The huge unwieldy carts of the Belgian farmer crept slowly along, drawn by great Flemish horses. In front walked the men, plodding along beside the splendid animals, with whose help they had ploughed their fields—fields they would never see again. In the carts was piled up all that they possessed in the world, all that they could carry of their homes wrecked and blasted by the Vandals, a tawdry ornament or a child's toy looking out pitifully from the heap of clothes and bedding. And seated on the top of the heap were the woman and the children.

But these were the well-to-do. There were other little groups who had no cart and no horse. The father and a son would walk in front carrying all that a man could lift on their strong backs; then came the children, boys and girls, each with a little white bundle over their shoulder done up in a towel or a pillowslip, tiny mites of four or five doing all they could to save the home; and last came the mother with a baby at her breast, trudging wearily through the dust. They came in an endless stream, over and over again, for mile after mile, always in the same pathetic little groups, going away, only going away.

At last, with a sigh of relief, we reached Boom, and the end of the lines of refugees, for the Germans themselves were not far beyond. At the *Croix Rouge* we asked for instructions as to where we were likely to be useful. Boom had been shelled in the morning, but it was now quiet, and there was no fighting in the neighbourhood. We could hear the roar of guns in the distance on the east, and we were told that severe fighting was in progress in that direction. The British had reinforced the Belgian troops in the trenches at Duffel, and the

HOMELESS

Germans were attacking the position in force. Taking the road to the left, we passed the great brick-fields which provide one of the chief industries of Boom, and we drove through the poorer portion of the town which lies amongst them. It was utterly deserted. It was in this part of the town that the shelling had been most severe, but a large number of the shells must have fallen harmlessly in the brickfields, as only a house here and there was damaged.

If, however, the object of the Germans was to clear the town of inhabitants, they had certainly succeeded, for there was not a man, woman, or child to be seen anywhere. It is a strange and uncanny thing to drive through a deserted town. Only a few days before we had driven the same way, and we had to go quite slowly to avoid the crowd in the streets. This time we crept along slowly, but for a very different reason. We distrusted those empty houses. We never knew what might be hiding round the next corner, but we did know that a false turning would take us straight into the German lines. It was the only way by which we could reach our destination, but we were beyond the main Belgian lines, and our road was only held by a few isolated outposts. After a mile or so we came upon a small outpost, and they told us that we should be safe as far as Rumps, about three miles farther, where their main outpost was placed. An occasional shell sailed over our heads to reassure us, some from our own batteries, and some from the enemy's. We only hoped that neither side would fire short.

At Rumps we found the headquarters of the regiment, and several hundred troops. At the sight of our khaki uniforms they at once raised a cheer, and we had quite an ovation as we passed down the street. At the *Etat Majeur* the colonel himself came out to see us, and his officers crowded round as he asked us anxiously about the British arrivals. He pulled out his orders for the day, and told us the general disposition of the British and Belgian troops. He told us that the road to Duffel was too dangerous, and that we must turn northwards to Contich, but that there might be some wounded in the *Croix Rouge* station there. He and his men were typical of the Belgian Army—brave, simple men, defending their country as best they could, without fuss or show. I hope they have come to no harm. If only that army had been trained and equipped like ours, the Germans would have had a hard struggle to get through Belgium.

We turned away from the German lines northwards towards Contich. Our road lay across the open country, between the farms which mean so much of Belgium's wealth. In one field a man was ploughing with three big horses. He was too old to fight, but he could do this much for his country. Surely that man deserves a place in his country's Roll of Honour. Shells were falling not four fields away, but he never even looked up. It must take more nerve to plough a straight furrow when the shells are falling than to aim a gun. I like to think of that man, and I hope that he will be left to reap his harvest in peace.

A little farther on we came upon the objective of the German shells—a battery so skilfully concealed that it was only when we were close to it that we realised where it was. The ammunition-carts were drawn up in a long line behind a hedge, while the guns themselves were buried in piles of brushwood. They must have been invisible from the captive balloon which hung over the German lines in the distance. They were not firing when we passed, and we were not sorry, as we had no desire to be there when the replies came. An occasional shell gives a certain spice to the situation, but in quantity they are better avoided.

As we approached Contich a soldier came running up and told us that two people had just been injured by a shell, and begged us to come to see them. He stood on the step of the car, and directed us to a little row of cottages half a mile farther on. At the roadside was a large hole in the ground where a shell had fallen some minutes before, and beside it an unfortunate cow with its hind-quarters shattered. In the garden of the first cottage a poor woman lay on her back. She was dead, and her worn hands were already cold. As I rose from my knees a young soldier flung himself down beside her, sobbing as though his heart would break. She was his mother.

Behind the cottage we found a soldier with his left leg torn to fragments. He had lost a great deal of blood, and he was still bleeding from a large artery, in spite of the efforts of a number of soldiers round who were applying tourniquets without much success. The ordinary tourniquet is probably the most inefficient instrument that the mind of man could devise—at least, for dealing with wounds of the thigh out in the field. It might stop haemorrhage in an infant, but for a burly soldier it is absurd. I tried two of the most approved patterns, and both broke in my hands. In the end I managed to stop it with a handkerchief and a stick. I would suggest the elimination of all tourniquets, and the substitution of the humble pocket-handkerchief. It, at least, does not pretend to be what it is not. Between shock and loss of blood our soldier was pretty bad, and we did not lose much time in transferring him to our car on a stretcher. The *Croix Rouge* dressing-station was more than a mile farther on, established in a large villa in its own grounds. We carried our man in, and laid him on a table with the object of dressing his leg properly, and of getting the man himself into such condition as would enable him to stand the journey back to Antwerp.

Alas! the dressing-station was destitute of any of the most elementary appliances for the treatment of a seriously wounded man. There was not even a fire, and the room was icy cold. There was no hot water, no brandy, no morphia, no splints, and only a minute quantity of dressing material. A cupboard with some prehistoric instruments in it was the only evidence of surgery that we could find. The Belgian doctor in charge was doing the best he could, but what he could be expected to do in such surroundings I do not know. He seemed greatly relieved to hear that I was a surgeon, and he was most kind in trying to find me everything for which I asked. From somewhere we managed to raise some brandy and hot water, and a couple of blankets, and with the dressings we had brought with us we made the best of a bad job, and started for home with our patient. Antwerp was eight miles away. It was a bitterly cold evening, and darkness was coming on. It seemed improbable that we could get our patient home alive, but it was perfectly certain that he would die if we left him where he was.

It seemed such a pity that a little more forethought and common sense could not have been expended on that dressing-station, and yet we found that with rare exceptions this was the regular state of affairs, whether in. Belgium or France. It seems to be impossible for our professional brethren on the Continent to imagine any treatment apart from a completely equipped hospital. Their one idea seems to be to get the wounded back to a base hospital, and if they die on the way it cannot be helped. The dressing-stations are mere offices for their redirection, where they are carefully ticketed, but where little else is done. Of course, it is true that the combatant forces are the first consideration, and that from their point of view the wounded are simply in the way, and the sooner they are carried beyond the region of the fighting the better; but if this argument were carried to its logical conclusion, there should be no medical services at the front at all, except what might be absolutely necessary for the actual transport of the wounded.

I am glad to say that our later experiences showed that the British influence was beginning to make itself felt, and that the idea of the wounded as a mere useless encumbrance was being modified by more humanitarian considerations. And in a long war it must be obvious to the most hardened militarist that by the early treatment of a wound many of its more severe consequences may be averted, and that many a man may thus be saved for further service. In a war of exhaustion, the ultimate result might well depend on how the wounded were treated in the field.

The road was crowded with traffic, and it was quite dark before we reached Antwerp. Our patient did not seem much the worse for his journey, though that is perhaps faint praise. We soon had him in our theatre, which was always warm and ready for cases such as this. With energetic treatment his condition rapidly improved, and when we left him to go to dinner we felt that our afternoon had not been entirely wasted.

CHAPTER 12

The Bombardment—Night

We had had plenty of notice that we might expect a bombardment. On Saturday a boat had left with most of the English Colony. On Tuesday morning the Germans sent in official notice that they intended to bombard the city, and in the evening the Government and the Legations left by boat with the remainder of our countrymen who lived in Antwerp. We had faced the prospect and made every preparation for it, and yet when it did come it came upon us as a surprise. It is sometimes fortunate that our capacities for anticipation are so limited.

It was almost midnight on Wednesday, the 7th of October, and two of us were sitting in the office writing despatches home. The whole building was in absolute silence, and lit only by the subdued light of an occasional candle. In the distance we could hear the dull booming of the guns. Suddenly above our heads sounded a soft whistle, which was not the wind, followed by a dull thud in the distance. We looked at one another.

Again it came, this time a little louder. We ran up to the roof and stood there for some moments, fascinated by the scene. From the dull grey sky came just sufficient light to show the city laying in darkness around us, its tall spires outlined as dim shadows against the clouds. Not a sound arose from streets and houses around, but every few seconds there came from the south-east a distant boom, followed by the whistle of a shell overhead and the dull thud of its explosion. The whole scene was eerie and uncanny in the extreme. The whistle changed to a shriek and the dull thud to a crash close at hand, followed by the clatter of falling bricks cutting sharply into the stillness of the night. Plainly this was going to be a serious business, and we must take instant measures for the safety of our patients. At any moment a shell might enter one of the wards, and—well, we had seen the hospital at Lierre. We ran downstairs and told the night nurses to get the patients ready for removal, whilst we went across to the gymnasium to arouse those of the staff who slept there. We collected all our stretchers, and began the methodical removal of all our patients to the basement.

In a few minutes there was a clang at the front-door bell, and our nurses and assistants who lived outside began to arrive. Two of the dressers had to come half a mile along the Malines road, where the shells were falling thickest, and every few yards they had had to shelter in doorways from the flying shrapnel. The bombardment had begun in earnest now, and shells were fairly pouring over our heads. We started with the top floor, helping down those patients who could walk, and carrying the rest on stretchers. When that was cleared we took the second, and I think we all breathed a sigh of relief when we heard that the top floor was empty. We were fortunate in having a basement large enough to accommodate all our patients, and wide staircases down which the stretchers could be carried without difficulty; but the patients were all full-grown men, and as most of them had to be carried it was hard work.

I shall never forget the scene on the great staircase, crowded with a long train of nurses, doctors, and dressers carrying the wounded down as gently and as carefully as if they were in a London hospital. I saw no sign of fear in any face, only smiles and laughter. And yet overhead was a large glass roof, and there was no one there who did not realise that a shell might come through that roof at any moment, and that it would not leave a single living person beneath it. It made one proud to have English blood running in one's veins. We had 113 wounded, and within an hour they were all in places of safety; mattresses and blankets were brought, and they were all made as comfortable as possible for the night. Four were grave intestinal cases. Seven had terrible fractures of the thigh, but fortunately five of these had been already repaired with steel plates, and their transport was easy; in fact, I met one of them on the staircase, walking with the support of a dresser's arm, a week after the operation!

Some of the patients must have suffered excruciating pain in being moved, but one never heard a murmur, and if a groan could not be kept back, it was passed over with a jest for fear we should notice it. It was a magnificent basement, with heavy arched roofs everywhere, and practically shell-proof. The long passages and the large kitchens were all tiled and painted white, and as the electric light was still running and the whole building was well warmed, it would have been difficult to find a more cheerful and comfortable place. Coffee was provided for everyone, and when I took a last look round the night nurses were taking charge as if nothing had happened, and the whole place was in the regular routine of an ordinary everyday hospital.

Upstairs there was an improvised meal in progress in the office, and after our two hours' hard work we were glad of it. It is really wonderful how cheerful a thing a meal is in the middle of the night, with plenty of hot coffee and a borrowed cake. It is one of the compensations of our life in hospital, and even shells are powerless to disturb it. After that, as we knew we should have a heavy day before us, we all settled down in the safest corners we could find to get what rest we could. The staircase leading up to the entrance hall was probably the safest spot in the building, covered as it was by a heavy arch, and it was soon packed with people in attitudes more or less restful.

A ward with a comfortable bed seemed to me quite safe enough, and I spent the night with three equally hedonistic companions. At first we lay listening to the shells as they passed overhead, sometimes with the soft whistle of distance, and sometimes with the angry shriek of a shell passing near. Occasionally the shriek would drop to a low howl, the note of a steam siren as it stops, and then a deafening crash and the clatter of falling bricks and glass would warn us that we had only escaped by a few yards. But even listening to shells becomes monotonous, and my eyes gradually glued together, and I fell asleep.

When I awoke it was early morning, and daylight had just come. The shells were still arriving, but not so fast, and mostly at a much greater distance. But another sound came at intervals, and we had much discussion as to what it might mean. Every three and a half minutes exactly there came two distant booms, but louder than usual, and then two terrific shrieks one after the other, exactly like the tearing of a giant sheet of calico, reminding us strongly of the famous scene in *Peter Pan*. Away they went in the distance, and if we ever heard the explosion it was a long way off. They certainly sounded like shells fired over our heads from quite close, and at a very low elevation, and we soon evolved the comforting theory that they were from a pair of big British guns planted up the river, and firing over the town at the German trenches beyond. We even saw a British gunboat lying in the Scheldt, and unlimited reinforcements pouring up the river. Alas! it was only a couple of big German guns shelling the harbour and the arsenal; at least, that is the conclusion at which we have since arrived.

But for some hours those shells were a source of great satisfaction and comfort. One can lie in bed with great contentment, I find, when it is the other people who are being shelled.

Chapter 13

The Bombardment—Day

We were up early in the morning, and our first business was to go round to the British Headquarters to find out what they intended to do, and what they expected of us as a British base hospital. If they intended to stay, and wished us to do likewise, we were quite prepared to do so, but we did not feel equal to the responsibility of keeping more than a hundred wounded in a position so obviously perilous. From shrapnel they were fairly safe in the basement, but from large shells or from incendiary bombs there is no protection. It is not much use being in a cellar if the house is burnt down over your head. So two of us started off in our motor to get news.

The headquarters were in the Hôtel St. Antoine, at the corner of the Place Verte opposite to the cathedral, so we had to go right across the town. We went by the Rue d'Argile and the Rue Leopold, and we had a fair opportunity of estimating the results of the night's bombardment. In the streets through which we passed it was really astonishingly small. Cornices had been knocked off, and the fragments lay in the streets; a good many windows were broken, and in a few cases a shell had entered an attic and blown up the roof. Plainly only small shells had been used. We did not realise that many of the houses we passed were just beginning to get comfortably alight, and that there was no one to put out the fires that had only begun so far to smoulder. A few people were about, evidently on their way out of Antwerp, but the vast bulk of the population had already gone.

It is said that the population of half a million numbered by the evening only a few hundreds. We passed a small fox terrier lying on the pavement dead, and somehow it has remained in my mind as a most pathetic sight. He had evidently been killed by a piece of shrapnel, and it seemed very unfair. But probably his people had left him, and he was better out of it.

We turned into the *Marche aux Souliers*, and drew up at the Hôtel St. Antoine, and as we stepped down from the car a shell passed close to us with a shriek, and exploded with a terrific crash in the house opposite across the narrow street. We dived into the door of the hotel to escape the falling debris. So far the shells had been whistling comfortably over our heads, but it was evident that the Germans were aiming at the British Headquarters, and that we had put our heads into the thick of it, for it was now positively raining shells all round us. But we scarcely noticed them in our consternation at what we found, for the British Staff had disappeared. We wandered through the deserted rooms which had been so crowded a few days before, but there was not a soul to be seen. They had gone, and left no address.

At last an elderly man appeared, whom I took to be the proprietor, and all he could tell us was that there was no one but himself in the building. Of all the desolate spots in the world I think that an empty hotel is the most desolate, and when you have very fair reason to believe that a considerable number of guns are having a competition as to which can drop a shell into it first, it becomes positively depressing. We got into our car and drove down the Place de Meir to the Belgian *Croix Rouge*, where we hoped to get news of our countrymen, and there we were told that they had gone to the Belgian *Etat Majeur* nearby. We had a few minutes' conversation with the President of the *Croix Rouge*, a very good friend of ours, tall and of striking appearance, with a heavy grey moustache. We asked him what the *Croix Rouge* would do. "Ah," he said, "we will stay to the last!" At that very moment a shell exploded with a deafening crash just outside in the Place de Meir. I looked at the president, and he threw up his hands in despair and led the way out of the building. The Belgian Red Cross had finished its work.

At last at the *Etat Majeur* we found our headquarters, and I sincerely hope that wherever General Paris, Colonel Bridges, and Colonel Seely go, they will always find people as pleased to see them as we were. They very kindly told us something of the situation, and said that, though they had every intention of holding Antwerp, they advised us to clear out, and they placed at our disposal four motor omnibuses for the transport of the wounded. So off we drove back to the hospital to make arrangements for evacuating. It was a lively drive, for I suppose that the Germans had had breakfast and had got to work again; at any rate, shells were coming in pretty freely, and we were happier when we could run along under the lee of the houses. However, we got back to the hospital safely enough, and there we held a council of war.

It was in the office, of course—the most risky room we could have chosen, I suppose—but somehow that did not seem to occur to anyone. It is curious how soon one grows accustomed to shells. At that moment a barrel-organ would have caused us far more annoyance. We sat round the table and discussed the situation. It was by no means straightforward. In the first place several members of the community did not wish to leave at all; in the second, we could not leave any of our wounded behind unattended; and in the third, it seemed unlikely that we could get them all on to four buses. After a long discussion we decided to go again and see General Paris, to ask for absolute instructions as a hospital under his control, and if he told us to go, to get sufficient transport. And then arose a scene which will always live in my mind. We had impressed into consultation a retired officer of distinction to whose help we owed much, and now owe far more, and whom I shall call our friend.

Perhaps he wished to give us confidence—I have always suspected that he had an ulterior motive—but he concluded the discussion by saying that he felt hungry and would have something to eat before he started, and from his haversack he produced an enormous German sausage and a large loaf of bread, which he offered to us all round, and he said he would like a cup of tea! The shells could do what they liked outside, and if one of them was rude enough to intrude, it could not be helped. We must show them that we could pay no attention to anything so vulgar and noisy. At any rate, the effect on us was electrical. The contrast between the German shells and the German sausage was too much for us, and the meeting broke up in positive confusion. Alas that sausage, the unparalleled trophy of an incomparable moment, was left behind on the table, and I fear the Germans got it.

General Paris had been obliged to shift his headquarters to the Pilotage, on the docks and at the farthest end of the city from us. He was very considerate, and after some discussion said that we had better leave Antwerp, and sent Colonel Farquharson with us to get six buses. The Pilotage is at the extreme north end of the Avenue des Arts, which extends the whole length of Antwerp, and the buses were on the quay by the Arsenal at the extreme south end, so that we had to drive the whole length of this, the most magnificent street of Antwerp, and a distance of about three miles. It was an extraordinary drive. In the whole length of that avenue I do not think that we passed a single individual. It was utterly deserted.

All around were signs of the bombardment—tops of houses blown off, and scattered about the street, trees knocked down, holes in the roadway where shells had struck. On the left stood the great *Palais de Justice*, with most of its windows broken and part of the roof blown away, and just beyond this three houses in a row blazing from cellar to chimney, the front wall gone, and all that remained of the rooms exposed. As I said, only small shells had been used, and the damage was nothing at all to that which we afterwards saw at Ypres; but it gave one an impression of dreariness and utter desolation that could scarcely be surpassed. Think of driving from Hyde Park Corner down the Strand to the bank, not meeting a soul on the way, passing a few clubs in Piccadilly burning comfortably, the Cecil a blazing furnace, and the Law Courts lying in little bits about the street, and you will get some idea of what it looked like. The scream of the shells and the crash when they fell near by formed quite a suitable if somewhat Futurist accompaniment.

But the climax of the entertainment, the *bonne bouche* of the afternoon, was reserved for the end of our drive, when we reached the wharf by the Arsenal, where the British stores and transport were collected. Here was a long row of motor-buses, about sixty of them, all drawn up in line along the river. Beside them was a long row of heavily loaded ammunition lorries, and on the other side of the road was the Arsenal, on our left, blazing away, with a vast column of smoke towering up to the sky. "It may blow up any minute," said Colonel Farquharson cheerily, "I had better move that ammunition." I have never seen an arsenal blow up, and I imagine it is a phenomenon requiring distance to get it into proper perspective; but I have some recollection of an arsenal blowing up in Antwerp a few years ago and taking a considerable part of the town with it.

However, it was not our arsenal, so we waited and enjoyed the view till the ammunition had been moved, and the colonel had done his best to get us the motor-buses. He could only get us four, so we had to make the best of a bad job. But. meanwhile the Germans had evidently determined to give us a really good show while they were about it, for while we waited a Taube came overhead and hovered for a moment, apparently uncertain as to whether a bomb or a shell would look better just there. A flash of tinsel falling in the sunlight showed us that she had made up her mind and was giving the range.

ANTWERP—AFTER THE BOMBARDMENT

But we could not stay, and were a quarter of a mile away when we looked back and saw the first shells falling close to where we had been two minutes before. They had come six miles.

The bombardment was increasing in violence, and large numbers of incendiary shells were being used, whilst in addition the houses set on fire during the night were now beginning to blaze. As we drove back we passed several houses in flames, and the passage of the narrow streets we traversed was by no means free from risk. At last we turned into our own street, the Boulevard Leopold, and there we met a sight which our eyes could scarcely credit. Three motor-buses stood before our door and patients were being crowded into them. Those buses and our own lives we owe to the kindness of Major Gordon. Without them some at least must have remained behind. The three were already well filled, for our friends thought that we had certainly been killed and that they must act for themselves. We sent them off under the escort of one of our cars, as it seemed foolish to keep them waiting in a position of danger.

On our own four we packed all our remaining patients and all the hospital equipment we could remove. One does not waste time when one packs under shell fire, and at the end of three-quarters of an hour there was not a patient and very little of value in the hospital. I took charge of the theatre as I knew where the things went, and I think the British working man would have been rather astonished to see how fast the big sterilizers fell apart and the operating-tables slid into their cases. The windows faced shellwards, and I must confess that once or twice when one of them seemed to be coming unpleasantly near I took the opportunity to remove my parcels outside. How the patients were got ready and carried out and into the buses in that time is beyond my comprehension.

But somehow it was managed. I took a last look round and drove out the last nurse who was trying to rescue some last "hospital comfort" for a patient, and in the end I was myself driven out by two indignant dressers who caught me trying to save the instrument sterilizer. The buses were a wonderful sight. Inside were some sixty patients, our share of the whole hundred and thirteen, and on top about thirty of our staff, and the strangest collection of equipment imaginable. The largest steam sterilizer mounted guard in front, hoisted there by two sailormen of huge strength, who turned up from somewhere. Great bundles of blankets, crockery, and instruments were wedged in everywhere, with the luggage of the staff. At the door of each bus was seated a nurse, like a conductor, to give what little attention was possible to the patients. It was a marvellous sight, but no cheerier crowd of medical students ever left the doors of a hospital for a Cup-tie.

Chapter 14

The Night Journey

There was only one way out—by the bridge of boats across the Scheldt. It was a narrow plank road, and as vehicles had to go across in single file at some distance apart, the pressure can be imagined. For an hour and a half we stood in the densely packed Cathedral Square watching the hands of the great clock go round and wondering when a shell would drop among us. We had seen enough of churches to know what an irresistible attraction they have for German artillery, and we knew that, whatever may be the state of affairs in Scotland, here at any rate the nearer the church the nearer was heaven. But no shells fell near, we only heard them whistling overhead.

The scene around us was extraordinary, and indeed these were the remains of the entire population of Antwerp. The whole city had emptied itself either by this road or by the road northwards into Holland. Crowds of people of every class—the poor in their working-clothes, the well-to-do in their Sunday best—all carrying in bundles all they could carry away of their property, and wedged in amongst them every kind of vehicle imaginable, from a luxurious limousine to coster's carts and wheelbarrows. In front of us lay the Scheldt, and pouring down towards it was on the left an endless stream of fugitives, crossing by the ferry-boats, and on the right an interminable train of artillery and troops, crossing by the only bridge. At last there was a movement forwards; we crept down the slope and on to the bridge, and slowly moved over to the other side. Perhaps we should not have felt quite so happy about it had we known that two men had just been caught on the point of blowing up the boats in the centre, and that very shortly after the Germans were to get the range and drop a shell on to the bridge. At five o'clock we were across the bridge and on the road to Ghent.

Of all the pitiful sights I have ever seen, that road was the most utterly pitiful. We moved on slowly through a dense throng of fugitives—men, women, and little children—all with bundles over their shoulders, in which was all that they possessed. A woman with three babies clinging to her skirts, a small boy wheeling his grandmother in a wheelbarrow, family after family, all moving away from the horror that lay behind to the misery that lay in front. We had heard of Louvain, and we had seen Termonde, and we understood. As darkness came down we lit our lamps, and there along the roadside sat rows of fugitives, resting before recommencing their long journey through the night. There was one row of little children which will live for ever in my memory, tiny mites sitting together on a bank by the roadside. We only saw them for an instant as our lights fell on them, and they disappeared in the darkness. Germany will have to pay for Louvain and Termonde. It is not with man that she will have to settle for that row of little children.

We had a few vacant seats when we left Antwerp, but they were soon filled by fugitives whom we picked up on the road. Strangely enough, we picked up two of our friends in Antwerp with their families. One was the doctor who had taken all our radiographs for us, and to whom we owed a great deal in many ways. He had left his beautiful house, with X-ray apparatus on which he had spent his fortune, incomparably superior to any other that I have ever seen, and here he was trudging along the road, with his wife, his two children, and their nurse. They were going to St. Nicholas, on their way to Holland, and were delighted to get a lift. Unfortunately, by some mistake, the nurse and children left the bus at Zwyndrecht, a few miles from Antwerp, the doctor came on to St. Nicholas, and his wife went right through with us to Ghent. It took him three days to find the children, and when we last heard from him he was in Holland, having lost everything he had in the world, and after two months he had not yet found his wife. And this is only an instance of what has happened all over Belgium.

We reached St. Nicholas about eight o'clock, having covered thirteen miles in three hours. It was quite dark, and as we had a long night before us we decided to stop and get some food for ourselves and our patients. There was not much to be had, but, considering the stream of fugitives, it was wonderful that there was anything. We hoped now to be able to push on faster, and to reach Ghent before midnight, for it is only a little over twenty miles by the direct road. To our dismay, we found that Lokeren, halfway to Ghent, was in the hands of the Germans, and that we must make a detour, taking us close to the Dutch border, and nearly doubling the distance. Without a guide, and in the dark, we could never have reached our destination; but we were fortunate enough to get a guide, and we set out on our long drive through the night. Twenty minutes later a German scouting party entered St. Nicholas. It was a narrow margin, but it was sufficient.

We were rather a downhearted party when we set out northwards towards the Dutch frontier, for we had been told that the three buses we had sent on in advance had gone straight on to Lokeren, and had undoubtedly fallen into the hands of the Germans, who had made certain of holding the road by destroying the bridge. We hoped that they might have discovered this in time, and turned back, but we could not wait to find out. We knew that the enemy were quite close. At first we used our lights, but a shrapnel whistling overhead warned us that we were seen, and for the remainder of the night we travelled in darkness. These were minor roads, with a narrow paved causeway in the centre, and loose sand on each side. Long avenues of trees kept us in inky darkness, and how the drivers succeeded in keeping on the causeway I really do not know.

Every now and then one of the buses would get into the sand; then all the men would collect, dig the wheels clear, and by sheer brute force drag the bus back to safety. Twice it seemed absolutely hopeless. The wheels were in the loose sand within a foot of a deep ditch, and the least thing would have sent the bus flying over on to its side into the field beyond; and on both occasions, while we looked at one another in despair, a team of huge Flemish horses appeared from nowhere in the darkness and dragged us clear. Think of an inky night, the Germans close at hand, and every half-hour or so a desperate struggle to shoulder a heavily loaded London bus out of a ditch, and you may have some faint idea of the nightmare we passed through.

As we crept along the dark avenues, the sky behind us was lit by an ever-increasing glare. Away to the south-east, at no great distance, a village was blazing, but behind us was a vast column of flame and smoke towering up to heaven. It was in the direction of Antwerp, and at first we thought that the vandals had fired the town; but though the sky was lit by many blazing houses, that tall pillar came from the great oil-tanks, set on fire by the Belgians lest they should fall into German hands. A more awful and terrifying spectacle it is hard to conceive. The sky was lit up as if by the sunrise of the day of doom, and thirty miles away our road was lighted by the lurid glare. Our way led through woods, and amongst the trees we could hear the crack and see the flash of rifle-fire. More than once the whiz of a bullet urged us to hurry on.

At Selsaete, only a mile from the Dutch frontier, we turned southwards towards Ghent, and for an interminable distance we followed the bank of a large canal. A few miles from Ghent we met Commander Samson, of the Flying Corps, and three of his armoured cars. The blaze of their headlights quite blinded us after the darkness in which we had travelled, but the sight of the British uniforms and the machine guns was a great encouragement. The road was so narrow that they had to turn their cars into a field to let us pass. We had just come up with a number of farm waggons, and the clumsy Flemish carts, with their huge horses, the grey armoured cars, with their blazing headlights, and our four red motor-buses, made a strange scene in the darkness of the night. At last we reached Ghent utterly tired out, though personally I had slept a sort of nightmare sleep on the top step of a bus which boldly announced its destination as Hendon.

It was five o'clock, and day was breaking as we got our patients out of the buses and deposited them in the various hospitals as we could find room for them. To our unspeakable relief, we found that the rest of our party had come through by much the same road as we had taken ourselves, but they had reached Ghent quite early the night before. Their earlier start had given them the advantage of clearer roads and daylight. With good fortune little short of miraculous, we had all come so far in safety, and we hoped that our troubles were over. Alas, we were told that though Germans were expected to enter Ghent that very day, and that all British wounded must be removed from the hospitals before ten o'clock. There was nothing for it but to collect them again, and to take them on to Ostend. One had died in the night, and two were too ill to be moved. We left them behind in skilled hands, and the others we re-embarked on our buses *en route* for Bruges and Ostend.

The First Act in the story of the British Field Hospital for Belgium was drawing to an end. Our hospital, to which we had given so much labour, was gone, and the patients, for whom we had grown to care, were scattered. Yet there was in our hearts only a deep gratitude that we had come unharmed, almost by a miracle, through so many dangers, and a firm confidence that in some other place we should find a home for our hospital, where we could again help the brave soldiers whose cause had become so much our own.

CHAPTER 15

Furnes

A week after we had reached London, we were off again to the front. This time our objective was Furnes, a little town fifteen miles east of Dunkirk, and about five miles from the fighting-line. The line of the Belgian trenches ran in a circle, following the course of the River Yser, the little stream which has proved such an insuperable barrier to the German advance. Furnes lies at the centre of the circle, and is thus an ideal position for an advanced base, such as we intended to establish. It is easy of access from Dunkirk by a fine main road which runs alongside an important canal, and as Dunkirk was our port, and the only source of our supplies, this was a great consideration. From Furnes a number of roads lead in various directions to Ypres, Dixmude, Nieuport, and the coast, making it a convenient centre for an organisation such as ours, requiring, as we did, ready means of reaching the front in any direction, and open communication with our base of supplies.

We crossed from Dover in the government transport, and arrived at Dunkirk about ten o'clock on Tuesday morning. There we met Dr. Munro's party, the famous Flying Ambulance Corps, with whom we were to enter on our new venture. They had not come over to England at all, but had come down the coast in their cars, and had spent the last few days in Malo, the seaside suburb of Dunkirk. The Belgian Government very kindly lent us a couple of big motor-lorries in which to take out our stores, and with our own motors we made quite a procession as we started off from the wharf of Dunkirk on our fifteen-mile drive to Furnes. It was late in the afternoon when we reached our new home. It was a large school, partly occupied by the priests connected with it, partly by officers quartered there, and one of the larger classrooms had been used as a dressing-station by some

The surgical staff, Furnes

Belgian doctors in Furnes.

For ourselves, the only accommodation consisted of a few empty classrooms and a huge dormitory divided into cubicles, but otherwise destitute of the necessaries for sleep. Several hours' hard work made some change in the scene, mattresses and blankets being hauled up to the dormitory, where the nursing staff was accommodated, while straw laid down in one of the classrooms made comfortable if somewhat primitive beds for the male members. Meanwhile, in the kitchen department miracles had been accomplished, and we all sat down to dinner with an appetite such as one rarely feels at home, and for which many of our patients over in England would be willing to pay quite large sums. The large room was lit by two candles and a melancholy lamp, there was no tablecloth, the spoons were of pewter, with the bowls half gone, and the knives were in their dotage. But the scales had fallen from our eyes, and we realised what trifles these things are. *Madame*, the genius who presided over our domestic affairs, and many other affairs as well, and her assistants, had produced from somewhere food, good food, and plenty of it; and what in the world can a hungry man want more? Truly there are many people who require a moral operation for cataract, that they might see how good is the world in which they live.

Next day we proceeded to unpack our stores, and to try to make a hospital out of these empty rooms, and then only did we discover that an overwhelming misfortune had overtaken us. By some extraordinary circumstance which has never been explained, we had lost practically the whole of the surgical instruments which we had brought out of Antwerp with such trouble and risk. They were tied up in sheets, and my own impression is that they were stolen. However that may be, here we were in as ludicrous a position as it is possible for even a hospital to occupy, for not only had we none of the ordinary instruments, but, as if Fate meant to have a good laugh at us, we had a whole series of rare and expensive tools. We had no knives, and no artery forceps, and not a stitch of catgut; but we had an oesophagoscope, and the very latest possible pattern of cystoscope, and a marvellous set of tools for plating fractures. It reminded one of the costume of an African savage—a silk hat, and nothing else. Some Belgian doctors who had been working there lent us a little case of elementary instruments, and that was absolutely all we had.

Scarcely had we made this terrible discovery, when an ambulance arrived with two wounded officers, and asked if we were ready to admit patients. We said, "No," and I almost think that we were justified. The men in charge of the ambulance seemed very disappointed, and said that in that case there was nothing for it but to leave the wounded men on their stretchers till an ambulance train should come to take them to Calais, which they might ultimately reach in two or three days' time. They were badly wounded, and we thought that at least we could do better than that; so we made up a couple of beds in one of the empty rooms, and took them in. Little did we dream of what we were in for. An hour later another ambulance arrived, and as we had started, we thought that we might as well fill up the ward we had begun. That did it. The sluice-gates were opened, and the wounded poured in. In four days we admitted three hundred and fifty patients, all of them with injuries of the most terrible nature. The cases we had seen at Antwerp were nothing to these. Arms and legs were torn right off or hanging by the merest shreds, ghastly wounds of the head left the brain exposed. Many of the poor fellows were taken from the ambulances dead, and of the others at least half must have died.

For four days and four nights the operating theatre was at work continuously, till one sickened at the sight of blood and at the thought of an operation. Three operating tables were in almost continuous use, and often three major operations were going on at the same time; and all the instruments we had were two scalpels, six artery forceps, two dissecting forceps, and a finger-saw. Think of doing amputations through the thigh with that equipment! There was nothing else for it. Either the work had to be done or the patients had to die. And there was certainly no one else to do it.

The rapid advance of the Germans had swept away all the admirable arrangements which the Belgian Army had made for dealing with its wounded. The splendid hospitals of Ghent and Ostend were now in German hands, and there had not yet been time to get new ones established. The cases could be sent to Calais, it was true, but there the accommodation was so far totally inadequate, and skilled surgical assistance was not to be obtained. For the moment our hospital, with its ludicrous equipment, was the only hope of the badly wounded. By the mercy of Heaven, we had plenty of chloroform and morphia, and a fair supply of dressings, and we knew by experience that at this stage it is safer to be content with the minimum of actual operative work, so that I think it was we, rather than our patients, who suffered from the want of the ordinary aids of surgery. In the wards there was a shortage, almost as serious, of all the ordinary equipment of nursing, for much

DINNER, FURNES

THE COURTYARD, FURNES

of this had been too cumbrous to bring from Antwerp; and though we had brought out a fair supply of ordinary requirements, we had never dreamt of having to deal with such a rush as this.

Ward equipment cannot be got at a moment's notice, and the bulk of it had not yet arrived. We only possessed a dozen folding beds, in which some of the worst cases were placed. The others had to lie on straw on the floor, and so closely were they packed that it was only with the greatest care that one could thread one's way across the ward. How the nurses ever managed to look after their patients is beyond my comprehension, but they were magnificent. They rose to the emergency as only Englishwomen can, and there is not one of those unfortunate men who will not remember with gratitude their sympathy and their skill.

During these first days a terrific fight was going on around Dixmude and Nieuport, and it was a very doubtful question how long it would be possible for the Belgian and French troops to withstand the tremendous attacks to which they were being subjected. The matter was so doubtful that we had to hold ourselves in readiness to clear out from the hospital at two hours' notice, whilst our wounded were taken away as fast as we could get them into what one can only describe as a portable condition. It was a physical impossibility for our wards to hold more than a hundred and fifty patients, even when packed close together side by side on the floor, and as I have said, three hundred and fifty were dealt with in the first four days.

This meant that most of them spent only twenty-four hours in the hospital, and as we were only sent cases which could not, as they stood, survive the long train journey to Calais, this meant that they were often taken on almost immediately after serious operations. Several amputations of the thigh, for example, were taken away next day, and many of them must have spent the next twenty-four hours in the train, for the trains were very tardy in reaching their destination. It is not good treatment, but good surgery is not the primary object of war. The fighting troops are the first consideration, and the surgeon has to manage the best way he can.

One of the most extraordinary cases we took in was that of the editor of a well-known sporting journal in England. He had shown his appreciation of the true sporting instinct by going out to Belgium and joining the army as a *mitrailleuse* man. If there is one place where one may hope for excitement, it is in an armoured car with a *mitrailleuse*. The *mitrailleuse* men are picked dare-devils, and their work takes them constantly into situations which require a trained taste for their enjoyment. Our friend the editor was out with his car, and had got out to reconnoitre, when suddenly some Germans in hiding opened fire. Their first shot went through both his legs, fracturing both tibiae, and he fell down, of course absolutely incapable of standing, just behind the armoured car. Owing to some mistake, an officer in the car gave the order to start, and away went the car. He would have been left to his fate, but suddenly realising how desperate his position was, he threw up his hand and caught hold of one of the rear springs. Lying on his back and holding on to the spring, he was dragged along the ground, with both his legs broken, for a distance of about half a mile.

The car was going at about twenty-five miles an hour, and how he ever maintained his hold Heaven only knows. At last they pulled up, and there they found him, practically unconscious, his clothes torn to ribbons, his back a mass of bruises, but still holding on. It was one of the most splendid examples of real British grit of which I have ever heard. They brought him to the hospital, and we fixed him up as well as we could. One would have thought that he might have been a little downhearted, but not a bit of it. He arrived in the operating theatre smiling and smoking a cigar, and gave us a vivid account of his experiences. We sent him over to England, and I heard that he was doing well. There is one sporting paper in England which is edited by a real sportsman. May he long live to inspire in others the courage of which he has given such a splendid example!

Chapter 16

Poperinghe

For a long week the roar of guns had echoed incessantly in our corridors and wards, and a continuous stream of motor-lorries, guns, and ammunition waggons had rumbled past our doors; whilst at night the flash of the guns lit up the horizon with an angry glare. The flood of wounded had abated, and we were just beginning to get the hospital into some sort of shape when the order came to evacuate.

It had been no easy task transforming bare rooms into comfortable wards, arranging for supplies of food and stores, and fitting a large staff into a cubic space totally inadequate to hold them. But wonderful things can be accomplished when everyone is anxious to do their share, and the most hopeless sybarite will welcome shelter however humble, and roll himself up in a blanket in any corner, when he is dead tired. For the first few days the rush of wounded had been so tremendous that all we could do was to try to keep our heads above water and not be drowned by the flood.

But towards the end of the week the numbers diminished, not because there were not as many wounded, but because the situation was so critical that the Belgian authorities did not dare to leave any large number of wounded in Furnes. Supplies were coming out from England in response to urgent telegrams, and, through the kind offices of the Queen of the Belgians, we had been able to obtain a number of beds from the town, in addition to twenty which she had generously given to us herself. So that we were gradually beginning to take on the appearance of an ordinary hospital, and work was settling down into a regular routine. The sleepy little town of Furnes had been for some weeks in a state of feverish activity.

After the evacuation of Antwerp and the retirement of the Belgian Army from Ostend, it had become the advanced base of the Belgian troops, and it was very gay with Staff officers, and of course packed with soldiers. The immense Grand Place lined with buildings, in many cases bearing unmistakable signs of a birth in Spanish times, was a permanent garage of gigantic dimensions, and the streets were thronged day and night with hurrying cars. We in the hospital hoped that the passage of the Yser would prove too much for the Germans, and that we should be left in peace, for we could not bear to think that all our labour could be thrown to the winds, and that we might have to start afresh in some other place. But one of the massed attacks which have formed such a prominent feature of this terrible war had temporarily rolled back the defence in the Dixmude district, and it was deemed unwise to submit the hospital to the risk of possible disaster.

We were fortunate in having Dr. Munro's ambulance at our disposal, and in rather over two hours more than a hundred wounded had been transferred to the Red Cross train which lay at the station waiting to take them to Calais. An evacuation is always a sad business, for the relations between a hospital and its patients are far more than professional. But with us it was tragic, for we knew that for many of our patients the long journey could have only one conclusion. Only the worst cases were ever brought to us, in fact only those whose condition rendered the long journey to Calais a dangerous proceeding, and we felt that for many of them the evacuation order was a death warrant, and that we should never see them again. They were brave fellows, and made the best of it as they shook hands with smiling faces and wished us "*Au revoir*," for though they might die on the way they preferred that to the danger of falling into the hands of the Germans. And they were right. They knew as well as we did that we are not fighting against a civilized nation, but against a gang of organised savages.

Three hours later we were mingling with the crowds who thronged the road, wondering with them where our heads would rest that night, and filled with pity at the terrible tragedy which surrounded us. Carts, wheelbarrows, perambulators, and in fact any vehicle which could be rolled along, were piled to overflowing with household goods. Little children and old men and women struggled along under loads almost beyond their powers, none of them knowing whither they went or what the curtain of fate would reveal when next it was drawn aside. It was a blind flight into the darkness of the unknown.

Our orders were to make for Poperinghe, a little town lying about fifteen miles due south of Furnes, in the direction of Ypres. For the first ten miles we travelled along the main road to Ypres, a fine avenue running between glorious trees, and one of the chief thoroughfares of Belgium. Here we made our first acquaintance with the African troops, who added a touch of colour in their bright robes to the otherwise grey surroundings. They were encamped in the fields by the side of the road, and seemed to be lazily enjoying themselves seated round their camp-fires. At Oostvleteren we parted company with the main road and its fine surface, and for the next six miles we bumped and jolted along on a bad cross-road till our very bones rattled and groaned.

There was no suggestion now of the horrors of war. Peaceful villages as sleepy as any in our own country districts appeared at frequent intervals, and easy prosperity was the obvious keynote of the well-wooded and undulating countryside. We were in one of the great hop districts, and the contrast with the flat and unprotected country round Furnes was striking. One might almost have been in the sheltered hopfields of Kent. Little children looked up from their games in astonishment as we rolled by, and our response to their greetings was mingled with a silent prayer that they might be spared the terrible fate which had befallen their brothers and sisters in far-off Louvain. The contrasts of war are amazing. Here were the children playing by the roadside, and the cattle slowly wending their way home, and ten miles away we could hear the roar of the guns, and knew that on those wasted fields men were struggling with savage fury in one of the bloodiest battles of the war.

In the great square of Poperinghe the scene was brilliant in the extreme. Uniforms of every conceivable cut and colour rubbed shoulder to shoulder; ambulance waggons, guns, ammunition trains, and picketed horses all seemed to be mixed in inextricable confusion; while a squadron of French cavalry in their bright blue and silver uniforms was drawn up on one side of the square, waiting patiently for the orders which would permit them to go to the help of their hard-pressed comrades. It seemed impossible that we could find shelter here, for obviously every corner must have been filled by the throng of soldiers who crowded in the square. But we were quite happy, for had we not got *Madame* with us, and had her genius ever been known to fail, especially in the face of the impossible? Others might go without a roof, but not we, and others might go to bed supperless, but in some miraculous way we knew that we should sit down to a hot dinner. We were not deceived. The whole nursing staff was soon comfortably housed in a girls' school, while the men were allotted the outhouse of a convent, and there, rolled up in our blankets and with our bags for pillows, we slept that night as soundly as we should have done in our own comfortable beds in England.

There was ample room in the courtyard for our heavily laden ambulances, for we had brought all our stores with us; and a big pump was a welcome sight, for grime had accumulated during the preceding twelve hours. By the side of the friendly pump, in a railed-off recess, a life-size image of Our Lady of Lourdes, resplendent in blue and gold, looked down with a pitying smile on a group of pilgrims, one of whom bore a little child in her arms; whilst a well-worn stone step spoke of the number of suppliants who had sought her aid.

We had fasted for many hours, and while we were doing our part in unpacking the small store of food which we had brought with us, *Madame*, with her usual genius, had discovered on the outskirts of Poperinghe an obscure cafe, where for a small sum the proprietor allowed us to use his kitchen. There we were presently all seated round three tables, drinking coffee such as we had rarely tasted, and eating a curiously nondescript, but altogether delightful, meal. There were two little rooms, one containing a bar and a stove, the other only a table. Over the stove presided a lady whose novels we have all read, cooking bacon, and when I say that she writes novels as well as she cooks bacon it is very high praise indeed—at least we thought so at the time.

Some genius had discovered a naval store in the town, and had persuaded the officer in charge to give us cheese and jam and a whole side of bacon, so that we fed like the gods. There was one cloud over the scene, for the terrible discovery was made that we had left behind in Furnes a large box of sausages, over the fate of which it is well to draw a veil; but *Madame* was not to be defeated even by that, and a wonderful salad made of biscuits and vinegar and oil went far to console us. And that reminds me of a curious episode in Furnes. For several days the huge store bottle of castor oil was lost. It was ultimately discovered in the kitchen, where, as the label was in English, it had done duty for days as salad oil! What is there in a name after all?

We had not been able to bring with us all our stores, and as some of these were wanted two of us started back to Furnes late at night to fetch them. It was a glorious night, and one had the advantage of a clear road. We were driving northwards, and the sky was lit up by the flashes of the guns at Nieuport and Dixmude, whilst we could hear their dull roar in the distance. All along the road were encamped the

Turcos, and their camp-fires, with the dark forms huddled around them, gave a picturesque touch to the scene. Halfway to Furnes the road was lit up by a motor-car which had caught fire, and which stood blazing in the middle of the road. We had some little difficulty in passing it, but when we returned it was only a mass of twisted iron by the roadside. There was no moon, but the stars shone out all the more brilliantly as we spun along on the great Ypres road. It was long after midnight when we reached the hospital, and it was not a little uncanny groping through its wards in the darkness. There is some influence which seems to haunt the empty places where men once lived, but it broods in redoubled force over the places where men have died. In those wards, now so dark and silent, we had worked for all the past days amid sights which human eyes should never have seen, and the groans of suffering we had heard seemed to echo through the darkness. We were glad when we had collected the stores we required and were again in the car on our way back to Poperinghe.

Next morning we called at the *Hôtel de Ville* in Poperinghe, and there we learnt that the queen, with her usual thoughtfulness, was interesting herself on our behalf to find us a building in which we could make a fresh start. She had sent the Viscomtesse de S. to tell us that she hoped to shortly place at our disposal either a school or a convent. On the following day, however, we heard that the situation had somewhat settled, and an order came from General Mellis, the chief of the medical staff, instructing us to return to Furnes. A few hours later found us hard at work again, putting in order our old home.

There was one rather pathetic incident of our expedition to Poperinghe. Five nuns who had fled from Eastern Belgium—they had come, I think, from a convent near Louvain—had taken refuge in the school in Furnes in which we were established. When we were ordered to go to Poperinghe, they begged to be allowed to accompany us, and we took them with us in the ambulances. On our return they were so grateful that they asked to be allowed to show their gratitude by working for us in the kitchen, and for all the time we were at Furnes they were our devoted helpers. They only made one request, that if we left Furnes we would take them with us, and we promised that we would never desert them.

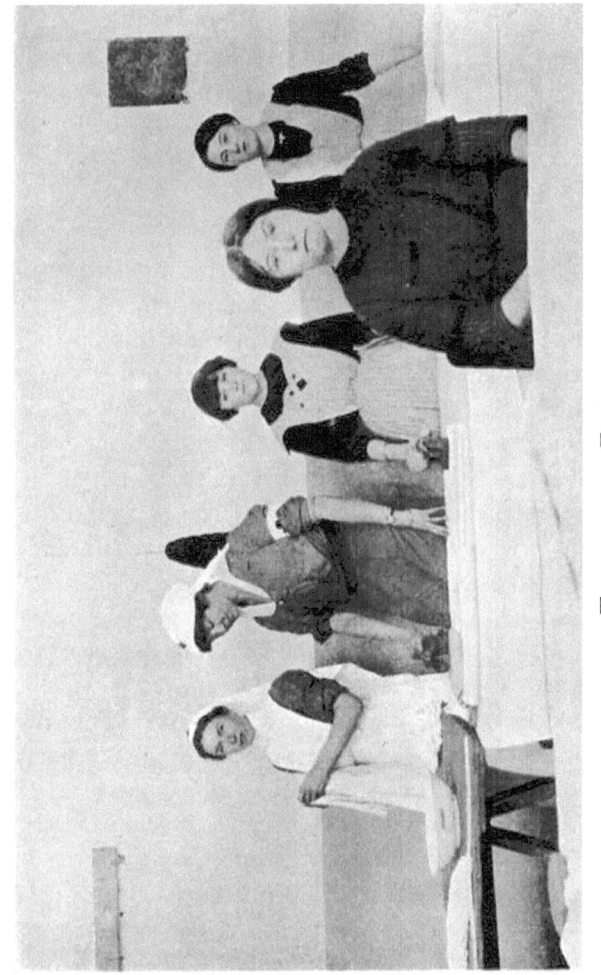

The laundry, Furnes

Chapter 17

Furnes Again

The position of the hospital at Furnes was very different from that which it had held at Antwerp. There we were in a modern city, with a water-supply and modern sanitary arrangements. Here we were in an old Continental country town, or, in other words, in medieval times, as far as water and sanitation were concerned. For it is only where the English tourist has penetrated that one can possibly expect such luxuries. One does not usually regard him as an apostle of civilization, but he ought certainly to be canonized as the patron saint of continental sanitary engineering. As a matter of fact, in a country as flat as Belgium the science must be fraught with extraordinary difficulties, and they certainly seem to thrive very well without it. We were established in the Episcopal College of St. Joseph, a large boys' school, and not badly adapted to the needs of a hospital but for the exceptions I have mentioned. Our water-supply came, on a truly hygienic plan, from wells beneath the building, whilst we were entirely free from any worry about drains. There were none. However, it did not seem to affect either ourselves or our patients, and we all had the best of health, though we took the precaution of sterilizing our water.

We were now the official advanced base hospital of the Belgian Army, and not merely, as in Antwerp, a free organisation working by itself. The advantage of this arrangement was that we had a constant supply of wounded sent to us whenever there was any fighting going on, and that the evacuation of our patients was greatly facilitated. Every morning at ten o'clock Colonel Maestrio made the tour of our wards, and arranged for the removal to the base hospital at Dunkirk of all whom we wished to send away. It gave us the further advantage of special privileges for our cars and ambulances, which were allowed to go practically anywhere in search of the wounded with absolute freedom. Formerly we had owed a great deal to the assistance of the Belgian *Croix Rouge*, who had been very good in supplementing our supply of dressings, as well as in getting us army rations for the patients. This, of course, had all come to an end, and we now had to rely on our own resources.

Our personnel had undergone considerable alteration, for while several of our original members had dropped out, we had joined forces with Dr. Hector Munro's Ambulance Corps, and four of their doctors had joined our medical staff. Dr. Munro and his party had worked in connection with the hospitals of Ghent till the German advance forced both them and ourselves to retreat to Ostend. There we met and arranged to carry on our work together at Furnes. The arrangement was of the greatest possible advantage to both of us, for it gave us the service of their splendid fleet of ambulances, and it gave them a base to which to bring their wounded. We were thus able to get the wounded into hospital in an unusually short space of time, and to deal effectively with many cases which would otherwise have been hopeless. Smooth coordination with an ambulance party is, in fact, the first essential for the satisfactory working of an advanced hospital. If full use is to be made of its advantages, the wounded must be collected and brought in with the minimum of delay, whilst it must be possible to evacuate at once all who are fit to be moved back to the base. In both respects we were at Furnes exceptionally well placed.

We were established in a large straggling building of no attraction whatever except its cubic capacity. It was fairly new, and devoid of any of the interest of antiquity, but it presented none of the advantages of modern architecture. In fact, it was extremely ugly and extremely inconvenient, but it was large. Two of the largest classrooms and the refectory were converted into wards. At first the question of beds was a serious difficulty, but by the kind intervention of the queen we were able to collect a number from houses in the town, whilst Her Majesty herself gave us twenty first-class beds with box-spring mattresses. Later on we got our supplies from England, and we could then find beds for a hundred patients. Even then we were not at the end of our capacity, for we had two empty classrooms, the floors of which we covered with straw, on which another fifty patients could lie in comfort until we could find better accommodation for them. We could not, of course, have fires in these rooms, as it would have been dangerous, but we warmed them by the simple plan of filling them with patients and shutting all the windows and doors. For the first few nights, as a matter of fact, we had to sleep in these rooms on straw ourselves, and in the greatest luxury. No one who has slept all his life in a bed would ever realise how comfortable straw is, and for picturesqueness has it an equal?

I went into the Straw Ward on my round one wild and stormy night. Outside the wind was raging and the rain fell in torrents, and it was so dark that one had to feel for the door. Inside a dozen men lay covered up with blankets on a thick bed of straw, most of them fast asleep, while beside one knelt a nurse with a stable lantern, holding a cup to his lips. It was a picture that an artist might have come far to see—the wounded soldiers in their heavy coats, covered by the brown blankets; the nurse in her blue uniform and her white cap, the stable lantern throwing flickering shadows on the walls. It was something more than art, and as I glanced up at the crucifix hanging on the wall I felt that the picture was complete.

Above the two larger wards was a huge dormitory, divided up by wooden partitions into some sixty cubicles, which provided sleeping accommodation for the bulk of our staff. They were arranged in four ranks, with passages between and washing arrangements in the passages, and the cubicles themselves were large and comfortable. It was really quite well planned, and was most useful to us, though ventilation had evidently not appealed to its architect. Two rows were reserved for the nurses, and in the others slept our chauffeurs and stretcher-bearers, with a few of the priests. Our friends were at first much shocked at the idea of this mixed crowd, but as a matter of fact it worked very well, and there was very little to grumble at. The only real disadvantage was the noise made by early risers in the morning, convincing us more than ever of the essential selfishness of the early bird. A few of us occupied separate rooms over in the wing which the priests had for the most part reserved for themselves, and these we used in the daytime as our offices.

But the real sights of our establishment were our kitchen and our chef; we might almost have been an Oxford college. Maurice had come to us in quite a romantic way. One night we took in a soldier with a bullet wound of the throat. For some days he was pretty bad, but he won all our hearts by his cheerfulness and pluck. When at last he improved sufficiently to be able to speak, he told us that he was the assistant chef at the Hôtel Métropole in Brussels. We decided that he ought to be kept in a warm, moist atmosphere for a long time, and he was installed in the kitchen. He was a genius at making miracles

MAURICE

A STRAW WARD, FURNES

out of nothing, and his soups made out of bacon rind and old bones, followed by *entrées* constructed from bully beef, were a dream. He was assisted by the nuns from Louvain who had accompanied us to Poperinghe, and who now worked for us on the sole condition that we should not desert them. They were very picturesque working in the kitchen in their black cloaks and coifs. At meal-times the scene was a most animated one, for, as we had no one to wait on us, we all came in one after the other, plate in hand, while Maurice stood with his ladle and presided over the ceremonies, with a cheery word for everyone, assisted by the silent nuns.

The getting of supplies became at times a very serious question. Needless to say, Furnes was destitute of anything to eat, drink, burn, or wear, and Dunkirk was soon in a similar case. We had to get most of our provisions over from England, and our milk came every morning on the government transport, from Aylesbury. For some weeks we were very hard up, but the officer in charge of the naval stores at Dunkirk was very good to us, and supplied us with bully beef, condensed milk, cheese, soap, and many other luxuries till we could get further supplies from home. We used a considerable quantity of coal, and on one occasion we were faced by the prospect of an early famine, for Furnes and Dunkirk were empty. But nothing was ever too great a strain for the resources of our housekeeper. She discovered that there was a coal-heap at Ramscapelle, five miles away, and in a few hours an order had been obtained from the *Juge d'Instruction* empowering us to take the coal if we could get it, and the loan of a government lorry had been coaxed out of the War Lords.

The only difficulty was that for the moment the Germans were shelling the place, and it was too dangerous to go near even for coal; so the expedition had to be postponed until they desisted. It seemed to me the most original method of filling one's coal-cellar of which I had ever heard. And it was typical of a large number of our arrangements. There is something of the Oriental about the Belgians and the French. If we wanted any special favour, the very last thing we thought of doing was to go and ask for it. It was not that they were not willing to give us what we asked for, but they did not understand that method of approach. What we did was to go to breakfast with the *juge*, or to lunch with the minister, or to invite the colonel to dinner. In the course of conversation the subject would be brought up in some indirect way till the interest of the great man had been gained; then everything was easy. And surely there is something very attractive about a system where everything is done as an act of friendship, and not as the soulless reflex of some official machine. It is easier to drink red wine than to eat red tape, and not nearly so wearing to one's digestion.

As we were fifteen miles from Dunkirk, and as everything had to be brought out from there, transport was a serious problem. Every morning one of our lorries started for our seaport soon after nine, carrying the hospital mailbag and as many messages as a village carrier. The life of the driver was far more exciting than his occupation would suggest, and it was always a moot point whether or not he would succeed in getting back the same night. The road was of the usual Belgian type, with a paved causeway in the middle just capable of allowing two motors to pass, and on each side was a morass, flanked on the right by a canal and on the left by a field.

The slightest deviation from the greasy cobbles landed the car in the mud, with quite a chance of a plunge into the canal. A constant stream of heavy army lorries tore along the road at thirty or more miles an hour, and as a rule absolutely refused to give way. It took a steady nerve to face them, encouraged as one was by numbers of derelicts in the field on the one side and half in the canal on the other. On one bridge a car hung for some days between heaven and earth, its front wheels caught over the parapet, and the car hanging from them over the canal—a heartening sight for a nervous driver. It was rarely that our lorry returned without some tale of adventure. The daily round, the common task, gave quite enough occupation to *one* member of the community.

Chapter 18

Work at Furnes

Our work at Furnes differed in many ways from that at Antwerp. All its conditions were rougher, and, as we had to deal with a number of patients out of all proportion to our size, it was impossible to keep any but a few special cases for any length of time. We admitted none but the most serious cases, such as would be instantly admitted to any London hospital, and when I mention that in five weeks we had just a thousand cases in our hundred beds, the pressure at which the work was carried on will be realised. There is no hospital in England, with ten times the number of beds, that has ever admitted to its wards anything like this number of serious surgical cases. We were essentially a clearing hospital, with this important proviso, that we could, when it was required, carry out at once the heaviest operative work, and retain special cases as long as we thought fit.

Our object was always to get each patient into such a condition that he could be transferred back to the base without injury to his chances of recovery, and without undue pain, and I believe we saved the life of many a patient by giving him a night's rest in the Straw Ward, and sending him on next day with his wound properly dressed and supported. The cases themselves were of a far more severe type than those we had at Antwerp. There, indeed, I was astonished at the small amount of injury that had in many cases resulted from both shrapnel and bullet wounds, and it was certainly worthy of note that we had never once in our work there had to perform an amputation. At Furnes, we drew our patients from the line between Nieuport and Dixmude, where the fighting was for the most part at close range and of a most murderous nature. There were no forts, and the soldiers had little or no protection from the hail of high-explosive shells which the enemy poured upon them.

In Nieuport and Dixmude themselves the fighting was frequently from house to house, the most deadly form of fighting known. The wounds we had to treat were correspondingly severe—limbs sometimes almost completely torn off, terrible wounds of the skull, and bullet wounds where large masses of the tissues had been completely torn away. It was difficult to see how human beings could survive such awful injuries, and, indeed, our death-roll was a long one. Added to this, the men had been working in the wet and the mud for weeks past. Their clothes were stiff with it, and such a thing as a clean wound was not to be thought of. Simple cases at Antwerp were here tedious and dangerous, and they required all the resources of nursing and of surgery that we could bring to bear upon them. Still, it was extraordinary what good results followed on common-sense lines of treatment, and we soon learnt to give up no case as hopeless. But each involved a great amount of work, first in operating and trying to reduce chaos to reason, and then in dressing and nursing. For everyone all round—surgeons, dressers, and nurses—it was real hard physical labour.

Our rapid turnover of patients involved a large amount of manual labour in stretcher work, clearing up wards, and so on, but all this was done for us by our *brancardiers*, or stretcher-bearers. These were Belgians who for one reason or another could not serve with the army, and who were therefore utilised by the government for purposes such as these. We had some eight of them attached to our hospital, and they were of the greatest use to us, acting as hospital orderlies. They were mostly educated men—schoolmasters and University teachers—but they were quite ready to do any work we might require at any hour of the day or night. They carried the patients to the theatre and to the wards, they cleaned the stretchers—a very difficult and unpleasant job—they tidied up the wards and scrubbed the floors, and they carried away all the soiled dressings and burned them. They were a fine set of men, and I do not know what we should have done without them.

Work began at an early hour, for every case in the hospital required dressing, and, as we never knew what we should have to deal with at night, we always tried to get through the routine before lunch. At ten o'clock Colonel Maestrio arrived, with two of his medical officers, and made a complete round of the hospital with the surgeons in charge of the various cases. They took the greatest interest in the patients, and in our attempts to cure them. They would constantly spend an hour with me in the operating theatre, and after any exceptional operation they would follow the progress of the patient with the keenest interest. Many of the cases with which we had to deal required a certain amount of ingenuity in the reconstruction of what had been destroyed, so that surgery had often to be on rather original lines. What interested them most was the fixation of fractures by means of steel plates, which we adopted in all our serious cases.

Apparently the method is very little used abroad, and as an operation it is distinctly spectacular, for in a few minutes a shapeless mass which the patient cannot bear to be touched is transformed into a limb almost as strong as the other, which can be moved about in any direction without fear of breaking, and, when the patient recovers consciousness, almost without discomfort. We almost always had an interested audience, professional, clerical, or lay, for the chauffeurs found much amusement in these feats of engineering.

In the afternoon we almost always had some distinguished visitor to entertain, and it is one of my chief regrets that we never kept a visitors' book. Its pages would one day have been of the greatest interest. Twice every week the Queen of the Belgians came round our wards. She came quite simply, with one of her ladies and one of the Belgian medical officers, and no one could possibly have taken a deeper interest in the patients. Her father studied medicine as a hobby, and had, indeed, become a very distinguished physician, and she herself has had considerable training in medicine, so that her interest was a great deal more than that of an ordinary lay visitor. She was quite able to criticize and to appreciate details of nursing and of treatment. She always spoke to every patient, and she had a kind word for every one of them, Belgian, French, or even German, for we had a few Germans.

There was something deeply touching in the scene. The dimly lit ward, with its crude furniture, the slim figure in black, bending in compassion over the rough fellows who would gladly have given their lives for her, and who now lay wounded in the cause in which she herself had suffered. The Germans may destroy Belgium, but they will never destroy the kingdom of its queen. Sometimes the king came to see his soldiers—a tall, silent man, with the face of one who has suffered much, and as simple, as gentle, and as kindly as his queen. It was good to see the faces light up as he entered a ward, to see heads painfully raised to gaze after no splendid uniform, but a man.

One of our most distinguished and most welcome visitors was Madame Curie, the discoverer of radium. She brought her large X-ray equipment to Furnes for work amongst the wounded, and we per-

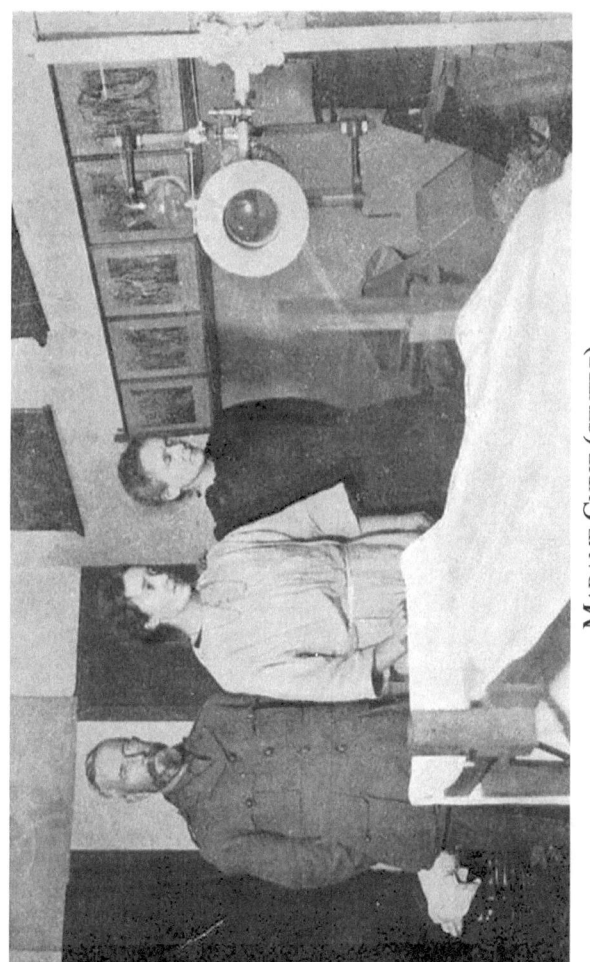

Madame Curie (centre)

suaded her to stay with us for a week. One of our storerooms was rapidly fitted up as an impromptu radiographic department, the windows painted over and covered with thick paper, a stove introduced, and a dark-room contrived with the aid of a cupboard and two curtains. Electric current was obtained from a dynamo bolted on to the step of a twenty-horse-power car, and driven by a belt from the flywheel of the engine.

The car stood out in the courtyard and snorted away, whilst we worked in the storeroom alongside. The coil and mercury break were combined in one piece, and the whole apparatus was skilfully contrived with a view to portability. Madame Curie was an indefatigable worker, and in a very short time had taken radiographs of all the cases which we could place at her disposal, and, indeed, we ransacked all the hospitals in Furnes, for when they heard of her arrival, they were only too glad to make use of the opportunity. Mademoiselle Curie developed the plates, and between them they produced photographs of the greatest utility to us.

Considering its obvious utility, whether in war or in civil practice, it has always been a source of wonder to me that there is no such thing as a car designed and built with a view to radiography. Perhaps it exists, but if so, I have never met It only means the building into the frame of suitable dynamo, and the provision of means for storing the rest of the equipment. It would place an X-ray equipment at the disposal of ever cottage hospital, or even of a country-house, and it would place the cottage hospital, not to mention the country-house, at the disposal of the enterprising radiographer.

As soon as our patients could be moved, we had to send them on to their base hospitals—the Belgians to Calais and the French to Dunkirk.

From Calais the Belgians were brought over the Channel, and distributed all over England and Scotland. I had a postcard from one of them from Perth. The French were taken on in hospital ships to Cherbourg and other seaports along the coast. From Furnes they were all carried in hospital trains, and the scene at the station when a large batch of wounded was going off was most interesting. Only the worst cases were ever brought to our hospital; all the others were taken straight to the station, and waited there until a train was ready to take them on. Often they would be there for twelve hours, or even twenty-four, before they could be got on, and the train itself would be constantly shunted to let troops and ammunition go by, and might take twelve hours to reach its destination.

There were no proper arrangements for the feeding of these men, all of whom were more or less badly wounded; and at first, when we heard at the hospital that a train was about to be made up, we took down all the soup and coffee we could manage to spare in big pails and jugs. But this was a mere makeshift, and was superseded very soon by a more up-to-date arrangement. A proper soup-kitchen was established at the station, with huge boilers full of soup and coffee always ready, and after that it was never necessary for a wounded soldier to leave Furnes hungry. All this was due to the energy and resource of Miss Macnaughtan, the authoress, who took it up as her special charge. She had a little passage screened off, and in this were fitted up boilers for coffee and soup, tables for cutting up meat and vegetables, and even a machine for cutting up the bread. It was all most beautifully arranged, and here she worked all day long, preparing for the inevitable crowd of wounded which the night would bring. How it was all managed was a mystery to me, for there was not enough food in Furnes to feed a tame cat, let alone a trainload of famished soldiers, and I am looking anxiously for her next book in the hopes of finding the solution.

The trains themselves were well equipped, though nothing to the hospital trains of England. The more severe cases were carried in long cars on a double row of stretchers, and they looked very comfortable on a cold night, with their oil-lamps and a coke stove in the centre of each car. A stretcher is, perhaps, not exactly a bed of roses for a wounded man, but when one considers what pain is involved in moving a man who is badly wounded, there is obviously a great advantage in placing him on a stretcher once for all on the battle-field, and never moving him again until he can be actually placed in bed in a hospital. On the train the men were looked after by the priests, splendid fellows who never seemed tired of doing all they could for the soldiers. One found the Belgian priest everywhere—in the trenches, in the hospitals, and in the trains—unobtrusive, always cheerful, always ready to help. From the brave Archbishop Mercier to the humblest village cure, regardless of their comfort and careless of their lives, they have stood by their people in the hour of their trial. May their honour be great in the hour of Belgium's triumph!

CHAPTER 19

Furnes—The Town

Like so many of the cities of Belgium, Furnes is a town of the past. To stand in the great square, surrounded by buildings which would delight the heart of any artist, is to travel back through three centuries of time. Spain and the Renaissance surround us, and we look instinctively towards the *pavillon* for the soldiers of Philip, or glance with apprehension at the door of the *Palais de Justice* for the sinister form of Peter Titelmann the Inquisitor. Around this very square marched the procession of the Holy Office, in all the insolent blasphemy of its power, and on these very stones were kindled the flames that were to destroy its victims. But all these have gone; the priest and his victim, the swaggering bravo and the king he served, have gone to their account, and Furnes is left, the record of a time when men built temples like angels and worshipped in them like devils.

The immense square, with the beautiful public buildings which surround it, speaks of a time when Furnes was an important town. As early as the year 850 it is said that Baldwin of the Iron Arm, the first of the great counts of Flanders, had established a fortress here to withstand the invasion of the Normans. After that Furnes appears repeatedly with varying fortunes in the turbulent history of the Middle Ages, until in the thirteenth century it was razed to the ground by Robert of Artois. In the next three hundred years, however, it must have entirely recovered its position, for in the days of the Spanish Fury it was one of the headquarters of the Inquisition and of the Spanish Army, and there is no town in Belgium upon which the Spanish occupation has left a greater mark. Since then, of no commercial or political importance, it has lived the life of a dull country town, and tradition says that there is plenty of solid wealth stored by its thrifty inhabitants behind the plain house-fronts which line its quiet streets.

St Walburga, Furnes

From the centre of the square one can see all that there is to be seen of Furnes. The four sides are lined by beautiful old houses whose decorated fronts and elaborate gables tell of the Renaissance and of Spanish days. Behind the low red roofs tower the churches of St. Walburga and St. Nicholas, dwarfing the houses which nestle at their base. In the corners of the square are public buildings, small when compared with those of Bruges and Ypres, but unsurpassed in exquisite detail of design. Behind one corner rises the tall belfry without which no Flemish town would be complete. On an autumn evening when the sun is setting, when the red roofs glow with a deeper crimson, and the tall churches catch the sun's last rays on their old brick walls, there can be few more perfect pictures than the square of Furnes.

The two oldest buildings in the square stand at the ends of the eastern side. At the north end is the *Pavillon des Officiers espagnols*, once the Town Hall, and, in the days of the Spanish occupation, the headquarters of the army for the district. It is an old Flemish building, solidly built, with high-pitched roof, and windows framed in ornamental stonework, ending in a big square tower with battlements and little turrets at its corners. A short outside staircase leads up to the entrance. The whole building gives the impression that in the days when it was built the Town Hall was also the fortress, and that the mayor had duties more strenuous than the eating of dinners. At the other end of the eastern side stands the old *Halle aux Vins*, where the night-watchmen had their quarters, a fine old gabled house with a loggia reached by a flight of steps in the centre, a row of plain stone columns supporting the floors above.

Directly opposite is the north-west corner of the square, with the *Palais de Justice* on the right and the *Hôtel de Ville* on the left. Both date from the Spanish occupation, but they are very different in their style of architecture. The first is classical and severe, the second has all the warmth of the Renaissance. The *Hôtel de Ville* is an elaborately decorated building, with two exquisite gables and a steep roof surmounted by a little octagonal tower. The loggia below, standing out from the building and supporting a balcony above, is perhaps its most charming feature, both for the beauty of its proportions and the delicacy of its carved stone balustrades. Inside, the rooms are as they were three hundred years ago, and the wonderful hangings of Cordova leather in the council chamber are still intact. Beside the *Hôtel de Ville* the straight lines of the *Palais de Justice*, with its pillars and its high narrow windows, form a striking contrast.

It was here, in the large room on the first floor, that the Inquisition held its awful court, and here were the instruments of torture with which it sought to enforce its will. Behind the *palais* rises the tall belfry, a big square tower from which springs an octagonal turret carrying an elaborate campanile. There is a quaint survival on this belfry, for upon it the town crier has a little hut. He is a cobbler, and from below one can hear the tap-tap of his hammer as he plies his trade. But at night he calls out the hours to the town below, together with any information of interest, concluding with the assurance that he and his wife are in good health. The office has descended from father to son from the earliest days of the history of Furnes, and its holder has always been a cobbler. Till early in last November the record was unbroken, but, alas the fear of German shells was too much for the cobbler, and he is gone.

Furnes is a town of contrasts, and though both its churches were built by the wonderful architects of the fourteenth century, there could hardly be two buildings more diverse. Behind the line of red roofs on the east of the square rises the rugged tower of St. Nicholas, a great square mass of old and weather-beaten brick, unfinished like so many of the Belgian towers, but rough, massive, and grand, like some rude giant. On the north, behind the *Palais de Justice* and the belfry, stands St. Walburga, with the delicate tracery of her flying buttresses and her spire fine as a needle. There is something fitting in the rugged simplicity which commemorates the grand old bishop, and in the exquisite fragility of the shrine of the virgin saint. The double flying buttresses of St. Walburga, intersecting in mid-air, and apparently defying the laws of gravity, are as delicate a dream as the mind of architect could conceive, and they give to the whole an airy grace which cannot be described.

The church was planned six hundred years ago on a gigantic scale, in the days when men built for the worship of God and not for the accommodation of an audience, and for six hundred years the choir stood alone as a challenge to future generations to complete what had been so gloriously begun. Only seven years ago the transept was added, and to the credit of its builders it is worthy to stand beside the choir. One wonders how many hundred years may have passed before the vision of the first great architect is complete. It is built for the most part of red brick, the rich red brick of Belgium, which grows only more mellow with age.

Inside, the tall pillars of a dark grey stone support at a great height a finely groined roof of the same red brick, lit by a clerestory so open that one wonders how it can carry the weight of the roof above. The tall windows of the transept, reaching almost from the floor to the roof, with their delicate tracery, carry on the same effect of airiness, while their light is softened by the really beautiful stained glass which they frame. The richly carved choir-stalls of dark mahogany and the fine organ furnish an interior of which any town in England might well be proud. And all this magnificence is in a little Flemish town of some six thousand inhabitants.

One is brought suddenly face to face with the tremendous difference which exists between the Protestant and the Catholic conception of what a church is and what it is for. To the one it is a place where men meet for mutual support and instruction, for united worship; to the other it is a place where men meet God. To the one some organised service is necessary; the other only requires the stones on which to kneel. The one will only go to church—in fact, he will only find his church open at certain appointed times; for the other it is only closed with darkness. Of course, I am using the words Protestant and Catholic to indicate broad conceptions of religion, and not as defining definite bodies of men; but even of those who call themselves by these names what I have said is largely true. And this difference in conception is reflected in the churches which they build. For the one a simple building will suffice which will seat in comfort those who may come; the other, though he alone should ever enter it, will raise to heaven the mightiest temple which mortal hands can frame.

Furnes still carries on a tradition of medieval times—the strange procession which passes through its streets and across the great square on the last Sunday in July. Its origin, in the twelfth century, is unknown, though many legends are woven around it. It is a long procession, in which are represented many of the episodes in the story of the Christ, some in sculptured groups of figures, some by living actors. Before each group walks a penitent, barefoot and heavily veiled in black gown and hood, carrying an inscription to explain the group which follows. Abraham appears with Isaac, Moses with the serpent, Joseph and Mary, the *Magi*, and the flight into Egypt. Then come incidents from the life of Jesus, and the great tragedy of its close.

The Host and its attendant priests conclude the procession. It is all very primitive and bizarre, but behind it there is a note of reality by which one cannot but be moved. For the figures concealed beneath the black hoods and dragging along the heavy wooden crosses are not actors; they are men and women who have come, many of them, long distances to Furnes, in the hope that by this penance they may obtain the forgiveness they desire.

Chapter 20

A Journey

The hospital had already been established in Furnes for ten days, and even in that time we had once had to escape to Poperinghe before the German advance, when, after a short visit to England, I left London to rejoin my friends on the last Friday in October. Crossing to the Continent is not at any time pleasant, and the addition of submarines and mines scarcely adds to its charms. But government had certainly done their best to make it attractive, for when we arrived at Dover on Friday night we found a comfortable boat waiting to take us over in the morning. We spent the night soundly asleep in her cabins, without the anxiety of feeling that we might miss her if we did not get up in time, and after an excellent breakfast we felt ready for anything. We were late in starting, for the Anglo-Belgian Ambulance Corps was going over, and their ambulances had to be got on board. We watched them being neatly picked up in the slings and planted side by side on deck. At half-past eight they were all on board, and we started off.

There was a moderate sea running, but our three screws made light work of it, and in an hour we were half-way over to our destination, Dunkirk. We were sitting in our cabin talking when suddenly the engines stopped, and there was considerable commotion on deck. We looked out to see what was the matter, and there met our eyes a sight which we are likely to remember—a huge man-of-war sinking. She was down by the stern, so far that every now and then the waves broke over her, and it was evident that she would soon go under. A submarine had attacked her an hour before, and struck her with two torpedoes. The first destroyed her screws, and she was then an easy prey; the second entered her saloon in the stern.

She was the *Hermes*, an old vessel, and of no great value at the present day, but it was tragic to see a great cruiser expiring, stabbed in the dark. Thanks to her buoyancy, she was only sinking slowly, and there was ample time for the whole of her crew to escape. Very different would be the fate of an unarmed vessel, for the explosion of a torpedo would probably blow such a large hole in the thin steel plates that she would go to the bottom like a stone. To torpedo a merchantman simply means the cold-blooded murder of the crew, for their chances of escape would be almost negligible, whilst it is impossible to find words to describe the attempts which have been made to sink hospital ships. About the last there is a degree of callous inhumanity remarkable even for Germany, for how could doctors and nurses make any efforts to save their own lives when it would be impossible for them to do anything to all at save the lives of their patients? And yet these things are not the unconsidered acts of a moment; they are all part of the campaign of frightfulness which has been so carefully planned for years, the consummation of the doctrines which learned professors have proclaimed for so long and with such astonishing success.

The order was given for our boats to be lowered, and down they went all six of them, manned partly by the crew and partly by the Ambulance Corps. We were surrounded by torpedo-boats, British and French, and most of the crew of the *Hermes* had already been transferred to them. A few minutes later there was a cheer, and we saw the Captain step down into one of the boats, the last man to leave his ship. Our boats had picked up twenty or so of the men, and the problem now was to get them on board again. A moderate sea was running, but it required all the skill of our sailors to haul them up without mishap. Standing by as we were, the ship rolled considerably, and several times one of the boats was within an ace of being broken up against her side. To get a boat out from a big liner in a heavy sea must be an almost miraculous feat, whilst to get her back again must be a sheer impossibility.

As it was, it took us at least an hour to get those six boats on board. All this time four torpedo-boats were racing in circles round and round us, on the lookout for the submarine, and ready to cut it down if it should appear. Indeed, a report went round that a torpedo was actually fired at us, but passed underneath the ship on account of her shallow draught. Standing at rest, we would have been an easy target, and but for our friends the torpedo-boats we should very likely have been attacked. It is not a good plan to hang about in the Channel just now.

Meanwhile the *Hermes* was steadily sinking. By the time all her crew were off her stern was awash, and in another half-hour she had a very marked list to port. She slowly, almost imperceptibly, listed more and more, and then the end came with startling suddenness. With a slow and gentle roll she heeled over till she was completely on her side and her great funnels under water; she remained there for a moment, and then slowly turned turtle and gradually sank stern first. For a long time about twenty feet of her nose remained above water, then this slowly sank and disappeared. It was all so quiet that it seemed like some queer dream. The fires must have been drawn with great promptness, for there was no explosion as her funnels went under, though we were standing some way off to be clear of flying fragments. She had been stabbed in the dark, and she passed away without a murmur.

There is something very moving in the end of a great vessel. It is so hard to believe that a thing of such vast bulk, and with organs of such terrific power, should be so utterly helpless because of a mere hole in her side. It is like watching the death of a god. We make such a turmoil about the end of our puny lives, and that great giant slides away into darkness without a murmur. Ah, but you will say, a man is of far more value than a ship. Is he? Is any single man in this world worth as much as the *Titanic?* And if so, how? He can make wealth, but so could she. He could bring happiness to others, and so could she. I have yet to find any ground on which any man can be put up in competition with that vessel in sheer worth to the world, and I am not speaking in any low sense of values. For I suppose the greatest man who ever lived might feel that his life was well spent if he had brought two continents nearer together. It was for that that she was created. The hard fact is that there are very few indeed of us, in spite of all the noise we make, who are worth to the world a thousand pounds, and if she could sell the bulk of us for that she would be positively drunk with fortune.

But, you will say, a ship has no soul. Are you quite so sure about that? Most people will maintain that their bodies contain a soul, and then they proceed to build up these same bodies with bread and bacon, and even beer, and in the end they possess bodies constructed without any shadow of doubt out of these ingredients. And if ten thousand men have toiled night and day, in blazing furnace and in dark mine, to build a mighty vessel, at the cost of years of labour, at the cost of pain and death, is not that vessel a part of them as much as their poor bodies, and do not their souls live in it as much as in their flesh and blood? We speak of the resurrection of the Body, and superior people smile at an idea so out-of-date and unscientific. To me the body is not mere flesh and blood, it is the whole complex of all that a man has thought and lived and done, and when it arises there will arise with it all that he has toiled for on earth, all that he has gained, and all that he has created by the sweat of his brow and the hunger of his soul. The world is not the dust-heap of the centuries, but only their storehouse.

It was late when we reached Furnes after a freezing drive in the dark, but all our thoughts were overshadowed by the tragedy we had seen. We felt that we had been present at the burial of a god.

Chapter 21

The Ambulance Corps

One of the most difficult problems for a medical service in war is the recovery of the wounded from the field of battle and their carriage back to hospital. In the old days men fought out a battle in a few hours, and the field at the end of the day was left to the conqueror. Then the doctors could go forward and attend to the wounded on the spot without any special danger to themselves. A man might lie out all night, but he would be certain to be picked up next day. But in this war everything is changed. It is one continuous siege, with the result that the removal of the wounded is a matter of extraordinary difficulty and danger. I have met with one officer who has been in a trench out at the extreme front for two and a half months. During the whole of that time he has never seen a German, and the nearest German trench is just one hundred yards away! Shell and shot have been pouring over his head all that time, and to raise one's head above the ground would be to court instant death.

Between the trenches the ground is a quagmire, and any advance by either side is out of the question. But a time will come when the ground is just solid enough for a man to stand, there will be a desperate struggle for a few yards of ground, again both sides will subside into new trenches; but now between those trenches will lie perhaps some hundreds of wounded, and how in the world are they to be got? This is the problem with which an ambulance is everywhere faced— the recovery of the wounded from disputed ground. It was to grapple with difficulties like these that the rules of the Geneva Convention were framed, so that men wearing a Red Cross on their arms might be able to go where no combatant of either side dare venture, and succour the wounded, whether they were friend or foe, in safety both for themselves and for the wounded. It is, after all, possible to fight as gentlemen.

Or at least it was until a few months ago. Since then we have had a demonstration of "scientific" war such as has never before been given to mankind. Now, to wear a Red Cross is simply to offer a better mark for the enemy's fire, and we only wore them in order that our own troops might know our business and make use of our aid. A hospital is a favourite mark for the German artillery, whilst the practice of painting Red Crosses on the tops of ambulance cars is by many people considered unwise, as it invites any passing aeroplane to drop a bomb. But the Germans have carried their systematic contempt of the rules of war so far that it is now almost impossible for our own men to recognise their Red Crosses. Time after time their Red Cross cars have been used to conceal machine-guns, their flags have floated over batteries, and they have actually used stretchers to bring up ammunition to the trenches.

Whilst I was at Furnes two German spies were working with an ambulance, in khaki uniforms, bringing in the wounded. They were at it for nearly a week before they were discovered, and then, by a ruse, they succeeded in driving straight through the Belgian lines and back to their own, Red Cross ambulance, khaki and all. The problems, then, that have to be faced by an ambulance corps in the present war are fairly perplexing, and they demand a degree of resource and cool courage beyond the ordinary. That these qualities are possessed by the members of the ambulance corps of which Dr. Hector Munro and Lady Dorothie Feilding are the leading members is merely a matter of history. They have been in as many tight corners in the last few months as many an old and seasoned veteran, and they have invariably come out triumphant.

They started in Ghent under the Belgian Red Cross with a party of four surgeons, five women, and three men for the stretchers, and two chauffeurs to drive the two ambulances. Now they have grown into an organisation which takes on a great part of the ambulance work of the Belgian Army. At Ghent they were attached to the big Red Cross hospital in the Flandria Palace Hotel, and at first it was dull, for most of the fighting was around Antwerp, and the wounded were taken there. We were in Antwerp just then, and it was by no means dull. We shared Alost and Termonde as a common hunting-ground, and we several times had a visit from Dr. Munro in the Boulevard Leopold. In fact, we were discussing the possibility of arranging to work together when the crash came and Antwerp fell.

For the next few days the ambulance corps had enough work and ran enough risks to satisfy even the members of that notorious organisation. The Germans were coming on with great rapidity, and if there is one dangerous job, it is to pick up the wounded of a retreating army. But here the interest for an English ambulance was doubled, for the British Army was covering the retreat of the Belgians and the French. On Sunday, the 11th of October, they were asked to go out to Melle, four miles south-east of Ghent, to help with some French wounded, and, after spending some time there, they met the British Staff, and were asked to help them in their retreat through Zwynarde, a town on the Scheldt about four miles south of Ghent and the same distance from Melle. It was a dangerous undertaking, as the intention was to blow up the bridge which crosses the Scheldt at Zwynarde and to fight a retreating battle covering the retirement of our allies.

The bridge was to be blown up at ten o'clock that evening, and though it was only four miles away, it was already dark and a mist was rising from the river. The main roads were in the hands of the Germans, and there was nothing for it but to get across by a small side-road. They started off in the mist, and promptly lost their way. It is a pleasing situation to be lost in the dark somewhere very close to the enemy's lines when you know that the only available bridge is just going to be blown up. A thick mist had risen all around, and they were midway between two batteries—British and German—engaged in an artillery duel. The crash of the guns and the scream of the shells overhead filled the darkness with terror. But there was nothing for it but to go straight on, and though they must have gone right through the German lines and out again, they reached the bridge just ten minutes before it was blown into the air.

We all met at Ostend, and decided to join forces at Furnes, and it worked out as a splendid arrangement for both parties. Though our organisations remained entirely distinct, we worked together, and they had the advantage of a hospital to which they could always bring their patients, whilst we had the services of the smartest ambulance corps on the Continent. The qualities required for the satisfactory working of a hospital and the successful running of an ambulance are so distinct that I am sure that the ideal arrangement is to have two entirely distinct organisations working in harmony.

The position of an ambulance up at the front is always a delicate one, for as it moves about from place to place its members have opportunities of picking up information about the position and movements of the troops of a very confidential nature. It was therefore a great advantage to Dr. Munro when his party was joined by M. de Broqueville, the son of the Minister for War; for it meant that they would have full information as to where wounded were likely to require their help, and that they possessed the full confidence of the Belgian authorities. Their position and our own had been very greatly affected by the fortunes of the war, for the Belgian *Croix Rouge* and Army Medical Services were for the moment in abeyance, and instead of obtaining from them the help which had hitherto been so generously given, we had now to undertake their work and to rely entirely on our own resources. We had not to wait long for an opportunity to show what we could do.

The Belgian Army, supported by a certain number of French troops, made its final stand on the line of the Yser, the little river which runs from Ypres through Dixmude and Nieuport to the sea. From this position they have never since been shaken, but they have never had to withstand more desperate attacks than those which took place in the end of October. The centre of these was Dixmude, and here the Germans threw against the little remnant of the Belgian Army forces which might have been expected to shatter it at a blow. Their efforts culminated in one of the fiercest and bloodiest engagements of the whole war, and at the height of the engagement word came that there were wounded in Dixmude, and that ambulances were urgently required to get them out. Getting wounded out of a town which is being shelled is not exactly a joke, and when the town is in rapid process of annihilation it almost becomes serious. But this was what the Corps had come out for, and two ambulances and an open car started off at once. As far as Oudecappelle the road was crowded with motor transport waggons carrying supplies of food and ammunition to the troops, but beyond that it was empty, unless one counts the shells which were falling on it in a steady hail.

Every now and then a Jack Johnson would fall and leave a hole in which one could bury a motor, and, apart from the shells, the holes made driving risky. There was over a mile of the road in this unhealthy state, and entirely exposed to the enemy's guns, before any shelter could be obtained; but the wounded must be fetched, and the cars pushed on as fast as they dared to drive. They were suddenly pulled up by an appalling obstacle. A Belgian battery advancing along the road to the front only twenty minutes before had been struck by a big shell. Several of the gunners were horribly mangled; ten horses lay dead, most of them in fragments; the gun was wrecked, and all its equipment scattered about the road. It was some minutes before the remaining soldiers could clear the road sufficiently for the cars to pass.

Dixmude itself was a roaring furnace, and shells were pouring into it in all directions. Practically every house had been damaged, many were totally demolished, and many more were on fire. The wounded were in the Town Hall on the square, and shells were bursting all over it. The upper portion was completely destroyed, and the church close by was blazing furiously, and must have set fire to the Town Hall soon after. On the steps lay a dead marine, and beside him stood a French surgeon, who greeted them warmly. The wounded were in a cellar, and if they were not got out soon, it was obvious that they would be burned alive. Inside the hall were piles of bicycles, loaves of bread, and dead soldiers, all in gruesome confusion. In the cellar dead and wounded were lying together. The wounded had all to be carried on stretchers, for everyone who could crawl had fled from that ghastly inferno, and only those who have shifted wounded on stretchers can appreciate the courage it requires to do it under shell fire. At last they were all packed into the ambulances, and even as they left the building with the last, a shell struck it overhead and demolished one of the walls. How they ever got out of Dixmude alive is beyond the ken of a mere mortal, but I suppose it was only another manifestation of the Star which shines so brightly over the fortunes of the Munro Ambulance.

How high is the appreciation of the Belgian Government for their work is shown in the fact that three of the lady members of the corps have just been decorated with the Order of Leopold—one of the highest honours which Belgium has to confer. It is not every honour which is so well earned.

Chapter 22

Pervyse—The Trenches

This is indeed the strangest of all wars, for it is fought in the dark. Eyes are used, but they are the eyes of an aeroplane overhead, or of a spy in the enemy's lines. The man who fights lives underground, or under water, and rarely sees his foe. There is something strangely terrible, something peculiarly inhuman, in the silent stealth of this war of the blind. The general sits in a quiet room far behind the lines, planning a battle he will never see. The gunner aims by level and compass with faultless precision, and hurls his awful engines of destruction to destroy ten miles away a house which is to him only a dot on a map. And the soldier sitting in his trench hears the shells whistling overhead and waits, knowing well that if he appeared for one instant above that rampart of earth he would be pierced by a dozen bullets from rifles which are out of his sight.

It is a war in the dark, and by far the most important of its operations are carried on, its battles are fought, in the literal sense of the word, underground. Perhaps the next war will be fought not merely underground, but deep in the bowels of the earth, and victory will rest, not with the finest shots or the expert swordsmen, but with the men who can dig a tunnel most quickly. The trenches may be cut by some herculean plough, deep tunnels may be dug by great machines, and huge pumping engines may keep them dry. Our engineers have conquered the air, the water, and the land, but it is still with picks and spades that our soldiers dig themselves into safety.

At Furnes the nearest point to us of the fighting line was Pervyse, and as the Ambulance Corps had a dressing-station there, we often went out to see them and the soldiers in the trenches close by. But the Belgian line was most effectively protected by an agency far more powerful than any trench, for over miles and miles of land spread the floods with which the Belgians, by breaking down the dykes, had themselves flooded the country. The floods were a protection, but they were also a difficulty, since they made actual trenches an impossibility. No ordinary pumps could have kept them dry. So they had built huts of earth behind a thick earth bank, and partly sunk in the very low embankment, only two or three feet above the fields, on which the railway ran. They were roofed with boards covered again with earth and sods, and behind each was a little door by which one could crawl in. Inside, the floor was covered with a bed of straw, and a bucket with holes in its sides and full of red-hot coke did duty as a stove, while narrow loopholes served for ventilation and for light, and were to be used for firing from in the event of an attack. Of course the huts were very cramped, but they were at least warm, they gave protection from the weather, and above all they were safe. The men only occupied them as a matter of fact for short periods of one or two days at a time, a fresh guard coming out from Furnes to take their places.

These huts, and all covered trenches, are only safe from shrapnel exploding in the air or near by. No ordinary trench is safe from a shell falling upon it; but this, as a matter of fact, has scarcely ever happened. For shells are as a rule fired from some considerable distance, and in most cases the opposing lines of trenches are so close together that there would be great danger of sending a shell into the back of your own trench, the most deadly disaster that can happen. The trenches are often so close together that their occupants can talk to one another, and a considerable amount of camaraderie may spring up.

I know of one instance where a private arrangement was made that they would not shoot on either side. One day a man on our side was wounded, and there was great annoyance till a note was thrown across apologizing profusely, and explaining that it was done by a man in a trench behind who did not know of the compact! A few days later a message came to say that an important officer was coming to inspect the German trench, and that they would be obliged to fire, but that they would give due warning by three shots fired in quick succession. The shots were fired, and our men lay low, under a storm of bullets, till firing ceased, and another message arrived to say that the danger was past. We really are queer animals!

Behind the trenches at Pervyse the fields were positively riddled with shot-holes. In one space, not more than twenty yards square, we counted the marks of over a hundred shells. The railway station was like a sieve, and most of the houses in the little town were absolutely destroyed. I do not believe that there was a house in the place which had not been hit, and the number of shells that must have rained on that small area would have sufficed not so many years ago for the siege of a large town. The church was destroyed beyond any possibility of repair. The roof was gone entirely, and large portions of the walls; a great piece of the tower had been blown clean out, and the tower itself was leaning dangerously. The bombardment of the church must have been terrific, for even the heavy pillars of the aisle had been snapped across. Of the altar only the solid stones remained, surrounded by fragments of what had once been the stained glass of the apse, and the twisted remains of the great brass candlesticks which had stood beside the altar. Only a few weeks ago this was an old parish church of singular beauty. Now even the graves in the churchyard have been torn open by the shells. These few battered walls, these heaps of stone and brick, are all that remain of a prosperous village and its ancient church.

The dressing station of the Ambulance Corps was one of their most daring and successful ventures. At first it was placed close to the trenches and just behind the railway station, in the house of the village chemist. At least there were evidences in the existence of portions of walls, roof, and floors that it had once been a house, and the chemist had left a few bottles behind to indicate his trade. But I do not think that anyone but a member of the corps would have ever thought of living there. There was plenty of ventilation, of course, since there were no windows left, part of the roof had gone, and the walls were riddled with holes through which shells had passed clean across the building. It could hardly be described as a desirable residence, but it had one incomparable advantage: it possessed a cellar. A couple of mattresses and a few blankets converted it into a palace, whilst the limits of luxury were reached when there arrived a new full-sized enamelled bath which one of the soldiers had discovered and hastened to present as a mark of gratitude. There was no water-supply, of course, and I do not think that there was a plug, but those were mere trifles. How such a white elephant ever found its way to Pervyse none of us will ever know. I do not believe that there was another for twenty miles around.

In this strange residence—it could hardly be called a house—lived two of the lady members of the corps. They were relieved from time to time, two others coming out to take their places, and every day they had visits from the ambulances which came out to pick up the

PERVYSE

YPRES

wounded. A room on the ground floor was used during the day, partly as a living-room, partly as a surgery, and here were brought any soldiers wounded in this part of the lines. At night they retired to the cellar, as the house itself was far too dangerous. The Germans shelled Pervyse almost every night, and sometimes in the day as well, and this particular house was the most exposed of any in the town. But shells were not the only trouble, and when a few weeks later the cellars were filled with water, it was evident that other quarters must be found.[1]

Pervyse was of course entirely deserted by its inhabitants, but it could scarcely be called dull. We went out one afternoon to see what was going on, and found a party of the corps at lunch. They seemed to be in particularly good spirits, and they told us that the house had just been struck by a shell, that the big Daimler ambulance had been standing outside, and that its bonnet had been riddled by the shrapnel bullets. We went outside to see for ourselves, and there we found a large hole in the side of the house, through which a shell had entered a room across the passage from that occupied by the corps, who had fortunately chosen the lee-side. The big six-cylinder Daimler had been moved into a shed, and there it stood with twenty or more holes in its bonnet, but otherwise uninjured. By a stroke of luck the driver had gone inside the house for a moment or he would undoubtedly have been killed. It is fortunate that the corps is possessed of such a keen sense of humour.

Shells may be amusing in the daytime, but they are not a bit amusing at night. Only two women with real solid courage could have slept, night after night, in that empty house in a ruined and deserted village, with no sounds to be heard but the rain and the wind, the splutter of the *mitrailleuse*, and the shriek of shells. Courage is as infectious as fear, and I think that the soldiers, watching through the night in the trenches near by, must have blessed the women who were waiting there to help them, and must have felt braver men for their presence.

Pervyse was protected by a wide screen of flood, and across this there was one way only—a slightly raised road going straight across six miles of water. No advance by either side was possible, for the road was swept by *mitrailleuses*, and to advance down it would have meant certain death. Half a mile down the road was a farmhouse held by a Belgian outpost, and beyond this, and perhaps half a mile away from it, were two other farms occupied by the Germans. We could see them

---

1. *The Cellar-House of Pervyse* by G. E. Mitton is also published by Leonaur.

moving amongst the trees. That piece of road between Pervyse and the Belgian farm was the scene of one of the very few lapses of the Germans into humanity.

It was known one morning in the trenches at Pervyse that several of their comrades in the farm had been injured in an outpost engagement. It was, however, impossible to reach them before nightfall as the road was swept by the German guns. Two Belgian priests, taking their lives in their hands, walked out to the farm, but they found that the wounded were beyond their powers of carriage. Nothing daunted, they went on to one of the German farms and asked for help, and a few minutes later the astounded Belgians saw a little procession coming up the road. In front walked the two priests, and behind them came four wounded Belgians, lying on stretchers carried by German soldiers. They came right into the lines, and they had a royal welcome. They all shook hands, and the little party of Germans walked back down the road amid the cheers of their opponents.

The spirit of chivalry is not dead in Germany; it is only stifled by her present rulers. Is it too much to hope that some day its voice may be heard and may command?

Chapter 23

Ypres

One morning early in December I was asked by Dr. Munro to run down with him in one of our motors to Ypres. A message had arrived saying that the town had been heavily shelled during the night, and that there were a number of children and of wounded there, who ought if possible to be removed to some less dangerous situation. So we started off to see what we could do for them. It was a dismal morning, and the rain was coming down in a steady drizzle which continued all day long, but fortunately we had a closed car, and we were protected from the elements. The road to Ypres is a broad avenue between long lines of tall trees, and today it was crowded with soldiers and transport motors. The French were moving up a large number of men to relieve and to support their lines between Dixmude and Ypres. Every little village seemed to be crowded with troops, for in this weather "the poorest village is better than the best bivouac," and the contrasts of the uniforms were very striking. Every type was represented—the smart French officer, the *Zouave*, the Turco, and the Arab, and one could not help wondering what the Senegalese and the Algerians thought of this soaking rain, or how they would fare in the rigours of a Belgian winter.

Like so many of the towns of Belgium, Ypres is a town of the past, and it is only in the light of its history that the meaning of its wonderful buildings can be realised, or an estimate formed of the vandalism of its destroyers. Its records date back to the year 900, and in the twelfth century it was already famous for its cloth. By the thirteenth century it was the richest and the most powerful city in Flanders, and four thousand looms gave occupation to its two hundred thousand inhabitants. These great commercial cities were also great military organisations, and there were few wars in the turbulence of the Middle

Ages in which Ypres did not have a share. In fact, it was almost always engaged in fighting either England, or France, or one of the other Flemish towns.

After a century of wars, to which Ypres once contributed no fewer than five thousand troops, the town was besieged by the English, led by Henry Spencer, Bishop of Norwich, with the help of the *burghers* of Ghent and Bruges. The town was surrounded by earthen ramparts planted with thick hedges of thorn, and by wide ditches and wooden palisades, and these were held by some ten thousand men. They were attacked, in 1383, by seventeen thousand English and twenty thousand Flemish. For two months Ypres was defended against almost daily attacks in one of the fiercest and most bloody sieges in history. At last Spencer saw that it was impossible to take the town by assault, and in view of the advance of a large French Army he withdrew. Ypres was saved, but its prosperity was gone, for the bulk of its population had fled. The suburbs, where large numbers of the weavers worked, had been destroyed by the besiegers and the looms had been burnt. The tide of trade turned to Bruges and Ghent, though they did not enjoy for long the prosperity they had stolen.

The commercial madness of the fourteenth century gave way to the religious madness of the sixteenth. Men's ideas were changing, and it is a very dangerous thing to change the ideas of men. For the momentum of the change is out of all proportion to its importance, and the barriers of human reason may melt before it. It is a mere matter of historical fact that no oppression has half the dangers of an obvious reform. At Ypres the Reformers were first in the field. They had swept through Flanders, destroying all the beauty and wealth that the piety of ages had accumulated, and here was rich plunder for these apostles of the ugly. There is real tragedy in the thought that the Reformer is sometimes sincere.

But at least the fanatics limited their fury to the symbols of religion. Philip of Spain could only be sated by flesh and blood, and for the next fifteen years Ypres was tossed to and fro in an orgy of persecution and war such as have rarely been waged even in the name of religion. At the end of that time only a miserable five thousand inhabitants remained within its broken ramparts.

With the seventeenth century commerce and religion made way for politics, and the wars of Louis XIV. fell heavily on Ypres. On four separate occasions the town was taken by the French, and the dismantled fortifications which still surround it were once an example of

The Cloth Hall, Ypres, after bombardment

the genius of Vauban. Yet with all these wars—commercial, religious, political—with all the violence of its history, Ypres had kept intact the glorious monuments of the days of her greatness, and it has been left for the armies of Culture to destroy that which even the hand of Philip spared.

The centuries have handed down to us few buildings of such massive grandeur as the great Cloth Hall, a monument of the days when the weavers of Ypres treated on equal terms with the powers of England and of France. This huge fortress of the Guilds is about a hundred and fifty yards long. The ground floor was once an open loggia, but the spaces between its fifty pillars have been filled in. Above this are two rows of pointed windows, each exactly above an opening below. In the upper row every second window has been formed into a niche for the figure of some celebrity in the history of the town. A delicate turret rises at each end of the facade, and above it rose the high-pitched roof which was one of the most beautiful features of the building. In the centre is the great square tower, reaching to a height of more than two hundred feet, and ending in an elegant belfry, which rises between its four graceful turrets.

The whole of this pile was finished in 1304; but in the seventeenth century there was added at its eastern end the Nieuwerck, an exquisite Renaissance structure supported entirely on a row of slim columns, with tiers of narrow oblong windows, and with elaborate gables of carved stone. The contrast between the strength and simplicity of the Gothic and the rich decoration of Spain is as delightful as it is bold. The upper part of this vast building formed one great hall, covered overhead by the towering roof. The walls were decorated by painted panels representing the history of the town, and so large were these that in one bay there was erected the entire front of an old wooden house which had been pulled down in the town, gable and all.

And all this is a heap of ruins. Whether any portion of it can ever be repaired I do not know, but the cost would be fabulous. The roof is entirely destroyed, and with it the whole of the great gallery and its paintings, for fire consumed what the shells had left. Only the bare stone walls remain, and as we stood among the pillars which had supported the floors above, it was difficult to realise that the heap of rubbish around us was all that was left of what had once been the envy of Europe. The only building which we have at all comparable to the Cloth Hall is the Palace of Westminster. If it were blasted by shells and gutted by fire, we might regret it, but what would be our feelings if it were the legacy of Edward the First, and had been handed down to us intact through six centuries?

Behind the Cloth Hall stands the Church of St. Martin, once for two and a half centuries the Cathedral of Ypres. It was largely built at the same time as the Cloth Hall, and it is a glorious monument of the architecture of the thirteenth century. Perhaps its most beautiful features are the great square tower, the lofty and imposing nave, and the exquisite rose window in the south wall of the transept, which is said to be the finest in Belgium. The tower was surrounded with scaffolding, and around its base were piles of stone, for the church was being repaired when the war began. I wonder if it will ever be repaired now. The Germans had expended on its destruction many of their largest shells, and they had been very successful in their efforts.

There were three huge holes in the roof of the choir where shells had entered, and in the centre of the transept was a pile of bricks and stone six feet high. Part of the tower had been shot away, and its stability was uncertain. The beautiful glass of the rose window had been utterly destroyed, and part of the tracery was broken. The old Parish Chapel on the south side of the nave had nothing left but the altar and four bare walls. The fine old roof and the great bronze screen which separated it from the nave had perished in the flames. The screen was lying in small fragments amongst the rubbish on the chapel floor, and at first I thought they were bits of rusty iron.

As I stood in the ruins of the Parish Chapel looking round on this amazing scene, there was a roar overhead, and one of the big 14-inch shells passed, to explode with a terrific crash amongst the houses a few hundred yards farther on. It was plain that the bombardment was beginning again, and that we must see to our business without any delay. Two more shells passed overhead as I came out of the church, with a roar very different from the soft whistle of a small shell. The destruction produced by one of these large shells is astonishing. One large house into which a shell had fallen in the previous night had simply crumpled up. Portions of the walls and a heap of bricks were all that was left, a bit of an iron bedstead and a fragment of staircase sticking out from the debris. The roof, the floors, and the greater part of the walls might never have existed.

In the Place in front of the cathedral were two holes where shells had fallen, and either of them would have comfortably held a motor-car. The children were all together in a little street a quarter of a mile west of the Cathedral, just where the last three shells had fallen. Fortunately they had hurt no one, though one had passed clean through the upper stories of a house where there were several children being got ready by one of our party for removal.

By good luck through some defect it did not explode, or the house would have been annihilated and everyone in it killed. Quite a collection of people had congregated in that little street, though why they considered it safer than the rest of the town I do not know. At first they were very unwilling to let any of the children go at all. But at last about twenty children were collected and were packed into ambulances. Some of them were without parents, and were being looked after by the neighbours, and the parents of some absolutely refused to leave. More children and a few adults to look after them were found later, and I think that in the end about a hundred were taken up to Fumes, to be sent on to Calais as refugees.

The children were as merry as crickets, and regarded it all as a huge joke; sitting in the ambulances, they looked for all the world like a school treat. But I have often wondered whether we were right to take them away or whether it would not have been better to have left them to take their chance. War is a very terrible thing, and the well-meant interference of the kind-hearted may do far more harm than good. What is going to happen to those children? I suppose that they are in some refugee home, to remain there till the war is over. And then? We did our best to identify them, but what are the chances that many of them will ever see their parents again? From what I have seen of these things I do not think that they are very large. Perhaps you will say that the parents ought to have gone with them.

It is easy for the well-to-do to leave their homes and to settle again elsewhere; but the poorer a man is the less can he afford to leave what little he possesses. In their own town they might be in danger, but at least they had not lost their homes, and they possessed the surroundings without which their individual lives would be merged in the common ocean of misery. The problem of the civil population, and especially of the children, in time of war is entirely beyond the scope of individual effort. It is a matter with which only a government or a very powerful organisation can deal, and it is a matter in which gvernments do not take a great deal of interest. Their hands are quite full enough in trying to defeat the enemy.

In all previous wars between civilized nations a certain regard has been paid to the safety of the civilian population, and especially of the women and children. But from the very first the German policy has been to utterly ignore the rights of non-combatants, tearing up the conventions which they themselves had signed for their protection. No government could be expected to be prepared for such a total apostasy from the elementary principles of civilized society, or to anticipate methods at which a Zulu might blush. If they had done so, it should have been their first care to remove all non-combatants from the area of fighting, and to make provision for them elsewhere. It is unfair that a civilian should be left with the hopeless choice of leaving a child in a house where it may at any moment be killed by a shell or taking it away with a considerable probability that it will be a homeless orphan. For life is a matter of small moment; it is living that matters.

The problem of the children of Belgium will be one of the most serious to be faced when the war is over. There will be a great number of orphans, whilst many more will be simply lost. They must not be adopted in England, for to them Belgium will look for her future population. There could be few finer ways in which we could show our gratitude to the people of Belgium than by establishing colonies over there where they could be brought up in their own country, to be its future citizens. It would form a bond between the two countries such as no treaty could ever establish, and Belgium would never forget the country which had been the foster-mother of her children.

But Ypres gave us yet another example of German methods of war. On the western side of the town, some distance from the farthest houses, stood the asylum. It was a fine building arranged in several wings, and at present it was being used for the accommodation of a few wounded, mostly women and children, and several old people of the workhouse infirmary type. It made a magnificent hospital, and as it was far away from the town and was not used for any but the purposes of a hospital, we considered that it was safe enough, and that it would be a pity to disturb the poor old people collected there. We might have known better. The very next night the Germans shelled it to pieces, and all those unfortunate creatures had to be removed in a hurry. There is a senseless barbarity about such an act which could only appeal to a Prussian.

Chapter 24

Some Conclusions

To draw conclusions from a limited experience is a difficult matter, and the attempt holds many pitfalls for the unwary. Yet every experience must leave on the mind of any thinking man certain impressions, and the sum of these only he himself can give. To others he can give but blurred images of all he may have seen, distorted in the curving mirrors of his mind, but from these they can at least form some estimate of the truth of the conclusions he ventures to draw. For myself, these conclusions seem to fall naturally into three separate groups, for I have met the experiences of the past three months in three separate ways—as a surgeon, as a Briton, and as, I hope, a civilized man. It is from these three aspects that I shall try to sum up what I have seen.

As a surgeon it has been my good fortune to have charge of a hospital whose position was almost ideal. Always close to the front, we received our cases at the earliest possible moment, and could deal with them practically first hand. Every day I realised more strongly the advantages of such a hospital, and the importance for the wounded of the first surgical treatment they receive. Upon this may well depend the whole future course of the case. No wounded man should be sent on a long railway journey to the base until he has passed through the hands of a skilled surgeon, and has been got into such a condition that the journey does not involve undue risk. And no rough routine treatment will suffice.

A surgeon is required who can deal with desperate emergencies and pull impossible cases out of the fire—a young man who does not believe in the impossible, and who can adapt himself to conditions of work that would make an older man shudder, and a man who will never believe what he is told until he has seen it for himself. For the conditions of work at the front are utterly different from those of civil practice, and it is impossible for any man after many years of regular routine to adapt himself to such changed environment. The long experience of the older man will be of far more use at the base, and he will have plenty of difficulties to contend with there.

I have often been told that there is no opening for skilled surgery at the front. In my opinion there is room for the highest skill that the profession can produce. It is absurd to say that the abdominal cases should be left to die or to recover as best they can, that one dare not touch a fractured femur because it is septic. To take up such an attitude is simply to admit that these cases are beyond the scope of present surgery. In a sense, perhaps, they are, but that is all the more reason why the scope of surgery should be enlarged, and not that these cases should be left outside its pale. I am far from advising indiscriminate operating. There are many things in surgery besides scalpels. But I do urge the need for hospitals close to the front, with every modern equipment, and with surgeons of resource and energy.

But for a surgeon this war between nations is only an incident in the war to which he has devoted his life—the war against disease. It is a curious reflection that whilst in the present war the base hospital has been given, if anything, an undue importance, in the other war it has been practically neglected. Our great hospitals are almost entirely field hospitals, planted right in the middle of the battle, and there we keep our patients till such time as they are to all intents and purposes cured. A very few convalescent homes will admit cases which still require treatment, but only a very few. The bulk of them expect their inmates to do the work of the establishment.

Now, this is most unreasonable, for a country hospital is cheaper to build and should cost less to run than one in town, and in many cases the patients will recover in half the time. Our hospitals in London are always crowded, the waiting-lists mount up till it seems hopeless to attack them, and all the time it is because we have no base hospital down in the country to which our patients might be sent to recover. I wonder how long it will be before each of the great London hospitals has its own base down in the country, with its own motor ambulances and its own ambulance coaches to carry its patients in comfort by rail to surroundings where they could recover as can never be possible in the middle of the London slums? And as to getting the staff to look after it, there would probably be a waiting-list for week-ends.

But there are more important considerations in this war than surgery, and one would have to be very blind not to perceive that this is a life-and-death struggle between Britain and Germany. The involvement of other nations is merely accidental. It is ourselves whom Germany is making this huge effort to crush, and but for one small circumstance she would have come within a measurable prospect of success. To swoop down on France through Belgium, to crush her in three weeks, to seize her fleet, and with the combined fleets of France and Germany to attack ours—that was the proposition, and who can say that it might not have succeeded? The small circumstance which Germany overlooked was Belgium, and it is to the heroic resistance of Belgium that we owe the fact that the German advance has been stopped.

At the cost of the desolation of their own country, Belgium has perhaps saved the flag of Britain, for where would it have flown on the seas if Germany had won? And at the very least she has saved us from a war beside which this is nothing—a war not now, but a few years hence, when she might have controlled half the Continent, and we should have stood alone. We owe an incalculable debt to Belgium, and we can only repay it by throwing into this war every resource that our country has to offer. For the only end which can bring peace to Europe is the total annihilation of Germany as a military and naval power. What other terms can be made with a nation which regards its most solemn treaties as so much waste paper, which is bound by no conventions, and which delights in showing a callous disregard of all that forms the basis of a civilized society? The only guarantees that we can take are that she has no ships of war, and that her army is only sufficient to police her frontier. The building of a war vessel or the boring of a gun must be regarded as a *casus belli*. Then, and then only, shall Europe be safe from the madness that is tearing her asunder.

But there is a wider view of this war than even that of Britain. We are not merely fighting to preserve the pre-eminence of our country; we are fighting for the civilization of the world. The victory of Germany would mean the establishment over the whole world of a military despotism such as the world has never seen. For if once the navy of Britain is gone, who else can stop her course? Canada, the United States, South America, would soon be vassals of her power—a power which would be used without scruple for her own material advantage. This is not a war between Germany and certain other nations; it is a war between Germany and civilization. The stake is not a few acres of land, but the freedom for which our fathers gave their lives.

Is there such a thing as neutrality in this war? Germany herself gave the answer when she invaded Belgium. It is the undoubted duty of many great nations, and of one before all others, to stand aside and not to enter the struggle; but to be neutral at heart, not to care whether the battle is won or lost, is impossible for any nation which values honour and truth above the passing advantages of worldly power. We do not ask America to fight on our side. This is our fight, and only Britain and her Allies can see it through. But we do ask for a sympathy which, while obeying the laws of neutrality to the last letter, will support us with a spirit which is bound by no earthly law, which will bear with us when in our difficult task we seem to neglect the interests of our friends, and will rejoice with us when, out of toil and sorrow, we have won a lasting peace.

This war is not of our choosing, and we shall never ask for peace. The sword has been thrust into our hands by a power beyond our own to defend from a relentless foe the flag which has been handed down to us unsullied through the ages, and to preserve for the world the freedom which is the proudest birthright of our race. When it is sheathed, the freedom of the world from the tyranny of man will have been secured.

ALSO FROM LEONAUR
AVAILABLE IN SOFTCOVER OR HARDCOVER WITH DUST JACKET

THE 9TH—THE KING'S (LIVERPOOL REGIMENT) IN THE GREAT WAR 1914 - 1918 by *Enos H. G. Roberts*—Mersey to mud—war and Liverpool men.

THE GAMBARDIER by *Mark Severn*—The experiences of a battery of Heavy artillery on the Western Front during the First World War.

FROM MESSINES TO THIRD YPRES by *Thomas Floyd*—A personal account of the First World War on the Western front by a 2/5th Lancashire Fusilier.

THE IRISH GUARDS IN THE GREAT WAR - VOLUME 1 by *Rudyard Kipling*—Edited and Compiled from Their Diaries and Papers—The First Battalion.

THE IRISH GUARDS IN THE GREAT WAR - VOLUME 1 by *Rudyard Kipling*—Edited and Compiled from Their Diaries and Papers—The Second Battalion.

ARMOURED CARS IN EDEN by *K. Roosevelt*—An American President's son serving in Rolls Royce armoured cars with the British in Mesopatamia & with the American Artillery in France during the First World War.

CHASSEUR OF 1914 by *Marcel Dupont*—Experiences of the twilight of the French Light Cavalry by a young officer during the early battles of the great war in Europe.

TROOP HORSE & TRENCH by *R.A. Lloyd*—The experiences of a British Lifeguardsman of the household cavalry fighting on the western front during the First World War 1914-18.

THE EAST AFRICAN MOUNTED RIFLES by *C.J. Wilson*—Experiences of the campaign in the East African bush during the First World War.

THE LONG PATROL by *George Berrie*—A Novel of Light Horsemen from Gallipoli to the Palestine campaign of the First World War.

THE FIGHTING CAMELIERS by *Frank Reid*—The exploits of the Imperial Camel Corps in the desert and Palestine campaigns of the First World War.

STEEL CHARIOTS IN THE DESERT by *S. C. Rolls*—The first world war experiences of a Rolls Royce armoured car driver with the Duke of Westminster in Libya and in Arabia with T.E. Lawrence.

WITH THE IMPERIAL CAMEL CORPS IN THE GREAT WAR by *Geoffrey Inchbald*—The story of a serving officer with the British 2nd battalion against the Senussi and during the Palestine campaign.

AVAILABLE ONLINE AT **www.leonaur.com**
AND FROM ALL GOOD BOOK STORES